LIVES OF THE MASTERS

Maitrīpa

INDIA'S YOGI OF NONDUAL BLISS

Klaus-Dieter Mathes

Shambhala

Shambhala Publications, Inc.
2129 13th Street
Boulder, Colorado 80302
www.shambhala.com

Cover art: Robert Fenwick May, Jr.
Cover design: Gopa & Ted2, Inc.

9 8 7 6 5 4 3 2 1

FIRST EDITION
Printed in Canada

♾ This edition is printed on acid-free paper that meets
the American National Standards Institute z39.48 Standard.
♻ This book is printed on 100% postconsumer recycled paper.
For more information please visit www.shambhala.com.

Shambhala Publications is distributed worldwide by
Penguin Random House, Inc., and its subsidiaries.

LIBRARY OF CONGRESS CATALOGING-IN-PUBLICATION DATA
Names: Mathes, Klaus-Dieter, author.
Title: Maitrīpa: India's Yogi of Nondual Bliss / Klaus-Dieter Mathes.
Description: Boulder: Shambhala, 2021. | Series: Lives of the masters |
Includes bibliographical references and index.
Identifiers: LCCN 2020048709 | ISBN 9781611806700 (trade paperback)
Subjects: LCSH: Mahāmudrā (Tantric rite) | Advayavajra, active approximately
11th century. | Emptiness (Philosophy) | Siddhas—Biography—Early works to 1800. |
Tantric Buddhism—India—Early works to 1800. |
Buddhist Literature—Translations into English.
Classification: LCC BQ7699.M34 M38 2021 | DDC 294.3/925092—dc23
LC record available at https://lccn.loc.gov/2020048709

Contents

Series Introduction

BUDDHIST TRADITIONS are heir to some of the most creative thinkers in world history. The Lives of the Masters series offers lively and reliable introductions to the lives, works, and legacies of key Buddhist teachers, philosophers, contemplatives, and writers. Each volume in the Lives series tells the story of an innovator who embodied the ideals of Buddhism, crafted a dynamic living tradition during his or her lifetime, and bequeathed a vibrant legacy of knowledge and practice to future generations.

Lives books rely on primary sources in the original languages to describe the extraordinary achievements of Buddhist thinkers and illuminate these achievements by vividly setting them within their historical contexts. Each volume offers a concise yet comprehensive summary of the master's life and an account of how they came to hold a central place in Buddhist traditions. Each contribution also contains a broad selection of the master's writings.

This series makes it possible for all readers to imagine Buddhist masters as deeply creative and inspired people whose work was animated by the rich complexity of their time and place and how these inspiring figures continue to engage our quest for knowledge and understanding today.

KURTIS SCHAEFFER, *series editor*

Preface

Somebody who wishes to know suchness does not find it
In the Yogācāra tenets;
Even Madhyamaka, which is not adorned
With the words of a guru, is only middling.

MAITRĪPA, *Ten Verses on True Reality*

Maitrīpa wished to compose pāramitā-based pith instructions that accord with the system of the secret mantra

SAHAJAVAJRA, introduction to his *Ten Verses on True Reality* commentary

Here, *mahāmudrā* stands for the pith instructions on the reality of Mahāmudrā

SAHAJAVAJRA, commentary on the *Ten Verses on True Reality*, verse 7

THESE LINES nicely reflect Maitrīpa's essential quality: as a genuine master of Mahāmudrā and emptiness, he could impart Madhyamaka teachings in terms of special pith instructions in such a way that qualified disciples could gain an immediate realization of reality's luminosity. It is precisely this direct access to the reality of Mahāmudrā that upgrades ordinary pāramitā-based teachings to the level of the mantra system. One could compare this approach to a mind-to-mind transmission on par with formal tantric empowerment.

Back in the '80s, when some of my Dharma friends were planning to join the first three-year retreat in Halscheid, Germany, I was told that, following the Maitrīpa lineage, it was also possible to practice

Mahāmudrā on the basis of a special form of *śamatha* and *vipaśyanā* that does not depend on the six dharmas of Nāropa. A direct realization of one's true nature of mind would not only be possible through formal tantric empowerment and practice in a three-year retreat, but also in a direct mind-to-mind transmission of realization that can happen, for example, through special pith instructions on otherwise exhausting philosophical texts. Maitripa's *Ten Verses on True Reality* (*Tattvadaśaka*) are enhanced by such instructions (as implied by verse 2) and open up, according to Maitrīpa's disciple Sahajavajra, a not-specifically-tantric access to Mahāmudrā. I vividly remember Khenpo Tsultrim Gyatsho Rinpoche's inspiring explanations of logic, Madhyamaka, and the Maitreya works that amounted to something similar to what must have been happening during such pith instructions.

Having written my doctoral thesis on Maitreya's *Distinguishing the Phenomenal World of Mental Representation from the True Nature of Phenomena* (*Dharmadharmatāvibhāga*) and my second book on the *Sublime Continuum* (*Uttaratantra*), Maitrīpa returned to my radar, as both of these Maitreya works are said to have been discovered and transmitted by Maitrīpa. My study of the *Sublime Continuum* (better known as *Ratnagotravibhāga* among Indologists) was mainly based on a newly discovered commentary by Gö Lotsāwa Zhönnu Pel (1392–1481) on this standard Indian treatise on buddha nature, in which Maitrīpa's *Ten Verses on True Reality* and Sahajavajra's commentary are repeatedly adduced in support of Sūtra Mahāmudrā. As the *Ten Verses on True Reality* and its commentary are intimately interwoven with the so-called *amanasikāra* (nonconceptual realization)[1] cycle of Maitrīpa's works, I embarked on a follow-up research project on Maitrīpa, and prepared a critical edition and translation of the amanasikāra cycle. The result of my endeavor was published in 2015 by the Austrian Academy of Sciences Press under the title

A Fine Blend of Mahāmudrā and Madhyamaka: Maitrīpa's Collection of Texts on Nonconceptual Realization (Amanasikāra).

Having realized the importance of Maitrīpa for the Kagyü schools and given the notorious understatement and even neglect of his contribution in the Western reception of Mahāmudrā, I felt compelled to make my translation and analysis of Maitrīpa's amanasikāra cycle more accessible and spread it to a broader audience. This new contribution on Maitrīpa in the Lives of the Masters series will also serve the more practice oriented, as Maitrīpa so elegantly blends Madhyamaka with Mahāmudrā approaches. In the spirit of Maitrīpa, the conceptual approach of the ascending tenet systems is reduced here to what is absolutely needed for a practitioner of Mahāmudrā: the effective deconstruction of any model of reality. As no such model has ever been found to withstand critical analysis, the only chance the yoginī or yogin has is then to leave all conceptual assessment of true reality behind and open up to a Mahāmudrā path of tantric creation and completion stage practice and/or directly realizing one's luminous nature in an immediate mind-to-mind transmission with the guru. Maitrīpa thus laid out a fascinating practice system that combines the profound Madhyamaka view of "nonabiding" or non-foundationalism (*apratiṣṭhāna*) with mainly *Hevajra Tantra*–based Mahāmudrā. In his *Presentation of Empowerment* (*Sekanirdeśa*), verses 29–31, Maitrīpa thus says:

> Not to abide in anything is known as *mahāmudrā*. . . .
> Effortless wisdom can be taken as inconceivable. Something "inconceivable"
> That one has been able to conceive cannot truly be inconceivable.
> Those who see suchness in accordance with Madhyamaka are fortunate,
> In that they realize true reality, provided that they are aware of it in a direct way.

Taking buddhahood to be truly free from mental elaboration, Maitrīpa interprets empowerment and the completion stage practice in the *Hevajra Tantra* in a way that allows one to identify the goal of buddhahood as coemergent joy at a moment that is entirely free from conceptuality. This unique tradition goes back to Saraha and was also practiced by Maitrīpa's Yogācāra teacher Ratnākaraśānti. It differs from the Kālacakra-dominated six dharmas of Nāropa and adds an often neglected yet important dimension to tantric Mahāmudrā in the Kagyü schools. Another refreshing point of his teachings is an element Maitrīpa inherited from Saraha's spontaneous songs of realization (*dohā*), namely, the immediate access to the true nature of mind. The possibility of such an instantaneous approach occasionally shines through the works of Maitrīpa and his circle. It is because Maitrīpa transmitted this spirit of the dohās to Marpa and Padampa Sangyé that the Kagyü schools continue to profit from a freshness that benefits numerous Mahāmudrā practitioners worldwide.

The main part of this book is a new analysis of Maitrīpa's amanasikāra cycle, which only ocassionally draws on a few of my previous papers listed in the bibliography. My translation of Maitrīpa's short life story from the *Dharma Treasure of the Drigung Kagyü* in the first chapter of this book (pp. 18–27) and Maitrīpa's main literary work, the amanasikāra cycle, in the third part (pp. 149–309) are reproduced with permission and thanks to the Austrian Academy of Sciences Press. My translations of the main part of the *Destruction of Wrong Views* (*Kudṛṣṭinirghātana*) and the first part of the *Presentation of Empowerment*, which I did not include in the Austrian Academy book, are also published here, so that the present publication contains for the first time a complete English translation of the amanasikāra cycle. Since the present publication aims to make Maitrīpa's life, philosophy, and works accessible to a general readership, I have removed brackets from my translations wherever possible and have avoided including transcriptions or alternative readings. I have also removed all asterisks indicating Sanskrit names or titles that were back translated from Tibetan, with the exception of the bibliography. Such information can be found in my Austrian Academy book for those who are more scholastically adventurous. It should also be noted that many of Maitrīpa's teachings include tantric instructions, which traditionally require receiving proper initiations and explanations from a qualified Buddhist teacher.

I would like to take the opportunity here to express again my sincere gratitude to Venerable Thrangu Rinpoche, who assisted me in my research and translation of the Maitrīpa texts continuously, whether in Kathmandu, Sarnath, or the West. Many thanks also to Philip Pierce (Nepal Research Centre) and Michele Martin (Buddhist Digital Resource Center) for reading parts of the manuscripts and improving my English.

Maitrīpa

Introduction

In this world, in the land of the Victorious One (i.e., India),
You are famous like a second buddha.
You are like a crown jewel on my head,
The victory banner of the never waning teaching.

Worthy recipient of universal worship and offering,
Banner of renown, your pleasing voice
Reaches all directions.
Are you not the venerable master Maitrīpa?

Your lotus feet, I respectfully touch.
Having drunk the elixir [of your teaching,]
I realized the pinnacle of the view, Mahāmudrā,
The natural state beyond extremes.

All my qualities have become thoroughly complete,
Untainted by any fault.
This is what the emanation of the Sugata in human form,
The noble being Marpa taught.[2]

THESE VERSES from Tsangnyön Heruka's (1452–1507) *Life Story and Songs of Milarepa* most fittingly introduce Maitrīpa (986–1063),[3] revered by the Kagyü schools as one of their most important Indian lineage holders. The name Maitrīpa, as this Indian master is usually referred to in Tibetan sources, is derived from vernacular Maitrīpā, which is a short form of Sanskrit Maitrīpāda ("Venerable Love"). It is the name Maitrīpa is said to have received during his ordination from Ratnākaraśānti (ca. 970–1045).[4] Sometimes his ordination name is also given as Maitrīgupta instead of Maitrīpāda.[5] In Indian texts, we more often find Maitrīpa's secret tantric name, Advayavajra, though.[6] Finally, Rāmapāla calls his teacher

Maitreyanātha—as found in the *Commentary on the Presentation of Empowerment* (*Sekanirdeśapañjikā*)—and in the *Pith Instructions on the Sublime Continuum* contained in the *Collected Works of the Kadampa*, Maitrīpa also goes by Maitreyanātha.

Maitrīpa is revered for standing in a lineage of transmission that goes back to the great Brahmin Saraha (ca. tenth century),[7] whose teaching and spontaneous songs of realization reached Maitrīpa through the tantric Nāgārjuna and mystical Śavaripa.[8] Later Tibetan doxographers referred to Saraha's songs as Essence Mahāmudrā, as they enable qualified disciples immediate access to the true nature of mind. This is considered possible through a direct mind-to-mind transmission of the guru's blessing, as expressed in a verse by Saraha that Śavaripa sang when granting Maitrīpa tantric empowerment:

> When the natural mind has been purified,
> The guru's qualities enter your heart.
> Realizing this, Saraha sang this song,
> Though he had not seen a single tantra, a single
> mantra.
> When the guru's words have entered your heart,
> It is like seeing a treasure in the palm of your hand.[9]

Such a direct introduction to one's true nature beyond tantra and mantra, or Essence Mahāmudrā, is considered challenging to practice and thus embedded in a gradual path based either on sūtras or on the tantric practice of the generation and completion stages.[10] In his *Twenty Verses on True Reality* (*Tattvaviṃśikā*), Maitrīpa thus says:

> To those unable to know
> The level of self-empowerment as it really is,
> The path is taught in gradual steps
> Toward the attaining of enlightenment.[11]

All life stories of Maitrīpa describe the hardships India's yogi of nondual bliss and emptiness underwent to obtain the extraordinary teachings of Śavaripa. Only after interrupting his career as a scholar at Vikramapura[12] did Maitrīpa meet his guru Śavaripa, or rather Śavaripa appeared to him several times in a supernatural way in the mountains of the central Indian Deccan. Śavaripa finally gave Maitrīpa empowerment and Mahāmudrā teachings and sent him back to teach in the north Indian monastic milieu. Pawo Tsuklak Trengwa (1504–1566) writes in his *Dharma History: A Feast of the Learned Ones* that at this time the king of Magadha venerated Śavaripa's disciple, calling him the great master Maitrīpa. Tsuklak Trengwa further reports that afterward, Maitrīpa composed in Jvālagiri Monastery his most crucial literary oeuvre, the amanasikāra cycle.[13]

In this cycle, Maitrīpa blends Śavaripa's Mahāmudrā with his favored Madhyamaka philosophy of nonabiding (*apratiṣṭhāna*), which aims at radically transcending any conceptual assessment of true reality. This goal is achieved by "withdrawing one's attention" (amanasikāra) from anything that involves the duality of perceived and perceiver. This is clear from Maitrīpa's *Justification of Nonconceptual Realization* (*Amanasikārādhāra*), namely, where amanasikāra is explained as a nonaffirming negation:

> In the case of amanasikāra, too, it is what is applicable—namely, mental engagement (*manasikāra*) resulting in something perceived, a perceiver, and the like—that is negated by the privative *a*, and not the mind itself.

Maitrīpa, however, takes amanasikāra not only in this ordinary sense of mental nonengagement but also analyzes the compound *a-manasikāra* as "luminous self-empowerment." In doing so, he understands the privative *a* as denoting luminous emptiness, with which one directly engages (*manasikāra*) in a nonconceptual way. This, in any case, is the conclusion in the *Justification of Nonconceptual Realization*:

> Moreover, *a* stands for the word "luminous," and *manasikāra* for the word "self-empowerment" (*svādhiṣṭhāna*). It is both *a* and *manasikāra*, so we get *amanasikāra*. Because of that, the words *a*, *manasikāra*, and so forth, refer to the inconceivable state of being luminous and the one of self-empowerment.

Maitrīpa thus introduces to the practice of not becoming mentally engaged a Mahāmudrā component (luminous emptiness) that allows him to continuously refrain from any form of reification and stabilize his nonconceptual realization of emptiness. In other words, amanasikāra not only means to refrain from projecting wrong notions (such as an independent existence or characteristic signs) onto anything arisen in dependence, whether *skandha*s, *dhātu*s, or *āyatana*s,[14] but also a sustained realization of the luminous nature of mind. This is what Maitrīpa intends when he says in *Ten Verses on True Reality*, verse 5, that phenomena are realized as luminous. Sahajavajra comments:

> What is called natural luminosity is self-awareness, in view of its being naturally free from stains. One may ask, How does one see the phenomena of true reality, whose nature is such a suchness? Therefore, Maitrīpa said, "through the *samādhi* of realizing true reality for what it is." The latter is a path that features śamatha and vipaśyanā united as a pair.[15]

Maitrīpa's collection of Mahāmudrā and Madhyamaka works was called the "amanasikāra cycle" with the above double meaning of amanasikāra in mind.

Blending Mahāmudrā and Madhyamaka

Even though elements of Sūtra Mahāmudrā must have been transmitted by Maitrīpa—this is most clear from Sahajavajra's commentary on the *Ten Verses on True Reality*—Maitrīpa mainly presents Mahāmudrā in a tantric context, namely, as the third seal (*mudrā*) in a sequence of four seals, which Maitrīpa introduces in *A Presentation of Empowerment*, another essential text of the amanasikāra cycle that explains empowerment on the basis of a sequence of the four seals:

> Having approached a *karmamudrā*,
> One should meditate on the *dharmamudrā*.
> Hereafter comes *mahāmudrā*,
> From which the *samayamudrā* arises.[16]

The tantric path outlined in this sequence is effectively initiated with the help of a *karmamudrā*. This first seal involves intercourse with an actual consort in order to generate a sequence of four joys, i.e., joy, supreme joy, coemergent joy, and the joy of no-joy, which provisionally helps to identify the goal of the path through such an artificially created image of coemergent joy. A good definition of karmamudrā is found again in Rāmapāla's commentary on Maitrīpa's *Presentation of Empowerment*:

> It is called action (*karma*) seal (*mudrā*) because in as much as it has the nature of the coemergent, it is the seal, i.e., the stamp, mark, of action, i.e., of the activity of body, speech, and mind. It is precisely woman who is expressed by the term action seal, because that term is used with synecdochal meaning, due to a metaphorical usage based on the fact that she is the physical support of that (the action seal, i.e., the four joys).[17]

Rāmapāla then explains the *dharmamudrā* as the only means of supreme joy, the *dharmadhātu*, which has the nature of nonabiding that comes from analysis.[18] The great seal (*mahāmudrā*), the technical term for the goal of buddhahood, is equated with the Madhyamaka view of nonabiding in *A Presentation of Empowerment*, verse 29, which is achieved by refraining from any reification. The nonconceptual character of *mahāmudrā* is most clear from Rāmapāla's commentary:

> Then, given that it impresses its seal (*mudrā*) on the three other mudrās, *mahāmudrā* is both great (*mahā*) and a seal. It is beyond analysis,[19] and its nature is nonabiding. It is made manifest by the diligent and continuous cultivation of the wisdom of the path. It is nonexistent (i.e., lacks an own nature), free of the hindrances of the knowable, and the basis of everything perfect. It has the identity of cyclic existence and nirvāṇa as its nature, consists of universal compassion, and has the unique form of great bliss.[20]

The convention seal (*samayamudrā*), the fourth seal, is by its nature the manifestation of the tantric *sambhogakāya* and *nirmāṇakāya*.[21] This sequence of the four seals provides the frame for both the third and fourth empowerments and the completion stage practice in the Yoginī Tantras. In *A Presentation of Empowerment*, Maitrīpa further claims that practitioners do not properly know his Mahāmudrā teachings of the four seals as long as they have not touched the dust on Śavaripa's feet:

> As long as they have not touched
> The dust on Lord Śavara's feet,
> They do not know
> The four seals and the four moments.[22]

This strongly expresses the inconceivable nature of Mahāmudrā realization, of which only a reflection shines through during the technical yoga practices of the sequence of gradual stages.

To go by Rāmapāla's commentary, Maitrīpa combines in his *Presentation of Empowerment* the tantric system of the four seals with the sūtra teachings of the *Magic Formula for Entering the Nonconceptual* (*Avikalpapraveśadhāraṇī*), the *Ornament of Manifested Wisdom* (*Jñānālokālaṃkāra*), and the *Ornament of Realization* (*Abhisamayālaṃkāra*) or the *Sublime Continuum*, and thus with thc Maitreya works.[23] In other words, Mahāmudrā is linked with the view of nonabiding and the practice of becoming mentally disengaged. This means that one refrains from abiding or getting fixed in any conceptually created extreme, such as the inherent existence of locally determined phenomena, by continuously withdrawing one's attention from such notions. Such an extreme state of nonconceptuality can only be sustained by a blissful Mahāmudrā realization of one's true nature of mind, which is clear from the tantric meaning of amanasikāra as luminous self-empowerment. The resulting bliss can only be stabilized by also realizing its emptiness. Otherwise, it will be reified as an object of desire and become a cause of suffering. This blend of Mahāmudrā and Madhyamaka considerably contributed to integrating the new teachings and practices of the Siddhas into mainstream Buddhism.[24] It is against this background that I call Maitrīpa a Master of Mahāmudrā and Emptiness.

Traces of Sūtra Mahāmudrā

Maitrīpa transmitted his Mahāmudrā-*cum*-Madhyamaka system not only to Marpa Lotsāwa (1012–1097) but also to Réchungpa (1084–1161), who studied with Maitrīpa's disciple Rāmapāla.[25] Padampa Sangyé (d. 1105), another disciple of Maitrīpa, called his teacher's Mahāmudrā system the "calming of suffering." The calming of suffering teachings were transmitted in three cycles.[26] Of particular interest is the last one, which Gö Lotsāwa Zhönnu Pel (1392–1481) characterizes in his *Blue Annals* as follows:

> The teachings of the later [calming of suffering] transmission were called "Cycle on the Method of the Drop of Stainless Mahāmudrā." The term *mahāmudrā* denotes here the very Mahāmudrā system of Maitrīpa, because Padampa Sangyé had been a personal disciple of Maitrīpa. "Stainless" refers to genuine teachings. "Method" means that there is a path of realization that slightly differs from the other instructions. [Padampa Sangyé] called it the pāramitā system in essence and in accordance with the secret mantra system. In the commentary on Maitrīpa's *Ten Verses on True Reality*, too, this tradition is found [and described to belong to] the pāramitā system; its conduct, which accords with the Secret mantra system, is similar to explanations in the *Hevajra Tantra*. Since it is not based on deity yoga and lacks the sequence of the four seals, [Sahajavajra] taught that it does not belong to the secret mantra system. It is evident that [the system of Padampa Sangyé] is in accordance with this.[27]

This points to an essential feature in the Kagyü schools, namely, sūtra- or pāramitā-based Mahāmudrā. Gö Lotsāwa Zhönnu Pel thus claims that Maitrīpa's system contains a form of Mahāmudrā that works outside of the strict tantric system of creation and completion stages. In other words, pāramitā-based Mahāmudrā was not an invention of Gampopa (1079–1153), as Sakya Paṇḍita (1182–1251) claims, but has an Indian origin within Maitrīpa's circle. The works of Maitrīpa and his disciples thus figure prominently in a controversy some Kagyüpas had with Sakya Paṇḍita. This is clear from the following passage in the *Blue Annals*:

> The basic text of this Mahāmudrā of ours is the *Treatise on the Sublime Continuum of the the Great Vehicle* (*Mahāyānottaratantraśāstra*) by the Venerable Maitreya. Phakmo Drupa in turn said the same thing to Jé Drigungpa (1143–1217), and for this reason many explanations of the *Treatise on the Sublime Continuum of the the Great Vehicle* are found in the works of Jé Drigungpa and his disciples. In this connection, the Dharma master Sakyapa (i.e., Sakya Paṇḍita) maintains that there is no conventional expression for *mahāmudrā* in the pāramitā system, and that the wisdom of *mahāmudrā* is only the wisdom arisen from empowerment. But in the *Entering True Reality* (*Tattvāvatāra*) composed by the Master Jñānakīrti it is said: "As for someone with sharp faculties who practices the *pāramitā*s diligently, by performing the meditations of calm abiding and deep insight, he becomes truly endowed with the *mahāmudrā* [already] in the state of an ordinary being; and this is the sign of the irreversible [state attained] through correct realization." And the commentary on the *Ten Verses on True Reality* composed by Sahajavajra clearly explains a wisdom that realizes suchness as possessing the following three particular features: in essence it is the pāramitā [system], it accords with the mantra [system], and its name is Mahāmudrā. Therefore, Götsangpa (1189–1258), too, explains that Jé Gampopa's pāramitā [system-based] Mahāmudrā is in line with the assertions of the master Maitrīpa.[28]

The Eighth Karmapa Mikyö Dorjé (1507–1554) lists three Tibetan receptions of Maitrīpa's amanasikāra cycle: (1) Mantra Madhyamaka, (2) Sūtra Madhyamaka, and (3) Madhyamaka of False Aspectarian (Alīkākāra)–Cittamātra.[29] The first two were transmitted by both Marpa Lotsāwa Chökyi Lodrö and Milarepa, though it was mainly Maitrīpa's cycle transmitted as Sūtra Madhyamaka that

Gampopa emphasized and spread. Gampopa called it *mahāmudrā*, but Mikyö Dorjé warns that the term *mahāmudrā* usually is reserved for the wisdom of bliss and emptiness in the mantra system, claiming that the calm abiding and deep insight of Sūtra Mahāmudrā should not be mistaken for the exemplifying and actual wisdoms of the unsurpassable mantra system.[30] It should be noted that Mikyö Dorjé's "Sūtra Madhyamaka reception of Maitrīpa's amanasikāra cycle" is referred to as Mahāmudrā by Gampopa. In the *Great Chariot* (*Shing rta chen po*), Mikyö Dorjé stresses that Mahāmudrā realization requires the tantric context of empowerment:

> These days, [so-called] Mahāmudrā realization,
> In the mountain solitude of Tibet,
> Is the current discursive form of awareness only.
> It depends on the study of and reflection on scriptures and
> reasoning
> And arises in the mind-stream
> Thanks to pointing-out instructions by the lama.
> . . .
> As for [genuine] Mahāmudrā realization,
> It is the distinguishing feature of Great Yoga.
> Other than that, it occurs upon accomplishment,
> Through the triad of empowerments,
> Vows, and conduct, and the like,
> How could Mahāmudrā be known?
> [Certainly not] through verbally or symbolically pointing out
> That one's mind is merely emptiness.[31]

Still, in support of Gampopa's *Discourse on the King of Meditation* (*Samādhirājasūtra*)-based Mahāmudrā, Mikyö Dorjé refers to the same passages from Jñānakīrti's *Entering True Reality* and Sahajavajra's commentary on it as does Gö Lotsāwa Zhönnu Pel. The way Gampopa reads Mahāmudrā into the *Discourse on the King of Meditation* follows Sahajavajra's commentary on the *Ten Verses on True Reality*, where a group of verses from the *Discourse on the King of Meditation*[32] are quoted, backing up Sahajavajra's Mahāmudrā pith instructions. The verses in question[33] teach that notions (*saṃjñās*), which Sahajavajra equates with characteristic signs (*nimittas*)[34] do not arise, are pure and of an inconceivable nature. This accords well with what Sahajavajra says about Mahāmudrā. Sahajavajra further points out that the inconceivable nature of this purity is equivalently expressed in *A Presentation of Empowerment*, verse 30.[35]

In his *Single Intent* (*Dgongs gcig*) commentary, Mikyö Dorjé expresses his concern about Zhönnu Pel's position on the matter of justifying Sūtra Mahāmudrā on the basis of Maitrīpa's *Ten Verses on True Reality*. Indeed, he accuses the Fourth Shamarpa Chökyi Drakpa (1453–1526) of uncritically following Zhönnu Pel:

> Later on Yizang Tséwa (i.e., Zhönnu Pel) said: "The Mahāmudrā maintained by the lord Nāropa is the Mahāmudrā of bliss and emptiness. The Mahāmudrā maintained by master Maitrīpa is the Mahāmudrā of the true nature [of mind]. The Mahāmudrā of bliss and emptiness is good Mahāmudrā. The Mahāmudrā of the true nature depends on it, and thus is a little inferior." Not being independent himself, our Shamarpa, Chökyi Drakpa, imitates him (i.e., Zhönnu Pel).[36]

Whether Maitrīpa taught Sūtra Mahāmudrā remains a contested issue, but Gö Lotsāwa Zhönnu Pel's definition of it as pāramitā system that accords with the mantra system finds support in Sahajavajra's commentary on Maitrīpa's *Ten Verses on True Reality*, a text that figures prominently in the amanasikāra cycle.

In other words, Sahajavajra introduces a form of Mahāmudrā

that differs from both the pāramitā system and the mantra system. The very possibility of Sūtra Mahāmudrā grew out of developments of the late phase of Indian Buddhism, when monastic communities started to integrate more readily elements of tantric Buddhism from the milieu of the Siddhas, which required empowerment (*abhiṣeka*) and subsequent tantric practices. Certain elements of these practices made an ordained practitioner choose between strictly following the monastic rules or profiting from the new, powerful, and effective techniques of tantric Mahāmudrā. Whether Maitrīpa and/or his disciples taught Sūtra Mahāmudrā or not boils down to the question whether advanced practices that are on par with tantric completion stage practices were considered possible without formal tantric empowerment, or at least the critical stages of it. In the Tibetan Buddhist mainstream, the second and third empowerments were replaced with less offensive ritual elements.[37] Sūtra Mahāmudrā, even though contested, helps to legitimize this substitution process.

Essence Mahāmudrā

Standing in the transmission lineage originating from Saraha, Maitrīpa should have also inherited aspects of Mahāmudrā that enable an immediate or sudden approach to enlightenment. In his commentary on the *Jewel Garland of True Reality*, Maitrīpa's disciple Vajrapāṇi distinguishes such a possibility from a gradual path:

> In order that sentient beings of inferior intellect may realize [true reality], I shall summarize all tenets on true reality, writing down just a little. But first of all, there are two types of persons, the monkey-like and the crow-like. The monkey-like enters upon [true reality] gradually, whereas the crow-like enters upon it instantaneously. It is in consideration of those who enter upon [true reality] gradually that the three

> vehicles are presented. These are the Śrāvakayāna, Pratyekabuddhayāna, and Mahāyāna.[38]

Summarizing these different approaches, Kongtrul Lodrö Tayé (1813–1899) distinguishes in his *Treasury of Knowledge* (*Shes bya kun khyab mdzod*), besides the generally accepted Mantra Mahāmudrā, a Sūtra Mahāmudrā and an Essence Mahāmudrā. Moreover, Kongtrul's disciple Tashi Chöpel claims that originally Mahāmudrā was a path of its own, only meant for those with sharp faculties, but when it was eventually combined with either sūtras or tantras, it became a helpful practice for many more.

Life

CHAPTER 1

Translation of Maitrīpa's Life Story

ONE OF THE OLDEST Tibetan records of Maitrīpa's life is contained in the *Great Dharma Treasure of the Glorious Drigung Kagyü Tradition.*[39] According to the present Chetsang Rinpoche, the main part of this collection must have been already compiled under the direction of the seventeenth Drigung abbot, Künga Rinchen (1475–1527).[40] Maitrīpa's life story is the first text[41] in a compendium called *A History of the Twenty-Five Texts of the Amanasikāra Cycle.* It is followed by the amanasikāra texts themselves, most of them introduced and summarized at the end of each text, and a topical outline with notes taken by Bumla Bar.[42] In the same volume we find a hitherto unknown subcommentary on Sahajavajra's *Commentary on the Ten Verses on True Reality* (*Tattvadaśakaṭīkā*) by Tipi Bumla Bar.[43] Butön Rinchen Drup (1290–1364) mentions in his "record of received teachings" a certain Drabo Bumpa Bar, and in the *Blue Annals* we find one Drao Bumla Bar,[44] who was one of the seven men from Ü and Tsang to receive Mahāmudrā teachings from Maitrīpa's disciple Vajrapāṇi (b. 1017).[45] Since I could not identify any other Bumla Bar, it is possible that the author of Maitrīpa's life story was a disciple of Vajrapāṇi, who was personally acquainted with Maitrīpa. The content is very similar to another old Tibetan Maitrīpa biography from the thirteenth century,[46] an English translation of which was published by Marco Passavanti.[47] The unique features of the Drigung biography include a description of Maitrīpa's previous incarnation Jvālapati and the circumstances under which Maitrīpa received empowerment from Śavaripa.[48]

Translation of Maitrīpa's Life Story in the *Dharma Treasure of the Drigung Kagyü*

In a former life, this venerable master Maitrīpa [was Nāgārjuna's disciple Jvālapati].[49] One of the two students of the teacher Nāgārjuna was Nāgabodhi.[50] Belonging to the *brahmin* caste, he was more potent in meditation and thus instructed to meditate. [The other student,] Jvālapati, was of *kṣatriya* caste and, therefore, instructed to explain [the Dharma] that tames sentient beings. Jvālapati then taught the Dharma, and through his practice, an extraordinary power arose in him. Since there were heretics on an island in the ocean, he thought to tame them and requested his teacher Nāgārjuna. The teacher replied: "Bring a vase full of water from the river Gaṅgā!" He brought it, and Nāgārjuna took a drop from this water just once and said: "Generally speaking, the entire Buddhist Dharma is like the river Gaṅgā. What I know resembles a vase full of it. What you know is like a drop of water. The time to tame the heretics has not come. Do not go!"

Not listening, Jvālapati and three servants left. They reached the shore of the ocean, and Jvālapati moved floating over the water just like that. Dhanarati thought: Now if I [simply] follow the teacher moving over the water, I will fall behind. He whispered the mantra of his chosen deity on a handful of soil and threw it onto the water. In doing so, he parted the sea and walked on the dry ocean ground. The teacher said: "You are a siddha. Since it is not proper to keep you as my servant, you must return!" The disciple requested: "My siddhis, indeed, have arisen from you the teacher. May I, therefore, be your servant!" [Jvālapati] replied "Do not proceed by all means and return!" And sent him back.

Then Jvālapati took the two [servants] Dhanga and Singdhapali and left. They reached the island of the heretics, and when it was time to eat, they took the fruit. A yoginī[51] said: "Are you not yogins? Perform the practice of making [the fruit] fall on its own!" Jvālapati brought down the fruit with a fixed gaze. When she caused the fruit to move up the tree again, floating and descending, her mother came and said: "Do not mistreat him, this noble being, and offer him the fruit!"

At this time, many paṇḍitas, who were engaged in study, had loaded many books on an elephant, and the yoginī sang the following song: "What is the use for you of carrying many texts? It is like in the example of the noble fruit and the bees. Attached to the external, you only find an image of what is essential. Now, what do you know at all?" Then she offered him the fruit with the words: "My fruit is this noble fruit: its three eyes are the three *kāya*s; its three edges are the three realms; and three sides indicate the withdrawal of one's attention from the three times." Jvālapati got angry and did not take the fruit. The yoginī got mad at him: "Being a male, you will win, so let us perform the practice of killing. I will first protect my body, and [then it will be my turn to] perform the practice of killing you. You must then protect your own body."

Jvālapati started, and nothing happened to her. Then, when she performed the practice of killing, he was suddenly raised from meditative concentration. His lungs, heart, and so forth came out of his mouth, and he died.[52] Jvālapati told his two disciples there, that having broken the command of the teacher, this was the result. Then he said: "Protect this corpse from being burned for seven days from now so that I can confess to the teacher with my mind." This yoginī over there went to the local king and said: "In our place, there is the corpse of a big dead yakṣa. If it is not burned, it will turn into a zombie after seven days and spread disease among the people all over the country." The king came, and [Jvālapati's] disciples could not even protect [the corpse] from being burned. Upon his return to this island, Jvālapati found himself without a body; without a chance of finding another body, he prayed to enjoy and practice what is essential for his next life. It is said that as a consequence of this, the teacher Maitrīpa was born.

In the Middle Country there was a town called Jhāḍakaraṇī. In it dwelled the brahmin father Nānūka with his wife Sāvitrī.[53] Maitrīpa was born as their son. He was handsome, excellent, liked by all, and naturally endowed with qualities such as insight and endeavor. When he was eleven years old, he rejoiced in the system of Brahmin with a single staff and became well learned in the entire heretical textual tradition, including the four great Vedas. In particular, at a place called Varendhrā,[54] he studied the Paninian grammar of Liṅgadeva for one year. Next, he debated with the venerable Nāropa at the Northern gate of Nālandā. Nāropa won, so Maitrīpa followed Nāropa and thoroughly learned Madhyamaka, Pramāṇa, and Prajñāpāramitā. He was given an empowerment of the secret mantra system and the secret name Rāgavajra. He studied the tantras and pith instructions.

Afterward, he studied for one year and mastered the tenets of the Mind-Only School under Ratnākaraśānti, who protected the eastern gate of Nālandā. Moreover, he studied both non-Buddhist and Buddhist Dharma under Jñānaśrīmitra. Then he requested the teacher Śāntipa (i.e., Ratnākaraśānti) to function as the preceptor, took higher ordination, and studied the Vinayapiṭaka for six years.

Thus he became a great and fully accomplished paṇḍita. Inclined to teachings of what is essential, he had internalized neither the *Pañcakrama*, which is a commentary on the father tantras, nor the *Caturmudrānvaya*, which is a commentary on the mother tantras (both were composed by the [tantric] Nāgārjuna).[55] [Maitrīpa] recited the ten-syllable mantra of Khasarpaṇa (a form of Avalokiteśvara), who has the essence of liberation;[56] he circumambulated [the statue of Khasarpaṇa] and made a prayer. Thereupon, Avalokiteśvara prophesied to him in a dream: "Hey paṇḍita, you do not have a peaceful, but wrathful nature. Go to the south, to Śrī Parvata! You will be looked after by the glorious Śavareśvara (i.e., Śavaripa), and your doubts of confusion will be dispelled."

Having met Sāgara on the way, they traveled together. In the land of Oḍradeśa[57] they searched for half a month but did not find [Śavaripa]. Having stayed for a year at a stūpa called Dhānyakaṭaka, they were told by Tārā: "Go from here for five days in the northwestern direction! The guru you are looking for will be there."

They went there and searched for ten days while living on fruits. Thinking that they had not met this noble being because they had not abandoned food, they stayed on a flat stone and fasted for seven days. Even though [Maitrīpa] met him in a dream, he searched but did not find him. He despaired and thought: "I will meet him in the next life. What is the use of this present existence?" When he was about to jump off a cliff engulfed by clouds, he was held back by the prince [Sāgara]: "You are not a heretic; committing suicide is wrong."

They went in search of him again and met him face to face at the place of encounter. [Śavaripa] said the following: "Seeing me, you will be liberated. Even if you do not see me, you will find liberation. Seeing me, you will be bound in saṃsāra. Even if you do not see me, you will be bound. Do not be obsessed by the desire to see me. Even if you see me, do not think you have." Then Śavaripa disappeared, and he searched again. At the place of symbolic teaching, there was a yoginī killing lice. The yoginī shot an arrow at a pig that came out of a thick forest, killed [the pig], and ate its flesh. The yoginī sang the following song:

From the dense forest that is the saṃsāra of the three realms
Came the wild pig of ignorance.

I shot the arrow of clear insight and killed the wild pig of
ignorance.
I devoured the flesh in an experience of nonduality,
And experienced its taste as great bliss.
I did not see any real flesh.[58]

Then she killed a deer and sang:

Born in the forest that is the saṃsāra of the three realms,
The deer of subject-object duality roams.
I shot the arrow of mahāmudrā,
And killed the deer of ignorance.

Then the yoginī disappeared. Still not convinced, Śavaripa sang the following song:

What has never been born
Will not die;
Nobody is bound by existence,
Or liberated from it.

The novice monk Sāgarasiṃha was without doubt and became a buddha without remainder. Śavaripa disappeared. Again [Maitrīpa] searched for the guru and at the place of testing the basis he found a yoginī giving Śavaripa a foot massage. Maitrīpa became jealous, and Śavaripa said: "I have the Buddha's intention, which is like the sky, and I will teach it to you." The yoginī said: "Sir, I am not sure whether he is a proper recipient. Do not teach him yet!" She hit Maitrīpa's head, pressed him down, and [Śavaripa] disappeared. Then, at the place of giving empowerment, Śavaripa held a golden vase in his hand and gave Maitrīpa an empowerment. Bal po Asu[59] said that after the empowerment, [Śavaripa] gave instructions on the four seals, but according to Tipupa, Śavaripa sang the following song of commitment (*samaya*):

> When the natural mind has been purified,
> The guru's qualities enter your heart.
> Realizing this, Saraha sang this song,
> Though he had not seen a single tantra, a single mantra.
> When the guru's words have entered your heart,
> It is like seeing a treasure on the palm of your hand.
>
> On the path of nonconceptual realization (*amanasikāra*)—
> mahāmudrā—
> Do not entertain any hopes for any fruition whatsoever.
> If you realize the true nature of mind by yourself, this is
> mahāmudrā.
> What appears in this way is nothing outside your own mind.[60]

The empowerment having been bestowed in such a way, Maitrīpa did not believe in it and harbored doubts. Sāgarasiṃha accepted immediately and sang the following song:

> The victorious Śavaripa, who abides on Śrī Parvata,
> The bow, the deer, and the pig are not real, but emanations.
> Like a full moon, they are beautiful in the eyes of the world.
> I rejoice in all these beings in the form of emanations.
> About what is wholesome and what are misdeeds,
> Do not rely on notions such as remedy and what is opposed
> to remedy.
> Your wisdom of self-awareness is powerful like a lion.

Still, Maitrīpa did not believe, and at the place for explaining the Dharma, [Śavaripa] explained it to him. He spoke a few words about the *Anāvila Tantra*, which is like the sky, the *Tantra of the Sum Total of Mysteries* (*Guhyasamāja Tantra*), which is like the ocean, the *Hevajra Tantra*, which is like wisdom, and the *Cakrasaṃvara Tantra*, which is like a blessing. Then he explained the Dharma of the dohās and so forth, and said: "Since you do not believe me and harbor doubts, you will not be a buddha in this life. You will be a buddha following a future prophecy by Vajrayoginī."

Maitrīpa then left the three mountains, went for a mile, got tired, and fell asleep at the base of a rock. As a consequence of this, he did not remember anything [of what had happened at Śrī Parvata] and prepared himself to commit suicide. Śavaripa came in the sky in front of him and asked: "Maitrīpa, what is wrong?" He answered, "I forgot everything and thought of committing suicide." Śavaripa said:

Advayavajra, Avadhūtīpa,
How is it possible to forget things that have not
arisen?
How is it possible to forget
Things that have not passed out of existence?
The primordial liberation of the three realms
Is obstructed by ignorance.
[Ultimate] *Cakrasaṃvara*, great bliss,
Is the nature of nonarising.

Thus Maitrīpa found realization. He reached an understanding of all outer and inner phenomena, including the three mountains, and described his view [to the guru for his assessment]:

All phenomena are empty.
Emptiness and compassion

Are not two, and this is the teacher.
Appearances of relative truth are the teacher.
Having investigated the meaning of the yoginī's [symbolic instructions]
I will find liberation in any case.

Moreover, he said:

I realize that the true state is natural, without mental engagement,
Without even a speck of recollection.
Now, I will not ask anybody anymore.

Then he returned home, and his fame spread everywhere. He became known as the teacher Maitrīpa who went to Śrī Parvata in the south, met the glorious Śavaripa, and is now in possession of a fantastic tenet based on nonabiding as view and nonconceptual realization as meditation.

At this time there was a heretical teacher called Matra Rudra who was surrounded by a following of great heretical teachers and two thousand heretical disciples. He defeated Buddhist paṇḍitas, one after the other, and took over their monasteries, and having come to Nālandā, he said to Maitrīpa: "If it is true that you have met Śavaripa, I will not prevail and so shall embrace your teaching. If I win, you shall not claim to have met Śavareśvara, and together with your following, you must bow to me."

For each of them, a huge throne was erected. On each side, there were thirteen people holding parasols. A great assembly consisting of the king, ministers, and the people gathered to witness the spectacle. To the non-Buddhist and Buddhist paṇḍitas who served as a witness, Maitrīpa presented four great propositions. Even though each of [the great teachers], who were headed by the heterodox teacher Sahajavajra,[61] challenged him, they found no way to confute him. The heretical teachers were fully convinced [by Maitrīpa] and said: "You may think the Buddha was great, but Maitrīpa here definitely is." The heterodox Sahajavajra offered up his retinue of two thousand followers including those holding parasols and all of them followed Maitrīpa.

Then, at the time of the anniversary commemoration of the Buddha, Śāntipa posted an announcement of a disagreement with Maitrīpa. Thinking that it was not appropriate to have a dispute with his former teacher Śāntipa, Maitrīpa did not debate, and many rumors spread that the tenet of Śavaripa did not match the reasoning of Śāntipa. The following day [Maitrīpa thought] he would be allowed to debate and so posted an announcement stating that he (i.e., Śāntipa) should come to debate. Everybody discussed this, and thrones were erected. Even though invited thirteen times, [Śāntipa] did not turn up. Everybody said that Maitrīpa was the winner, and half of the offering to Bodhgayā was given to him. Thus he became known as a sovereign master.

At this time, the students requested the teacher, whose view was that of Apratiṣṭhāna-Madhyamaka, to compose a treatise that teaches the unique subtleties of his tenet, which is at the peak of all tenets. Thereupon he wrote the *Jewel Garland of True Reality*.

Then, similarly, Maitrīpa enjoyed without obstruction the infinite sky of knowable objects. Surrounded by a hundred thousand sun rays of scripture and reasoning, he drove the owls of bad views far away, and at this time, the sun of the teaching alone was shining. It rose on the snow mountain of omniscient mind. Realization, wisdom, and energy—all three—were complete in his body. He spread the roar of essencelessness and emptiness in the ten directions. This is what the supreme lion of speech taught:

The lion who conquers the elephant of
Knowledge that arises through causes—this is my treatise.

The answer to the question of the reason for that is self-evident.

This concludes the translation of Maitrīpa's life story in the Dharma Treasure of the Drigung Kagyü.

CHAPTER 2

Conversion, Monkhood, Expulsion Stories, and Legacy

QUITE A FEW ELEMENTS of Maitrīpa's life are noteworthy. Having lost in debate with Nāropa, Maitrīpa did not follow the stages of a normal Buddhist career but became ordained only after his extensive philosophical and tantric studies. In this chapter, we will also have a closer look at the stories in some Tibetan sources about Maitrīpa's expulsion from Vikramaśīla Monastery. The expulsion story is absent in the only Sanskrit biography, and going by Indian sources, tantric practice, which also includes controversial elements, was much less a problem in Buddhist monasteries of Maitrīpa's time than described in some Tibetan material. His role as a Mahāmudrā master is often underestimated; this chapter concludes with a description Maitrīpa's legacy on the basis of the pertinent Tibetan historigraphical sources.

Conversion

Maitrīpa's life as a Brahmin must have been exemplary, the young man being described as excellent, naturally endowed with good qualities such as insight and endeavor, and handsome. He mastered Sanskrit and the four Vedas,[62] studied the Paninian grammar of Liṅgadeva, and received, from his eleventh year onward, high esteem in the Brahmin tradition with a single staff. It is difficult to say what made this successful young man turn to Buddhism.[63] From the available material, we can simply gather that he must have shown up at the northern gate of the famous Buddhist university of Nālandā, where he lost a debate with Nāropa. In those days, anybody could turn up at the gates of a monastic university and challenge the Buddhist doctrine in philosophical discussion. A defeat would have meant that everybody had to convert to the philosophical or religious system of the unbeaten challenger. This could have been the reason why Maitrīpa converted to Buddhism and started to study Madhyamaka, Pramāṇa, and tantra under Nāropa, receiving from this great Nālandā master the secret tantric name Rāgavajra. According to Padma Karpo, Maitrīpa did not follow Nāropa's order to practice with a consort in the forest, because he wanted to stay on in the monastery and continue his studies.[64] Gö Lotsāwa Zhönnu Pel informs us in his *Blue Annals*, however, that Maitrīpa had a wife called Gaṅgādharā, a daughter of the king of Malabar.[65] Mahākāla looked after Maitrīpa and brought him Gaṅgādharā as a consort. She became a wisdom *ḍākinī* and an accomplished tantric teacher in her own right.[66] The founder of the Shangpa Kagyü, the Tibetan yogin Kyungpo Naljor, is said to have presented her gold for having received instructions.[67]

Monkhood

One would expect that under these circumstances Maitrīpa took monk's vows relatively late, namely, as reported in the Sanskrit life story, after twenty-eight years of studying Buddhism and at least seven studying Brahmanical texts,[68] and not at the age of eighteen as Padma Karpo asserted.[69] According to the Sanskrit life story, Maitrīpa became a monk in the Saṃmatīya order when he reached the capital Vikramapura, presumably from Vikramaśīla.[70] The Tibetan life story from the Tucci Collection reports, however, that

Matitrīpa received ordination from Ratnākaraśānti in Vikramaśīla,[71] not Vikramapura.[72] After his late ordination as a Buddhist monk, Maitrīpa studied the three traditional baskets of Vinaya, Sūtra, and Abhidharma for four years, which is, at such a late stage of life, quite unusual, especially after his extensive Mahāyāna and tantric studies. However, this deviation from a stereotypical biography, if anything, makes the Sanskrit life story more trustworthy.[73]

Expulsion Stories

Some of the Tibetan historical literature contains different, to a certain extent even contradictory versions of Maitrīpa's expulsion from the monastery. It is noteworthy that neither the Sanskrit biographical source nor the Tibetan life stories in the *Dharma Treasure of the Drigung Kagyü* contain any such story. Harunaga Isaacson and Francesco Sferra opine that the Tibetan expulsion stories of Maitrīpa "have predominantly Tibetan sectarian concerns, and cannot be given much weight."[74] Karl Brunnhölzl oberseves that "records of expulsion from monasteries are almost stereotype features in many Tibetan biographies of great masters."[75] The earliest sources for the expulsion story are probably the Atiśa biographies, of which the earliest are from the middle of the twelfth century.[76] In the extensive biography of Atiśa, we find:[77]

> Venerable Atiśa had twenty monks gathered around him who acted as they liked accumulating unwholesome deeds. Among them in particular was Maitrīpa, whom Ratnākaraśānti accused of mistakes with regard to view, conduct, and fruition in a letter attached to a beam above a door. In order to atone for that he wrote the *Destruction of Wrong Views* together with the *Discourse on Dream* (*Svapnanirukti*) and the *Discourse on Illusion* (*Māyānirukti*). Moreover, Maitrīpa had

> been seen to secretly carry alcohol as a samaya substance for [his *yidam* practice of *Vajra*] *yoginī*.[78] Having been expelled [from Vikramaśīla Monastery], he did not use the door but walked through the wall. Atiśa then had doubts about the decision of expelling Maitrīpa.[79]

In his *Destruction of Wrong Views*, Maitrīpa situates his amanasikāra cycle within the more general Mahāyāna context of the six perfections (*pāramitā*). Even though the first five perfections of generosity, discipline, patience, diligence, and meditation may be performed automatically by those who are realized, they need to be intentionally performed by those who are still learning. Maitrīpa thus shows the necessity of conventional Dharma practice. Putting this text at the beginning of his cycle indeed protects the reader from faulty conduct. A gradual path is also laid out in the *Discourse on Dream*, as the dream example is explained in the ascending tenet systems.

The early explusion story in Atiśa's biography is almost identical with the one of Atiśa expelling Kamalarakṣita. Brunnhölzl thinks that the two accounts became conflated later. In Padma Karpo's *Lotus Opening Sun that Teaches the History of the Dharma* (*Chos 'byung bstan pa'i padma rgyas pa'i nyin byed*) the reason for Maitrīpa's expulsion is rather a departure from his former Yogācāra teacher Ratnākaraśānti on philosophical grounds:

> There, in the country of Kapika, Maitrīpa upheld the Madhyamaka of Nonabiding, and Ratnākaraśānti False Aspectarian Yogācāra. Having discussed, Maitrīpa won. His teacher got angry, stripped off his robes, and threw them out of the door. Maitrīpa picked up some parts of his robe from a pile of sweepings in the doorway, and then stayed close by at the temple Pleasant Tārā praying for seven days

> to Tārā. In a dream at dawn a sixteen-year-old girl appeared, telling him: "Avadhūtipa! Do not stay here. Go to the east, where Avalokiteśvara dwells at Khasarpaṇa Temple. He will give you a prophecy." Then the girl disappeared.[80]

This marked the beginning of Maitrīpa's journey in search of Śavaripa. It seems the narrative element of Maitrīpa grasping a bit of his stripped-off robes stands for Ratnākaraśānti's unsuccessful attempt to disrobe Maitrīpa. In any case, Padma Karpo reports another event of expulsion, this time from Vikramaśīla, where Maitrīpa, so it seems, still had been a monk, and after his return from Śavaripa:

> After a long time Maitrīpa got drunk on the alcohol of the samaya substances. Being a disciplined monk, Atiśa saw this, became concerned about the decline of the order, and sent the king a letter. The king dispatched an envoy to investigate the matter. Having reported that there is a case, the king assembled scholars and went to Maitrīpa saying: "You must be removed for having drunk alcohol." Maitrīpa replied: "I have not drunk, but you all have drunk. Vomit and we will know!" Having been forced to vomit, Maitrīpa used a *Hevajra* pith instruction to make them vomit alcohol.[81] He himself vomitted milk. Maitrīpa gently walked unobstructed from the middle of the monks through a wall. He left Vikramaśīla floating on the Gaṅgā on an antelope skin. Everybody on the shore begged him to stay, but he did not accept.[82]

In the accounts of Pawo Tsuklak Trengwa and Tāranātha, the expulsion story occurs before Maitrīpa had left in search of Śavaripa and not after he had returned from the jungle to a monastic environment.[83]

That Ratnākaraśānti had accused Maitrīpa on doctrinal grounds, is, as we will see in the next chapter, plausible, but it is hard to see how a monk could be disrobed simply for holding an opposing Buddhist philosophical position. Indian Buddhist monasteries were very tolerant in doctrinal issues, as long as its monks abided by the monastic vows and refrained from splitting the Saṅgha. To be sure, Yoginī Tantras and their practice in themselves cannot have been something outrageous at Vikramaśīla Monastery at Maitrīpa's time. A palmleaf manuscript of a *Hevajra Tantra* commentary, which was written in the end of the twelfth century in an eastern Indian Māgadhī script, found its way to the Kaiser Library in Kathmandu.[84] The last folio of the manuscript tells us that it was an official copy for the monastic library at Vikramaśīla.[85] As the extensive commentary contains numerous secrets regarding performance, it is safe to say that this Yoginī Tantra (i.e., *Hevajra*), which is the main tantric source for Maitrīpa, was also practiced by the mainstream at Vikramaśīla. Moreover, in his *Abbreviated Empowerment Ritual* (*Saṃkṣiptābhiṣekavidhi*), Vāgīśvarakīrti writes that sexual intercourse is also permitted in ritual for monks if they see their partner as mind-only (*cittamātra*) and as identical in nature with a deity, and therefore feel no defiled desire for her. And Abhayākaragupta states in his *Vajra Garland* (*Vajrāvalī*) that if a monk is firmly convinced that all phenomena are like an illusion or a dream (i.e., are of the single taste of emptiness), there is no problem with him taking the *prajñā*-wisdom empowerment or secret empowerment.[86] In other words, Maitrīpa could have remained a monk while engaging in tantric practice. It is difficult to say, though, whether one would have been officially allowed an actual tantric consort in a monastery during this latest phase of Indian Buddhism. It is more likely that Maitrīpa engaged in practice with a consort on charnel grounds or while roaming the forests in eastern India.

Final Years and Legacy

There is not much known about Maitrīpa's last years. At the end of the Tibetan life story from the Tucci Collection, it is said that after he met Śavaripa and received from him instructions, Maitrīpa acted for the benefit of beings for thirty-nine years. During this time he taught a vast range of Mahāyāna teachings.[87] When feeling that his time had come, Maitrīpa told his student Vajrapāṇi to gather all the students and perform a tantric feast (*gaṇacakra*). He gave each student a blessed item and taught them his final, testamentary instructions. Rejecting his disciples' wish to stay on for many more years, he said: "I have the power to stay, but it is not appropriate, since I would then miss the time for accomplishing the [highest] siddhi [of Mahāmudrā]."[88] As Maitrīpa had initial doubts about Śavaripa's teaching, his guru prophesied that he would not attain the highest siddhi in this lifetime, but only in the intermediate state after having been received by Vajrayoginī.[89]

The Tibetan chronicles, such as the ones by Gö Lotsāwa Zhönnu Pel,[90] Pawo Tsuklak Trengwa,[91] and Padma Karpo,[92] record twenty-one Indian disciples. The four greater ones among them were Sahajavajra, Dīvakāracandra, Vajrapāṇi, and Rāmapāla. Sahajavajra recognized Maitrīpa's *Ten Verses on True Reality* as Pāramitā-based pith instructions in accord with the mantra system and distinguished in them a special Mahāmudrā path eventually called Sūtra Mahāmudrā. However, Dīvakāracandra elaborates in his *Elucidation of the Wisdom from a Prajñā* (*Prajñājñānaprakāśa*) that it is impossible to attain Mahāmudrā without the erotic bliss of karmamudrā practice.[93] Vajrapāṇi authored the *Instructions on the Stages Handed Down By the Lineage of Gurus* (*Guruparamparākramopadeśa*), in which he combines extensive commentaries on his guru's *Jewel Garland of True Reality* (*Tattvaratnāvalī*), *Summary of the Meaning of Empowerment*

(*Sekatātparyasaṃgraha*), and *Presentation of Empowerment* (*Sekanirdeśa*) into a gradual path that leads from study, reflection, and meditation of the four philosophical tenets to tantric empowerment and practice. Vajrapāṇi's text also provides the framework for my presentation of Maitrīpa's gradual path further down. Rāmapāla is mostly known for his extensive commentary on the *Presentation of Empowerment*, in which he defends his guru's uncommon interpretation of the *Hevajra Tantra* of putting coemergent joy in the third position in the sequence of four joys (a point we will come back to further down).

To sum up Maitrīpa's life and legacy, Tāranātha, who received Maitrīpa's lineage through Rāmapāla, provides the following positive comparison with Nāropa:

> At the time of elder brother Nāropa's demise, this professor's (i.e., Maitrīpa's) act of value for creatures had just begun. Compared with Nāropa, his reputation and his gathering of disciples were not large, yet his benefit to others, like lightning, was the greater. He had many disciples in India during his lifetime, but there were not so many afterward. They spread more widely in the north—in Nepal, Tibet, and so forth.[94]

Philosophy

CHAPTER 3

Between Yogācāra, Madhyamaka, and Mahāmudrā

ALL SOURCES AGREE that Maitrīpa abandoned his life as a monk-scholar in search of the siddha Śavaripa at a relatively late stage in his life. It was only after this turning point that he could write about Mahāmudrā and Madhyamaka the way he did, namely from a position of having realized the subject matter directly. It is of interest that he still held Yogācāra in high esteem. Not only does he present Yogācāra as a necessary step to his Madhyamaka of Nonabiding, but he also makes ample use of the more experiential terms of Yogācāra, such as self-awareness and luminosity, to describe and explain his realization. It is in this sense that we must understand Maitrīpa's claim in the *Explaining the Seals of the Five Tathāgatas* (*Pañcatathāgatamudrāvivaraṇa*) that a Madhyamaka tenet based on self-awareness is supreme. To be sure, Maitrīpa does not reify emptiness, awareness being, like anything else for him, subject to dependent origination.

All this accurately reflects Maitrīpa's early exposure to Yogācāra and Madhyamaka doctrines, which he coordinated in his amanasikāra cycle, probably under the influence of Śavaripa. Ratnākaraśānti, Maitrīpa's old Yogācāra teacher, and Nāropa were famous paṇḍitas, both entrusted with the vital duty of gatekeeper of this great Buddhist center of learning. One thus wonders whether Nāropa's Madhyamaka and Ratnākaraśānti's Yogācāra were considered compatible tenets at Nālandā, and whether a synthesis of the two was the mainstream, with a certain degree of tolerance toward scholars leaning more to the one or other camp. In the Tibetan life stories, Maitrīpa is said to have eventually abandoned his reluctance to challenge his former teacher, Ratnākaraśānti, in debate, for fear that Śavaripa's Dharma would be considered unable to counter Ratnākaraśānti's reasoning. In other words, it is mainly according to the Tibetan tradition that Maitrīpa eventually had issues with his former teacher's Yogācāra.

As for tantric Mahāmudrā, Maitrīpa is entirely in line with Ratnākaraśānti's presentation of the sequence of the four moments in empowerment, in that both take *vilakṣaṇa* to be the third moment, thus understanding it in the sense of "freedom from defining characteristics."[95] In other words, Ratnākaraśānti and Maitrīpa disagree with the majority of scholars, such as Kamalanātha, Abhayākaragupta, Raviśrījñāna, and Vibhūticandra, who put vilakṣaṇa in the fourth position. Maitrīpa also lines up with his Yogācāra teacher, again against the mainstream, in holding that the goal of buddhahood is marked in the third position as coemergent joy. Still, Maitrīpa's understanding of correctly ascertaining the third moment involves not only the realization of nondual awareness (i.e., the Akṣobhya seal or Yogācāra emptiness), but also the simultaneous ascertainment of this awareness as being empty of an own nature (i.e., the Vajrasattva seal or Madhyamaka emptiness). For Maitrīpa, Yogācāra tenets are necessary steps and helpful if presented in such a way that their temporary realizations can be further refined in accordance with Madhyamaka. In other words, as the third joy marks the goal of buddhahood, it not only needs to be sealed by the Akṣobhya seal of nonduality but also the Vajrasattva seal of realizing that nondual joy is also empty of an own nature.

In Ratnākaraśānti's buddhology, Yogācāra is at the core, though. He even goes so far as to read an idealist position into Nāgārjuna's Madhyamaka.[96] In his commentary on *Hevajra Tantra*,[97] Ratnākaraśānti thus quotes Nāgārjuna's *Sixty Verses on Reasoning* (*Yuktiṣaṣṭikā*), verse 34, in support of his idealist position:

> Such things spoken of as the great elements
> Are contained in consciousness.
> They disappear in wisdom,
> Being indeed falsely imagined.[98]

Moreover, Ratnākaraśānti reads his Yogācāra interpretation of the three natures into the *Main Verses of the Middle Way* (*Mūlamadhyamakakārikā*):

> That which is dependent origination—
> That we call emptiness;
> The latter is dependent designation.
> This is the right middle path.[99]

Ratnākaraśānti equates dependent arising with the dependent nature (*paratantrasvabhāva*) and emptiness with the absence of imagined nature (*parikalpitasvabhāva*). This kind of emptiness still allows for an existing remainder, namely, the dependent in the form of false imagining, and it is this type of Yogācāra emptiness that still has the capacity to designate and make the dependent nature appear as skandhas:[100]

> Nāgārjuna taught [in his *Main Verses of the Middle Way*]: "That which is dependent arising—that we call emptiness. The latter is dependent designation. This is the right middle path." That which is dependent arising (i.e., the dependent nature)—in it the imagined nature does not exist. How should there then be a misplaced denial of dependent arising? Dependent designation, too, is dependent arising.

> When false imagining (*abhūtaparikalpa*) exists, the skandhas of appropriation and so forth are designated/imputed by it. This is the idea. The verse "That which is dependent arising . . . this is the right middle path" is meant in this way. Nothing that is of an imagined nature exists, but what has a dependent nature is not nonexistent. Therefore, this system is called the middle path. It is because of these appearances of nonexistent duality that false imagining exists; and given its existence, it also exists in that which is empty of duality (i.e., the perfect nature).[101] This establishes the three-nature theory. It is thus settled that the imagined nature does not exist, whereas the dependent is not nonexistent. And this is the middle path. Because some do not accept the existence of false imagining, we must reply that everything would then be a falsity.[102]

To be sure, the dynamic process of the dependent nature, which is responsible for false duality having manifested, is real in this Yogācāra system. The *Analysis of the Middle and Extremes* (*Madhyānta-vibhāga*), Ratnākaraśānti's often quoted source, describes the entire process of dependent arising, or the dependent nature,[103] as false imagining.[104] In Yogācāra, there is no external world apart from that, wherefore everything is but a product of false imagining. This translates into an ontological distinction between an only nominally existing (*prajñaptisat*) imagined nature, which emerges from a substantially existing (*dravyasat*) dependent nature.[105]

Ratnākaraśānti does not take Nāgārjuna's move from dependent arising to emptiness and back to dependent designation in the sense that everything exists only nominally (*prajñaptisat*). To be sure, in the eyes of Ratnākaraśānti, emptiness only negates the imagined nature, and not the substantially existing (*dravyasat*) dependent nature. On this point, Ratnākaraśānti follows the *Analysis of the*

Middle and Extremes, in which a saṃsāric state of mind is said to function as false imagining when enriched with mental imprints. False imagining thus exists and causes within itself the manifestation of the unreal imagined nature.[106] Candrakīrti, however, deconstructs this ontological distinction between the imagined and dependent, and presents the three natures in his autocommentary on the *Entering the Middle Way* (*Madhyamakāvatāra*)[107] as the conclusion to his refutation of arising from other:

> A snake, for example, is imagined on the basis of a dependently arisen coiled rope, for there is no snake in it, while the perfect is found in what the snake actually is (i.e., the rope), inasmuch as it is not imagined. Likewise, an own nature is imagined on the basis of what is dependent, (i.e., created). An own nature, however, is not created, for it is said [in the *Main Verses of the Middle Way*]:
>
> > An own nature is not artificial; it does not depend on something else.[108]
>
> > What is imagined on the basis of something created—something like a perceived dependently arising reflection—is [only] real insofar as it is the experiential object of a buddha, because then it is not imagined. A buddha is so named because he awakens to the [true nature of entities] alone, since he actualizes, without touching created entities, their own nature directly.[109] A correct understanding of the presentation of the three natures called the imagined, dependent, and perfect, having thus been facilitated, the intention of the [related] discourses must be explained. Since neither the perceived object nor the perceiving subject exists as something different from the dependent, the fact that these two (i.e., the perceived and the perceiver) are imagined must be understood in terms of their being the dependent[110] [nature].[111]

In other words, both the perceived object and the perceiving subject are imagined and dependent at the same time.[112]

Unfortunately, Ratnākaraśānti does not address this directly in his writing, but since he was doctrinally close to the *Analysis of the Middle and Extremes*, it is difficult to see how he could have accepted this. In the colophon of his *Instructions That are an Ornament of the Middle Way* (*Madhyamakālaṃkāropadeśa*) we find, though:

> [Ratnākaraśānti] was the greatest among the four gatekeepers [of Vikramaśīla] during his time, because he faultlessly realized the real intent of Ārya Asaṅga and Nāgārjunagarbha and clarified their teachings most excellently. The monk Candrakīrti and others deviated from Nāgārjuna's intent and abandoned nihilism and composed commentaries on the profound tantras later in their life.[113]

Ratnākaraśānti thus did not view Candrakīrti's philosophical works in high esteem, and Maitrīpa would have challenged his former teacher on these grounds, had Ratnākaraśānti accepted Maitrīpa's invitation to debate. If the account of Maitrīpa's challenge is accurate (and it is neither mentioned in the Sanskrit biography nor the Tibetan one from the Tucci Collection), Ratnākaraśānti and his disciples would have been forced to adopt Maitrīpa's Madhyamaka of Nonabiding and accept it as superior to Yogācāra.

CHAPTER 4

Sudden versus Gradual Paths

HAVING BEEN not only empowered and instructed by Śavaripa but also ordered by this legendary great siddha to teach, Maitrīpa mustered the necessary authority to teach Mahāmudrā as a realized guru. Saraha's central message that the only meaningful practice is to directly access one's *sahaja*-bliss, or wisdom, shines through the works of the amanasikāra cycle. In his *Twenty Verses on True Reality*, Maitrīpa thus explains that a direct approach to Mahāmudrā is possible for those with sharp faculties. In contrast, practitioners of inferior or average faculties must rely on more traditional forms of tantra, such as practicing with a consort (*karmamudrā*).

The possibility of a sudden realization harbors the danger of overestimating one's realization and cultivating wrong views, such as that one does not need to engage in generosity and the other initial perfections, which Maitrīpa calls "initial activity" (*ādikarman*). The annotated list of amanasikāra texts from the *Dharma Treasure of the Drigung Kagyü* thus contains the short note that Maitrīpa composed the *Destruction of Wrong Views* to show that a conventional Dharma practice must not be neglected.[114]

The way Maitrīpa deals with the conventional gradual path is exquisite. First, everybody, of course, needs to unfold the initial activity of the first five perfections of generosity, discipline, patience, diligence, and meditation. However, when realized, or as Maitrīpa puts it, when on the level of no more learning (i.e., the level of a buddha), this happens automatically without effort. If this does not occur, one is still in need of learning on the path of accumulating merit and wisdom. In his *Destruction of Wrong Views*, Maitrīpa further elaborates on initial activity in terms of the daily routine of an excellent adept (obviously still on the level of learning). One thus starts the day by taking refuge, avoiding the ten unwholesome deeds, washing one's face with clean water, recalling the three jewels, mantra recitations, and meditation. The meditation includes the visualization, worship, and praise of a maṇḍala of the five buddha families with Akṣobhya in the center. Through these many details, Maitrīpa shows the necessity of conventional Dharma practice.

The amanasikāra cycle is thus embedded within the more general Mahāyāna context of the six perfections, or the causal vehicle of the sūtra path. Maitrīpa describes in the *Destruction of Wrong Views* an extreme performance of the perfections, such as even giving one's own life. He calls it "mad conduct" (*unmattavrata*)—that is, conduct that appears to be mad. In the *Ten Verses on True Reality*, Maitrīpa says that such is the conduct of a practitioner who moves at will, like a lion, on the strength of having realized true reality. Maitrīpa's fellow monks could have seen in such conduct transgressions.

Of interest also is how Vajrapāṇi, one of the four chief disciples of Maitrīpa,[115] writes, in the introduction to his commentary on Maitrīpa's *Jewel Garland of True Reality*, the four philosophical tenets and three vehicles were only taught for the benefit of gradualists, who are considered inferior:

> So that sentient beings of inferior intellect may realize [true reality], I shall summarize all tenets on true reality, writing down just a little. But first of all, there are two types of persons, the monkey-like and the crow-like. The monkey-like enters upon [true reality] gradually, whereas the crow-like enters upon it instantaneously. Thinking of those who enter upon [true reality] gradually, the three vehicles are

> presented. They are the Śrāvakayāna, Pratyekabuddhayāna, and Mahāyāna.[116]

Going by this explanation, Maitrīpa taught the gradual path of philosophical tenets and generation and completion stages as teachings of provisional meaning that offer rungs for those who need a ladder. In other words, Maitrīpa combines Essence Mahāmudrā with the sūtras and tantras to create easier gradual paths.

CHAPTER 5

Maitrīpa's Gradual Path

IN AN ATTEMPT to reconstruct the gradual path, Maitrīpa would teach, it is safe to say, a beginner should first gain a precise understanding of the four philosophical tenets. They are not only laid out in the *Jewel Garland of True Reality*, but are also addressed in the *Discourse on Illusion*, *Discourse on Dream*, and *Pith Instruction on Reality Called A Treasure of Dohās* (*Dohānidhināmatattvopadeśa*). The *Madhyamakaṣaṭka* discusses the Middle Way in the Yogācāra and Madhyamaka tenets, which feature significantly the role in the description of the five-buddha maṇḍala and the yoga of the subtle drops in empowerment and the completion stage practice. Vajrapāṇi wrote the *Instructions on the Stages Handed Down by the Lineage of Gurus*, a detailed commentary on the *Jewel Garland of True Reality*, the *Summary of the Meaning of Empowerment*, and the *Presentation of Empowerment*. A similar sequence is found in the *Compendium of Tenets* (*Sthitisamāsa*) by Sahajavajra, another of the four chief disciples of Maitrīpa.

A Canonical Source and the *Jewel Garland of True Reality*

In his *Half-Metrical Commentary on True Reality, Which Teaches the Nonabiding of All Phenomena*,[117] a certain Avadhūtipa or Advayavajra[118] (likely Maitrīpa) quotes the *Discourse on the Illuminating Appearance of All Things Distinctly Without Departing from Their True Nature*,

Emptiness (*Āryadharmatāsvabhāvaśūnyatācalapratisarvālokasūtra*) in support of the superiority of the Madhyamaka tenet of nonabiding:

> Mañjuśrī, you asked whether all five ways of investigating phenomena are correct and whether some are correct and some others not. All of these five ways of investigating phenomena I consider right.
>
> Some think that we teach phenomena in the sense that all phenomena exist the way they appear. Why? Because the four elements and what is made up by them exist conventionally like an illusion.
>
> Or some think that we teach that phenomena are mind-only and that there are no phenomena apart from that. Why? By virtue of the fact that imprints of imputations of manifold phenomena that the mind constantly imagines are being placed in the mind, the latter always manifests distinct appearances of a self and phenomena. Still, ultimately they lack an own nature, for they are but mind-only.
>
> Or some think that we teach phenomena in the sense that mind itself has not arisen. Why? Because it lacks shape, color, the three times, as well as a border and center.
>
> Or some think that we teach phenomena to them in the sense that all phenomena manifest like an illusion and do not exist, just like an illusion. Why? Because all phenomena arise and emerge from causes and conditions.
>
> Or some think that we teach that all phenomena have not arisen in terms of their own nature, do not abide in terms of their own essence, transcend all extreme views on action and result, transcend concepts and their objects, and are the primordial qualities when mental elaborations are purified. Why? Because this is the unmistaken nature of all phenomena.[119]

In fact, the way this sūtra summarizes five ways of investigating phenomena is surprisingly similar to Maitrīpa's tenets, especially the last two Madhyamaka tenets of everything being like an illusion (*māyopamādvaya*) and nonabiding (*apratiṣṭhāna*), and can be rightfully considered a canonical support.

The *Jewel Garland of True Reality* not only describes the four tenet traditions but also summarizes the respective conduct and possible faults committed during meditation. This means that Maitrīpa does not want us only to study and analyze the different Buddhist models of reality, but also adopt the respective conduct and form of meditation. The majority of his audience in Nālandā and Vikramaśīla must have been well acquainted with the four tenet traditions, and reading Maitrīpa's description of them mainly served to refresh the subject matter, a memory of one's previous understanding after years of study and debate. Such must have been the preparation for tantric study and practice outlined in Maitrīpa's texts on empowerment, and the creation and completion stage practices as well.

In other words, before successfully embarking on the tantric path, one would do well to update one's study, analysis of, and meditation on Buddhist philosophy, outlined along the ascending steps of the four tenet traditions of Vaibhāṣika, Sautrāntika, Yogācāra, and Madhyamaka, which gradually enable a finer, more profound understanding of true reality. Maitrīpa interestingly relates the Vaibhāṣika position to the paths of the śrāvakas and pratyekabuddhas, while including the Sautrāntika within the Mahāyāna.

The Vaibhāṣika Tenets

We are supposed to start our analytical meditation along the lines of the "Vaibhāṣikas of the West,"[120] by looking into one of the most severe obstacles cyclic existence poses: attachment to our body. Based on Śāntideva's fundamental Mahāyāna work on *Engaging in the Bodhisattva Deeds* (*Bodhicaryāvatāra*) we are encouraged to mentally separate the sack-like skin from our body and remove, with the scalpel of insight, the flesh from the skeleton. And indeed, one of the most effective ways to overcome bodily attachment is the cultivation of the repulsive, which rests on the certainty that the body is but a collection of feces, urine, semen, blood, phlegm, mucus, intestines, joints, and organs. Apart from remedying this coarse form of attachment, the existence of external objects, and the notion of a personal self are still accepted on the level of inferior and average śrāvakas. The tenet of the western Vaibhāṣikas is similar to the one of the Vātsīputrīya-Sāṃmatīyas, who maintain the existence of an inexpressible personal self, which is beyond both the conditioned and unconditioned.[121]

Other Buddhists widely criticized this position for its proximity to the *ātman* theory of a soul. Whatever the historical value of Maitrīpa's description, it makes sense to deal with the most pressing issue immediately—a beginner's destructive obsession with the body—before addressing the more philosophical problems surrounding the notions of external matter and a personal self. In other words, during the time a beginner is mainly occupied with the cultivation of the repulsive, it is enough to simply abandon the notion of a permanent personal self without excluding also the possibility of an inexpressible self beyond permanence and impermanence. This latter possibility is still accepted by average śrāvakas, whose meditation practice is focused on exhaling and inhaling. Concerning the process, the latter are cautioned not to become senseless through breath retention.

An inexpressible self beyond permanence and impermanence is then excluded on the next level of analysis, namely that of superior śrāvakas, the Vaibhāṣikas from Kashmir. As one concentrates now on the four noble truths, the view of emptiness in the sense of lacking a personal self must be cultivated. This cultivation constitutes the noble truth of the path. In contrast, the first three truths are the recognition that suffering is the nature of the five skandhas, that the arising of this suffering is a mental construct. That cessation is deep insight (vipaśyanā). As one ascends the levels of śrāvakas, one increasingly feels drawn to work for the sake of others. Maitrīpa reports that notwithstanding some who claim that inferior śrāvakas attain the awakening only of a śrāvaka because of their fixed potential and lack of compassion, there is also the position that all of them will be buddhas. Going by the way things are presented, Maitrīpa prefers the thought underlying buddhanature (even though he never uses this term in his writings) over the traditional Yogācāra theory of fixed potentials, which exclude śrāvakas from the possibility of becoming a buddha. At this level, the practicing śrāvaka is able to cultivate the first two of the three types of compassion, namely, the ones created by focusing on sentient beings' suffering of suffering and suffering of change.

Pratyekabuddhas

The pratyekabuddhas resemble the superior śrāvakas. They share the same realization of emptiness, even without a teacher. If the description of this vehicle is more than just for the sake of doxographical completeness and thus taken as a further step on a gradual path, at this point, one mainly controls body, speech, and mind through a meditation of calm abiding. The risk of this practice is to get trapped in the meditative bliss of a mind close to falling asleep and a mind that is fast asleep. In the first case, one falls away from Buddhism into the Vedānta system of Bhāskara, and in the latter into the Vaiśeṣika mode.

The Sautrāntika Tenets

The summary of the Sautrāntika position heralds the presentation of the Mahāyāna systems. Once the level of a Sautrāntika is attained, conduct is henceforth characterized by the six perfections. This means that one trains in the perfections of generosity, discipline, patience, effort, and meditation in a state of perfect insight (*prajñāpāramitā*). At this point, one not only cultivates compassion but also wishes to take along sentient beings that have the potential for it to buddhahood. Just as in Yogācāra, Sautrāntikas believe that different groups of sentient beings have different potentials or even no potential for spiritual development at all. Even though this concept renders the Sautrāntika and Yogācāra vehicles inferior, they belong to Mahāyāna, inasmuch as the group with a bodhisattva potential already consists on its own of an incalculable number of sentient beings. To include this single group in one's aspiration qualifies as Mahāyāna *bodhicitta*.[122]

The underlying analysis includes now, for the first time, a comprehensive deconstruction of the entire external world into accumulations of momentary subtle atoms, whose continuous flows give the wrong impression that there are such things as permanent objects. Being too remote to be directly accessible to perception, one takes them, on the Sautrāntika level, as only being able to produce a cognition that consists of a mental form of the object. In support of this position, Dharmakīrti asks in his *Commentary on Valid Cognition* (*Pramāṇavārttika*), how a momentary thing could be perceived when the cognition of it occurs at a different time. In other words, the moment the mental form of an object is produced, the object may exist differently, or not at all. Even though the periods involved are on an entirely different scale, the situation can be compared to the perception of the stars in the night sky, whose light has traveled thousands or even millions of years before reaching our eyes. Even though we naively assume that stars in the night sky exist as we see them, some of them may have already exploded into a supernova or fallen into a black hole a long time ago.

Because of such an analysis, one's attention is withdrawn from the mental form of experiential objects. But when the mind turns to itelf it does not find anything either. Maitrīpa speaks of meditation through a mind realizing no-mind. This prepares the ground for the Yogācāra analysis and meditation, in which all external appearances are recognized as the vibrant radiance of one's mind. The realization that external objects are impossible triggers a process of deconstruction that also leads to the abandonment of a perceiving subject and, eventually, all reifying notions.

Up to the Sautrāntika level, we have still accepted momentary, yet independent material and mental factors of existence that constitute body and mind. This raises the question of how these two ontological categories interact in order to form the functioning complex of our psychophysical existence, or more simply, how is it possible that mind perceives matter. Either mind and matter are both denied inherent existence and only accepted as relational or complementary in a dynamic process of dependent arising (as in Madhyamaka), or one accepts only one fundamental category: mind.[123] The doxographical unfolding of tenets requires us to investigate the latter option, the system of Yogācāra.

The Yogācāra Tenets

On this level, one must ponder the question of how something material that exists independent of mind can cause a mental representation of it in one's mind. If mind and matter existed as two independent categories, how could they interact? This is admittedly a Madhyamaka argument, because, in Abhidharma and Yogācāra, conditioned factors of existence are attributed in their momentary existence an own nature (*svabhāva*) and still interact. The Yogācāras inherited from the Ābhidharmikas the notion that factors of existence have an own nature because they do not depend on parts for their existence.[124] Still, the Yogācāras claim that even if external matter existed in terms of atoms and the like, it could never transmit a representation of itself into the mind, let alone become a direct object of perception. In other words, something mental can only have a mental cause.[125]

Maitrīpa divides Yogācāra into Sākāravijñānavāda ("the tenet that [everything is] consciousness accompanied by mental forms") and Nirākāravāda ("the tenet that [consciousness] is without mental forms"). Sākāravāda is not further divided. At this point, Maitrīpa simply explains that the mind bears the forms of the complex world without any external correlate at all, it being free from any relation of perceived object and perceiving subject. In Sākāravāda, the mental forms are as real as the mind itself. Quoting Vasubandhu's crucial argument against material atoms,[126] the learned audience is expected to recapitulate Vasubandhu's line of reasoning in support of the *Discourse on the Ten Bodhisattva Levels* (*Daśabhūmikasūtra*) statement that the threefold world is mind only (*cittamātra*). The objection that there would then be no locally and temporally determined objects is addressed with reference to the dream example, and the perception of the same external world is explained through the simultaneous activation of a complex set of mental imprints that a group of sentient beings share due to their similar former intentional deeds.[127] As imprints of a specific group ripen, they mutually strengthen each other and become capable of creating a common environment. Human beings thus share the collective imprints for the manifestation of drinking water. For a fish, however, water must be what the troposphere is for land animals, for hungry ghosts water manifests as puss and blood, and for gods as nectar. In other words, there is no such thing as an ultimately existing body of water with inherent qualities. What one experiences depends on one's mental imprints or seeds. In his *Twenty Verses* (*Viṃśikā*), Vasubandhu claims that the Buddha, in reality, meant mental seeds and the cognitive content emerging from them, when he taught the sense spheres (*āyatanas*, i.e., sense faculties and their respective objects) to the śrāvakas:

> The perception, which manifests an image of matter, emerges from its own seed as soon as it has reached a specific state of transformation. This seed and the mental form it manifests, the Illustrious One taught as the sense spheres of the eyes and matter, respectively. The same goes for all types of perception up to the perception, which manifests the semblance of something tangible. This seed and mental form it displays, these two the Illustrious One taught as the sense spheres of the body and the tangible, respectively. This is the intent.[128]

This Yogācāra hermeneutics is accompanied by the deconstruction of any possible model of reality for an external material world. A whole is not accepted because it could never be more than its parts. A smallest indivisible atom cannot be found, because its spatial arrangement with other atoms, which is necessary in order to form gross visible objects, yields six parts, namely, the sides of the atom facing other atoms in the four cardinal directions along with the top and bottom sides.[129] This is, in fact, what Maitrīpa wants us to remember when he quotes the *Twenty Verses*:

> The instantaneous union of a subtle atom
> With six [others shows that] it has six parts.[130]

As further support of the idealist Yogācāra position, Maitrīpa quotes again Dharmakīrti, who questions in his *Commentary on*

Valid Cognition the necessity of external objects to account for the display of mental forms. Without mental forms, one would not know anything about an external world, and even when there are mental forms—one does not need external objects[131] for them to emerge:

> If the mind has forms of something blue or the like,
> What is then the justification for an external object?[132]
> If the mind does not have forms of something blue or the like,
> What is then the justification for an external object?[133]

Based on such reasoning, the meditation on the level where mind is still taken to have real mental forms (Sākāravijñānavāda) is centered on the direct actualization of the mind beyond the duality of perceived and perceiver, yet together with its numerous forms. To be sure, although the mental forms are accepted as real as the mind itself, one avoids construing them as external objects perceived by an internal subject. The danger at this level is to follow a tenet maintained by the proponents of Vedānta, namely the Bhagavatsiddhānta, which means taking the world as a transformation of, and thus as not different from, *brahman*, in the form of one's own ultimate and permanent mind.

After that, on the level of Nirākāravāda, mental forms come under scrutiny as well. The whole world is now again realized as mind only, but this time mind is self-awareness beyond mental forms. The meditation of the Nirākāravādins is to actualize wisdom[134] directly, without appearances—which is nondual inconceivable bliss free from mental fabrication. There is the danger, however, of cultivating the wrong notion of a permanent, self-aware consciousness, which is devoid of both appearances and mental fabrication. In this case, one would be following the Vedānta tradition of Bhāskara.

The Madhyamaka Tenets

Maitrīpa sees in these two types of Yogācāra analysis and meditation a necessary step toward Madhyamaka. To some extent, this reflects his development from Ratnākaraśānti's False Aspecterian Yogācāra to his favored Madhyamaka of Nonabiding. In a traditional Indian way, he did not turn directly against the position of his former teacher, but integrated Yogācāra as a meaningful preparation for Madhyamaka, a strategy Paul Hacker called inclusivism.[135] In an analytical approach, Madhyamaka tenets outshine, in the eyes of Maitrīpa, the lower Mahāyāna tenets of Yogācāra, because the latter cannot thoroughly remove subtle forms of superimposition, such as an ultimately existing nondual mind. Maitrīpa divides Madhyamaka into Māyopamādvayavāda ("the tenet of nonduality that conveys the sense that everything is like an illusion") and Apratiṣṭhānavāda ("the tenet of not abiding in any extreme").

The Madhyamaka of Nonduality in the Sense that Everything Is Like an Illusion

Nonduality (*advaya*) in the tenet name *māyopama-advaya* ("like an illusion-nonduality") means that everything shares the same ontological status of being like an illusion, there being no second category that would constitute a duality. Emptiness in Māyopamādvaya is now not only the absence of a perceived and perceiver or mental forms but includes a nondual mind as well. In his *Six Verses on the Middle Path* (*Madhyamaṣaṭka*), verses 3–4, Maitrīpa says that the followers of the Māyopamādvaya still maintain mere clarity or awareness. In the *Treasure of Dohās* (*Dohānidhi*), verse 10, the self-awareness of this first Madhyamaka system is beyond the four extremes, though; there, the abandonment of self-awareness is called nihilism and a stain on meditation. Thus it seems that the object of negation does not differ from the preceding tenet of False

Aspectarian Yogācāra. Still, since the four extremes of a tetralemma formed with existence and nonexistence are negated, self-awareness in Madhyamaka must be taken as being neither existent nor nonexistent, nor a combination of both, nor neither one nor the other. In comparison, in both Yogācāra tenets, self-awareness truly exists. In his *Jewel Garland of True Reality* presentation of Māyopamādvayavāda, Maitrīpa tells us to avoid the extreme of existence, otherwise the complex world would truly exist the way it appears. According to the Tibetan translation of this phrase, we need to focus only on the present moment of the world, without taking past and future into account. This recalls Nāgārjuna's refutation of motion, namely, that motion has ceased in the past and not yet started in the future. However, motion in the present moment alone cannot be construed in a meaningful way.[136] Nonexistence is excluded because (again, according to the Tibetan translation of the *Jewel Garland of True Reality*) appearances manifest through the power of mental imprints.

The Madhyamaka of Nonabiding

This leads to Maitrīpa's ultimate tenet, the Madhyamaka of Nonabiding (Apratiṣṭhānavāda), which aims at radically transcending any conceptual assessment of true reality. This goal is achieved by withdrawing one's attention from anything conceptually created.[137] Philosophically this amounts to the Prāsaṅgika attitude of avoiding postulating anything of one's own.[138] No model of reality works without flaws. So our only chance is to refrain from any form of reification, be it superimposition or wrong denial. In the *Saptaśatikā Prajñāpāramitā*, we find a passage with the past participle *apratiṣṭhita* ("not fixed/placed"), which Rāmapāla quotes in his commentary on the *Presentation of Empowerment* to illustrate the close relation between the grammatically related negated noun *apratiṣṭhāna* ("nonabiding") and the Mahāmudrā practice of amanasikāra:

> The Ilustrious One asked: "When you, Mañjuśrī, cultivate (i.e., meditate on) the perfection of insight, on what do you rely?" Mañjuśrī answered: "Illustrious one, when I cultivate the perfection of insight, I do this without being fixed (*apratiṣṭhita*) on anything." The Illustrious One asked: "Mañjuśrī, what is the cultivation of the perfection of insight for you who are not fixed on anything?" Mañjuśrī answered: "Illustrious One, this precisely is the cultivation of the perfection of insight (i.e., the nonabiding in anything)."[139]

The practice in Apratiṣṭhānavāda is amanasikāra. As we have already seen above, for Maitrīpa, the term *amanasikāra* not only means "withdrawing one's attention" or "not becoming mentally engaged" but also self-empowerment within luminous emptiness. This presupposes the direct insight of a state free from superimposition and wrong denial. It is in view of this that Maitrīpa favors the Madhyamaka "tenet of not abiding in any phenomena." Not to abide in any phenomena means that there is no ground in any phenomenon upon which the latter can be reified in any conceivable way. This goal is achieved by intellectually refraining from projecting wrong notions, such as an own nature or characteristic signs, onto anything arisen in dependence, whether skandhas, dhātus, or āyatanas.[140] Philosophically, this amounts to the Prāsaṅgika attitude of not postulating any position of one's own, as maintained by a number of Tibetan masters, such as Chomden Rikpé Reldri (1227–1305), Barawa Gyeltsen Pelzang (1310–1391), Taktsang Lotsāwa (1405–1477), Khédrup Jé (1385–1438) and Ju Mipham Namgyel Gyatso (1846–1912).[141]

Maitrīpa accepts dependent arising as a mere appearance, which is free from mental fabrication. This includes any notion of a locally determined factor of existence. In other words, one cannot single out from the interdependent world any smallest building block with a clear-cut borderline and independent existence. If such factors of existence (*dharmas*) were taken in terms of an own nature (*svabhāva*), their arising and passing out of existence would be impossible.[142] The open, dynamic process of dependent arising presupposes the absence of a *svabhāva* in any of the involved components. In a Tibetan commentary on the *Jewel Garland of True Reality*, probably written by Vajrapāṇi's disciple Tipi Bumla Bar,[143] the apparent and ultimate truths are taken as aspects of the same true reality:

> The goal of comprehension is the two inseparable truths. As for true reality, it is appearances in their entirety—namely, the mind—and what is simply beyond all mental fabrication. The appearance aspect of it is what is called "apparent truth" and the aspect of it that is free from mental fabrication is called "ultimate truth." And these two are connected with one another to the point of constituting an identity, just as what is created and what is impermanent are.[144]

This is also clear from Maitrīpa's *Elucidation of Nonabiding* (*Apratiṣṭhānaprakāśa*), where the arising of phenomena is inconceivable but not negated altogether:

> The very arising of phenomena is inconceivable,
> Even through original awareness.
> This very arising is called emptiness,
> Without falling into [the extreme of] nihilism.[145]

This points to the seeming contradiction in Nāgārjuna's *Main Verses of the Middle Way*, where dependent origination is prominently endorsed in the initial homage to the Buddha, yet described as not arising from self, other, and so forth:

I pay homage to him, the best of all teachers who, fully
awakened,
Taught dependent arising as being without cessation and
arising;
Without annihilation and eternity; without one thing and
many things;
And without coming and going—that is, the auspicious
pacification of mental fabrication.

Nowhere are any things found that have arisen
From themselves, something else, a combination of both, or
without a cause.[146]

Some have argued that the initial homage is a later addition and not by Nāgārjuna. Maitrīpa's understanding resolves the seeming contradiction by taking dependent origination as an inconceivable dynamic process that is beyond, in Nāgārjuna's words, one thing and many things. This means that dependent origination cannot be broken down into locally determined causes and effects, so that an arising from self, other, or a combination of both, or without a cause, is excluded. Dependent origination thus refers to complex open systems emerging from similarly complex systems. This calls into question our common-sense view of a universe built up from locally determined real entities. In this regard, Niels Bohr came to the conclusion that "isolated material particles are abstractions, their properties being definable and observable only through their interaction with other systems."[147] The interdependence of dependent origination is best compared to entangled systems, whose components cannot exist independently, inasmuch as they share, upon measurement, the same state of polarization or spin, for example.

One may argue that these discoveries in quantum physics, impressive as they are, do not have any bearing on the macroscopic scale of daily life. It should be considered, however, that everything is made up of subatomic particles. A lot of quantum effects may cancel themselves out on macroscopic or even mesoscopic levels, but Matthieu Ricard reckons, with regard to the Einstein-Podolsky-Rosen paradox (i.e., entanglement),[148] that since all "particles" in the universe were tightly bound together in the singularity of the Big Bang, they could still be so now.[149] Such a universal entanglement could be, in fact, an intelligent way of interpreting the strange behavior of Foucault's pendulum. Léon Foucault hung a pendulum from the roof of the Panthéon in Paris in order to prove that the Earth rotates on its axis. It slowly seemed to change the direction in which it was swinging. But it always swung in the same direction; it was only the Earth that was turning. But what is motionless? After a few weeks, even the sun has moved slightly from the course of the pendulum's direction. Only the most distant galaxies did not drift away from the first plane of its swing.

In his dialogue with Matthieu Ricard, Trinh Xuan Thuan draws the conclusion that the pendulum's behavior depends on the entire universe, including the most distant galaxies.[150] In support of this conclusion, one could refer to the Austrian philosopher and physicist Ernst Mach, who declared that the amount of resistance to movement comes from the influence of the whole universe (Mach's principle). However, such interactions cannot be based on the exchange of energy, resembling as they do the interaction between entangled photons or electrons. Trinh Xuan Thuan concludes that "each part contains the whole, and each part depends on all the other parts."[151]

In yet another domain of inquiry well beyond the microscopic scale, neuroscience, the amazing synchronization of widely distributed assemblies of cortical neurons correlates with conscious processing. The neuroscientist Wolf Singer made the noteworthy prediction at the end of his presentation at the Vienna symposium

Mind and Matter: New Models of Reality,[152] "we shall have to make the same transition as physics did when extending classical physics to quantum physics." This involves thinking in terms of "self-organizing systems with non-linear dynamics and very high dimensionality, in which relationships in phase space[153] have the status of objects." Such a dynamic system of interrelatedness reminds one of the above-mentioned quantum states of entangled systems whose components do not exist in a locally determined way.

This calls for the introduction of a new concept of existence, one that does not require a locally determined entity with an "own nature," but a dynamic system of mutual interrelationship and interconnectedness. It is this absence of "own nature" (i.e., own nature) and "other-being" from the standpoint of dependent origination that is called emptiness. In keeping with Maitrīpa's philosophy, entities with an own nature would then be viewed as reified constructions of the mind, which simplify phenomena at the cost of misrepresenting their irreducibly complex interconnectedness. This perspective would not only conform to the Madhyamaka definition of the object of negation as "own nature" but also provide a model that can more readily accommodate the strange observations of quantum physics, and the anticipated transition or paradigm shift in neuroscience.

It is with this analysis in mind that one best understands Maitrīpa's refutation of the four ontological possibilities of reifying or denying the phenomenal world based on a tetralemma formed with the pair "existent and "not existent" (*ucchedin*). In his *Jewel Garland of True Reality*, Maitrīpa defines Māyopamādvaya Madhyamaka with the following tetralemma:

> The Mādhyamikas know true reality
> As being free from four positions, that is to say,
> True reality is neither existent, nor is it not existent, nor is it a
> combination

Of existence and non-existence,
Nor can it be that neither is the case.[154]

The first position "existent" is ruled out on the grounds that the manifold world would really exist as it appears. Given the power of its appearance, though, "not existent" does not work either. Tipi Bumla Bar's Tibetan commentary on the tetralemma in the next verse,[155] which is formed with the pair "eternal" (*śāśvata*) and "annihilated" (*ucchedin*), explains that the first position does not apply, for nothing is established in its own right.

The third possibility can be ruled out because the combination of two impossible positions is likewise unacceptable. Finally, the neither-nor part of the tetralemma does not apply, for this would be incomprehensible (*bodhābhāva*). For Maitrīpa, this does not negate an ultimate characterized as inconceivable bliss, wisdom or the like. In other words, we have here a fifth value of an inconceivable reality that is reached after refuting, on a semantic level, the four values of the tetralemma.[156] Needless to say that this harbors the danger of reifying emptiness as an ultimate category, and this is probably also the reason why Nāgārjuna and his followers avoided introducing anything ultimate beyond the tetralemma, even though they may have intended it. In any case, Maitrīpa repeatedly speaks of the realization of true reality beyond the four extremes of mental fabrication. This is clear from the *Twenty Verses on Mahāyāna* (*Mahāyānaviṃśikā*), where Maitrīpa adds into his introduction to his Mahāyāna presentation of the fruit the following explanation:

Knowers of reality know true reality,
Which is free from the four extremes.[157]

Such a true reality is, for example, taken as the luminous nature of phenomena in the *Ten Verses on True Reality*,[158] luminous emptiness in the final analysis of amanasikāra in the *Justification of Nonconceptual Realization*,[159] or the original/natural kāya (*nijakāya*), which is the nature of the three kāyas (sometimes equated with the *svābhāvikakāya*). In Maitrīpa's *Twenty Verses on Mahāyāna*, we thus find:

> The seeing of this natural kāya is deep insight (*vipaśyanā*),
> Given that nothing is superimposed.
> This will be explained now,
> In accordance with the mantra system.[160]

To see (without superimposition) the original kāya is then equated with knowing a reality, which is beyond the ontological possibilities expressed in the tetralemma. In the following verse of the Apratiṣṭhāna explanation in the *Jewel Garland of True Reality*, true reality is said to be known beyond conceptual analysis:

> The wise know the true reality of things
> As the nonabiding in anything.[161]
> Now, this is not just conceptual analysis, for a
> conceptualizing mind
> Does not know the nature of mind.[162]

Before elaborating on the positive description of this true reality as effortless wisdom in the fourth verse of the Apratiṣṭhāna portion, Maitrīpa cautions us one more time that all conceptual reification of it does not exist at all:

> All superimposition, whatever there is—
> All this does not exist in any respect;
> The meaning of Madhyamaka is thus the absence of
> superimposition;
> Where is, then, the denial or establishing of anything?

This effortless wisdom
Is called inconceivable;
Something "inconceivable" that one has been able to
conceive
Cannot truly be inconceivable.[163]

In his *Commentary on the Presentation of Empowerment* (*Sekanirdeśa-pañjikā*),[164] Rāmapāla explains inconceivable wisdom as follows:

> And that wisdom without fixed abiding is "inconceivable wisdom," which does not come through analysis, but rather is effortless, emerging in its own sphere.[165]

In other words, as long as one deconstructs mental elaboration on the path, the neither-nor lemma excludes any positive assessment beyond the extremes. However, on the level of the fruit, with a privileged access to true reality, inconceivable wisdom is disclosed as something primordially present. Maitrīpa summarizes his final Madhyamaka view of nonabiding, stressing this crucial point:

When free from all superimpositions,
True reality appears of its own accord.
Expressions such as emptiness,
Remove superimpositions from it.[166]

This is then also the meditation: to actualize without attachment the result of this analysis. The goal of being without superimposition, Maitrīpa warns us, is not a state of dull nothingness. Even though the revealed reality is inconceivable, it is described as a wisdom without fixed abiding. The related conduct is to practice the six perfections without superimposition. How this works is spelled out in the *Great Vehicle Discourse Called The Questions of Brahmaviṣeśacintin*

(*Brahmaviśeṣacintiparipṛcchānāma Mahāyānasūtra*), which Rāmapāla quotes in the Mahāmudrā section of his *Commentary on the Presentation of Empowerment*, in the context of explaining how to abandon reified characteristic signs through the practice of not becoming mentally engaged:

> Giving up all defilements is generosity;
> Being free from mental effort is discipline;
> Being free from defining characteristics is patience;
> Not making distinctions is diligence;
> Nonabiding is meditation;
> Being free from mental fabrication is insight.[167]

With a direct access to true reality, one is in the state of indivisible compassion and emptiness.

Once this nature of mind is directly realized, the practitioner naturally rejoices in the fact that everybody, including themselves, already possesses the amazing qualities of true reality. Feeling compassion for all sentient beings who have not yet realized their profound nature, the bodhisattvas try their level best to help others to discover their true nature. In other words, compassion and the related buddha activity unfold automatically upon the realization of emptiness, which is, in its direct experience, inconceivable wisdom. This is best understood against the backdrop of emptiness being inseparably linked to dependent origination. The factors of existence (*dharmas*) thus constitute in their interconnectedness true reality. In the *Discourse on the King of Meditation*, which is an important source text for Sahajavajra's Sūtra Mahāmudrā, these dharmas are eventually realized as *buddhadharmas* (i.e., Buddha qualities, such as wisdom and compassion).[168]

To put it another way, once it is understood that one's existence is in one way or the other interwoven in open dynamic systems, it becomes clear that one's own and everybody's goal of attaining enduring happiness is best served by helping others and not by singling out, and clinging to, a self, which is wrongly conceived of as existing independent of the rest of the world. Understanding oneself and the things and beings around us—not only in natural science but also society, ecology, or economy—as dynamic systems of mutual interrelationship will draw attention to our responsibilities as engaged, embedded agents. This is what Maitrīpa's spiritual forefather Nāgārjuna claims in his *Exposition of the Enlightened Attitude* (*Bodhicittavivaraṇa*):

> When yogins have cultivated
> This emptiness in such a way,
> Their mind will no doubt be devoted
> To the welfare of others.[169]

In his *Destruction of Wrong Views*, Maitrīpa explains that the first five perfections of generosity, discipline, patience, diligence, and meditation (i.e., "initial activity") are performed automatically by those who have nothing more to learn. In other words, once a yogin rises to the level of a buddha, their "initial activity" unfolds without effort. If this does not happen, they are obviously still in need of learning on the gradual path of accumulating merit and wisdom. The successive analysis and related forms of meditation and conduct precisely are such a gradual path.

CHAPTER 6

Nonconceptual Realization (Amanasikāra)

THE ORIGINAL MEANING of the term *amànasikāra*, "to become mentally disengaged," is already well attested in early Buddhism. During the Samyé debate, Kamalaśīla (ca. 700–750) used it as a label for the teachings of the Chan master Mo-ho-yen.[170] As we have already seen above, Maitrīpa combined the primary meaning of *amanasikāra*, "mental nonengagement," with his tantric interpretation of the term, in the sense of self-empowerment within luminous emptiness, thus adding to it the cognizant element of direct realization. This is clear from the *Justification of Nonceptual Realization*, where the compound's initial *a-* not only represents the simple negation of a privative *a*, but also stands for a profound Madhyamaka type of negation, such as nonarising or emptiness, which Maitrīpa also understands positively as luminosity. Such an interpretation, so Maitrīpa explains, requires taking amanasikāra as a compound in which the component *pradhāna* ("the main thing") between *a* and *manasikāra* has been dropped.[171] When it is understood thus—that one directs one's attention (*manasikāra*) to the letter *a* as the main focus—*a* can no longer be the simple privative, but must stand for a more profound negation, such as the one implied by emptiness or nonorigination (*anutpāda*). In other words, the first *Commentary on the Grammar Used in Vārāṇasī* (*Kāśikāvṛtti*)-based analysis indicates a second analysis of amanasikāra, in which *a* is taken in the sense of nonarising (*anutpāda*) or emptiness. We thus get "realization" (*manasikāra*) of emptiness (*a*),[172] and in Maitrīpa's final analysis, self-empowerment within luminosity, which is, for Maitrīpa, a synonym of emptiness.

This twofold analysis of amanasikāra is not a mere grammatical philosophical exercise but essential for Maitrīpa's Apratiṣṭhāna Madhyamaka. In order to be able to sustain a genuinely nonconceptual state through the absence of reification, one needs the enlightened bliss of directly realizing the nature of mind. In other words, one needs to complement the path of radical deconstruction through mental nonengagement with nonconceptual realization. With this double meaning, *amanasikāra* became Maitrīpa's favored description of both the practice and the goal of Mahāmudrā. This must have been also the intent of Saraha (or Śavaripa), when he equated mahāmudrā with amanasikāra in the *Mahāmudrā Instructions Called A Treasure of Dohās* (*Dohākośanāmamahāmudropadeśa*).[173]

In its long history, the practice of withdrawing one's attention has always been combined with the mental engagement or realization of something else. Thus, according to the *Lesser Discourse on Emptiness* (*Cūḷasuññatasutta*),[174] monks first need to attend to the solitude grounded in the notion of the forest, after becoming mentally disengaged from any notion of a village or human beings. Next, they abandon the notion of forest and attend to the solitude grounded in the notion of earth, until they have successively withdrawn their attention from the notions of the four spheres of infinite space, infinite consciousness, nothingness, and neither-perception-nor-nonperception. In a final step, the monks combined their practice of mental disengagement with the direction of their attention to a mind, which is beyond characteristic signs.[175] Even though these stages of meditation were initially considered a path of liberation, the mainstream of early Buddhism did not believe in a liberation without insight (*prajñā*) and thus rejected the soteric function of such steps of mental disengagement.[176]

In a way similar to the *Lesser Discourse on Emptiness*, the *Stage of the Listener* (*Śrāvakabhūmi*) of the basic section of the *Stages of Yoga Conduct* (*Yogācārabhūmi*) combines the withdrawal of attention from cognitive notions or characteristic signs (*nimitta*) with a certain type of mental engagement, namely, the directing of one's attention (*manasikāra*) to space or the like. Such a combination is found, for example, in the following passage from the third state of yoga (*yogasthāna*) of the *Stages of the Listener* (which is on the focusing of the mind):

> Becoming mentally engaged by focusing on the element of space as a remedy for clinging to forms is the mental engagement of employing a remedy. Withdrawing one's attention from any characteristic sign and directing one's attention to the sphere beyond characteristic signs is the mental engagement of focusing on the sphere beyond characteristic signs.[177]

In the nirvāṇa section of the *Compilation of Ascertainment* (*Viniścayasaṃgrahaṇī*), too, amanasikāra is combined with manasikāra: the *arhat* in nirvāṇa with remainder is said to become mentally engaged, experiencing the sphere beyond characteristic signs by becoming mentally disengaged, in the sense of not focusing on a single characteristic sign.[178] In the *Stages of Meditation* (*Samāhitā Bhūmi*), which is also contained in the basic section of the *Stages of Yoga Conduct* (*Yogācārabhūmi*), the practitioner performs śamatha meditation through amanasikāra during the nine stabilizations of the mind:

> How does one perform the practice of not being mindful

> and becoming mentally disengaged? By bringing the mind to rest within, and the like.[179]

In other words, one withdraws one's focus from characteristic signs already at an early stage of the path, either by directing one's attention (*manasikāra*) to the sphere beyond characteristic signs or simply by śamatha meditation.

In Mahāyāna, the negation of manasikāra is taken as an attribute of the Buddha, along with other negative predicates, such as the absence of thoughts, mindfulness, or cognitive objects.[180] This is at least what we find in the *Ornament of Manifested Wisdom*, a Mahāyāna sūtra that plays an essential role in the Indian commentary on the *Sublime Continuum*. Both the *Ornament of Manifested Wisdom* and the *Sublime Continuum*, as we will see further down, enable bridging the gap between Mahāmudrā and the amanasikāra of Maitrīpa's Madhyamaka. A further Mahāyāna source for that is the *Magic Formula for Entering the Nonconceptual*, in which four sets of "characteristic signs" (*nimitta*) are abandoned "by becoming mentally disengaged" (*amanasikārataḥ*).[181]

Similarly, in the *Distinguishing the Phenomenal World of Mental Representation from the True Nature of Phenomena*, the same four sets of characteristic signs are abandoned by cultivating nonconceptual wisdom.[182] This, however, requires one to become mentally engaged (*manasikāra*) by focusing on the mind, whose imprints cause duality, and by realizing the nonexistence of this duality in four steps.[183] The *Distinguishing the Phenomenal World of Mental Representation from the True Nature of Phenomena* even defines nonconceptual wisdom by explicitly excluding amanasikāra:

> As to the comprehension of the defining characteristics, [nonconceptual wisdom is known] by its specific characteristic, which excludes five points: amanasikāra....[184]

Vasubandhu makes it clear that nonconceptual wisdom is not merely amanasikāra; otherwise, the knowledge possessed by small children and fools would be nonconceptual.[185] Still, one could argue (as Gö Lotsāwa Zhönnu Pel did) that the abandoning of the four types of characteristic signs in the *Distinguishing the Phenomenal World of Mental Representation from the True Nature of Phenomena* must be understood against the backdrop of the *Magic Formula for Entering the Nonconceptual*; that is, the characteristic signs must be abandoned by becoming mentally disengaged.[186] The obvious solution to this problem is to see in the amanasikāra of the *Magic Formula for Entering the Nonconceptual* not merely a complete absence of mental engagement, such as the one found at times in small children or fools. This is clear from the following passage in the *Magic Formula for Entering the Nonconceptual*, where the path first requires "correct mental engagement" (*samyaṅmanasikāra*):

> In this way, a bodhisattva, a great being, abandons the characteristic signs of all kinds produced by thoughts by becoming mentally disengaged, and is thus well connected with the nonconceptual. But first, he does not touch the nonconceptual sphere.... As a result of proper mental engagement, he touches the nonconceptual sphere "without the wish to acquire it" or [without any other] effort and purifies it gradually.[187]

The subsequent sentence in the *Magic Formula for Entering the Nonconceptual* (which is also quoted in Maitrīpa's *Justification of Nonceptual Realization*) explains that the nonconceptual sphere is called nonconceptual (*avikalpa*) or amanasikāra (according to the Gilgit manuscript) in virtue of being beyond all characteristic signs. In other words, the amanasikāra practice of the *Magic Formula for Entering the Nonconceptual* goes hand in hand with proper mental engagement, in a way similar to the mental engagement of focusing on the sphere beyond characteristic signs in the *Stages of the Listener*. This latter practice could be seen as a forerunner of the mental engagement of cultivating nonconceptual wisdom in the *Distinguishing the Phenomenal World of Mental Representation from the True Nature of Phenomena*, which is, of course, not merely the abandonment of characteristic signs by becoming mentally disengaged.

In his commentary on the *Magic Formula for Entering the Nonconceptual*, Kamalaśīla restricts the literal meaning of amanasikāra to the fruit of one's deep insight (*vipaśyanā*) practice—an insight that must be brought about by the logical inferences common to mainstream Madhyamaka. Analytic meditation turns into nonconceptual abiding in the same way as a fire kindled by rubbing pieces of wood burns the pieces of wood themselves:

> It is the characteristic signs of precise investigation that is intended by the expression "to become mentally disengaged." It has the nature of being conceptual, but it is burnt by the pure wisdom-fire arising from it, in the same way as a fire kindled by rubbing two pieces of wood burns those very pieces.[188]

When Saraha called his Mahāmudrā practice amanasikāra, he most surely did not have such a purely logical path in mind. While Kamalaśīla's approach to the nonconceptual rests on inferential reasoning, Saraha propagated a direct, revolutionary means of access to the true nature of mind with the help of pith-instructions. The term *amanasikāra* is thus used in a more literal sense, as implying that we should become as natural and unaffected as a small child, but with the cognizant element of coemergent wisdom.[189]

CHAPTER 7

The *Ten Verses on True Reality* in the Light of Sahajavajra's Commentary

THE MARPA KAGYÜ TRADITION attributes a crucial role to Maitrīpa's *Ten Verses on True Reality* and Sahajavajra's commentary to it,[190] which combines Apratiṣṭhāna Madhyamaka with Mahāmudrā. The bridging link is the *Sublime Continuum*–influenced concept of a true reality that can be only negatively determined in Madhyamaka analysis but positively described as luminous in meditative concentration, which realizes true reality as it is (*yathābhūtasamādhi*). At the beginning of the text, Maitrīpa venerates suchness (a synonym of true reality), which is not only taken as transcending existence and nonexistence, but also enlightenment (*bodhi*) after it has become stainless. The *Sublime Continuum*, a text that Maitrīpa is said to have rediscovered, similarly combines a *via negationis* with a *via eminentiae*:

> Homage to you, Dharma Sun, who cannot be thought of
> as nonexistent, existent, both existent and nonexistent
> together, and as being different from both existent and
> nonexistent together;
> To you who is beyond explanation, and whose calmness must
> be directly realized by self-awareness;

> To your brilliance of stainless wisdom light;
> O you who dispels the darkness of attachment and aversion
> toward the entire basis of cognition.[191]

The definition of enlightenment as stainless suchness becomes clear in Asaṅga's commentary on *Sublime Continuum* I.25:

> Suchness apart from stains is precisely this *dhātu* (buddha nature), which is called the *dharmakāya* of a tathāgata, when it has the defining characteristic of fundamental transformation on the level of a buddha.[192]

It is very likely that Maitrīpa was influenced by this Indian standard work on buddhanature, even though the technical term itself (i.e., *tathāgatagarbha* or *buddhadhātu*) is not found in his works. Of particular interest is Maitrīpa's turn from Madhyamaka-style negations to a positive description of reality in *Ten Verses on True Reality*:

> They (i.e., phenomena) are all realized as being luminous
> Through the samādhi of experiencing reality as it is,
> And this form of samādhi occurs
> In virtue of engaged bodhicitta.[193]

In his commentary, Sahajavajra clearly contrasts the bodhicitta of the samādhi in which phenomena are experienced as luminous from the bodhicitta of Kamalaśīla's *Stages of Meditation* (*Bhāvanākrama*), which is produced from analysis:

> No such an engaged bodhicitta is intended here [in the *Ten Verses on True Reality*, however,] since in the *Stages of Meditation* it must be produced by analysis, and is thus not pure.

But here [in the *Ten Verses on True Reality*], one must cultivate engaged bodhicitta right from the beginning with a non-analytical mind. When somebody who possesses pith instructions of the pāramitā system, which are adorned with the words of the guru, internalizes Yuganaddha Madhyamaka, then the very insight into the ultimate, namely, emptiness endowed with all excellent forms, [spontaneously] continues within a continuum of moments.[194] This is calm abiding and nothing else, for it has been said [in the *Hevajra Tantra*]:

Meditation is actually nonmeditation (or nonproduction[195]
by the mind),
The thorough knowledge of all phenomena.[196]

For this reason, the path is characterized by such a union of calm abiding and deep insight;[197] and here, to be sure, an engaging bodhicitta together with devotion toward a goal different from this path is not being asserted. This is also taught in Maitrīpa's *Twenty Verses on Mahāyāna*:

Well, one may realize emptiness
In the thousand collections of teachings;
[But] it is not realized through analysis.
The meaning of emptiness[198] is learned, rather, from the guru.[199]

It is further stated in the *Twenty Verses on Mahāyāna*:

He whose practice of continuous meditation [remains
undisturbed, even]
When apprehending forms, such as a vase,

> Will become a great buddha,
> Whose single body [of compassion and emptiness pervades]
> all forms.[200]
>
> To elucidate these two verses, [it should be remembered that Maitrīpa] said [in the *Ten Verses on True Reality*]:
>
> [This samādhi of realizing true reality as it is, for its part,
> Comes from engaging bodhicitta,][201]
> Because true reality arises without interruption,
> For those who are aware of its abode.[202]
>
> For those who, thanks to the pith instructions of the genuine guru, are aware of the basis of this engaging bodhicitta, whose nature is the suchness of the two truths united as a pair, there arise uninterruptedly—that is, in every moment—emptiness and compassion inseparable, these being the defining characteristics of ultimate bodhicitta. They are called yogins because they are of this very nature.[203]

In other words, Sahajavajra propagates initial vipaśyanā sessions that can be performed by resorting to direct cognition based on pith instructions. Such a vipaśyanā of direct insight into the ultimate is at the same time śamatha, the two being the same. As doctrinal support for this direct approach, Sahajavajra quotes the second part of a verse from the *Hevajra Tantra*,[204] whose first part is adduced in Maitrīpa's *Justification of Nonconceptual Realization* as proof that the practice of amanasikāra is also found in the tantras. It should be noted that the initial use of direct cognitions does not exclude noninferential types of analysis.[205] Moreover, pith instructions may, of course, contain analytical statements, and thus may also be accompanied by analysis. Sahajavajra quotes numerous instances of Madhyamaka reasoning himself, especially at the beginning of his commentary. In his explanation of *Ten Verses on True Reality*, verse 7, he explains amanasikāra as the "nonapprehension of things, achieved either by precise analysis or the pith instructions of a guru,"[206] which shows not only that Madhyamaka reasoning is relied upon to provide the doctrinal foundations of his tradition, but also that it may be used during meditation practice. Still, it does not play the same crucial role as in purely analytical approaches to initial vipaśyanā, such as of Kamalaśīla.[207]

In his commentary on *Ten Verses on True Reality*, verse 7, in which these pith instructions and the reality they reveal are called mahāmudrā, Sahajavajra defines nonduality in terms of his so-called Yuganaddha Madhyamaka as being "bodhicitta, which is the reality of nondual knowledge."[208] Before his explanation of the second part of the verse, the following objection is addressed: to define reality in the above-mentioned way has the fault of bearing the characteristic sign of an interpretative imagination of reality, in the same way as the practice of the samādhi of realizing true reality is accompanied by the characteristic sign of the interpretative imagination of remedies, and such characteristic signs must be abandoned through nonconceptual realization, as urged in the *Magic Formula for Entering the Nonconceptual*. The remaining part of verse 7, then, is taken as Maitrīpa's answer to such a possible objection. It says that nothing, not even such things as the characteristic signs of attainment, is really abandoned, but everything is simply realized as natural luminosity:

> The sentence "the suchness of the nondual world is bodhicitta" is the characteristic sign of an interpretative imagination of true reality. Likewise, the expression "the samādhi that experiences reality exactly as it is" is the characteristic sign of an interpretative imagination of the remedy,[209] and

the sentence "when realized, it has the nature of enlightenment" is the characteristic sign of an interpretative imagination of attainment. Somebody may then object: "If the Illustrious One [repeatedly] taught in the *Magic Formula for Entering the Nonconceptual* that even the characteristic signs of the remedy, etc., namely, those which become appearances and manifest, are completely abandoned through amanasikāra, how do these sentences then not contradict [what has been taught] here [in the *Ten Verses on True Reality*]?" [The possible answers are as follows.]

First of all, some say in this regard, concerning apparent entities, the reality of what must be accomplished and what accomplishes must be expressed first, since otherwise, it would follow that the teaching has no result. It has been taught, though, that later, after one has become familiar with the result, the characteristic signs of what must be accomplished, etc., will be abandoned. This follows from the practice of the abandonment of even the knowledge that is without characteristic signs. If inferential knowledge is taken first, how is there a contradiction? This is not the best answer, for it is insufficient. Therefore, another response has been taught [in *Ten Verses on True Reality*]:

But even the vain clinging to a state free from duality
Is taken, in like manner, to be luminous.[210]

The underlying intention here is as follows: so that those who do not know true reality might thoroughly realize that reality, it was taught that one must give up the three interpretative images and likewise wholly give up the four extremes. This is because it has been said [in *Presentation of Empowerment*]:

They who do not abide in [the domain of] the
remedy
Are not attached to reality,
And who do not even desire the fruit,
Find mahāmudrā.[211]

Here mahāmudrā stands for the pith instructions on the reality of mahāmudrā.[212] For those who thoroughly know the reality of entities there is no contradiction [with the *Magic Formula for Entering the Nonconceptual*], for [the interpretative imaginations of the remedy and the like] do not have to be abandoned in terms of the reality [of their luminous nature], as has been said [in *Twenty Verses on Mahāyāna*,] with regard to any of the three interpretative [forms of imagination]:

In order to purify the four extremes
[In any of the three interpretative forms of imagination],
They abide evenly in these four extremes.[213]

As to being free from duality, even the vain adherence to nonduality, namely, the interpretative imagination of reality, is luminous since it lacks an own nature and is pure by nature. Likewise, vain adherence to what must be accomplished and that which accomplishes must be realized as being luminous.[214]

The main point here is that, following *Presentation of Empowerment*, verse 36, both the pith instructions and the revealed reality are called mahāmudrā. This means that mahāmudrā in terms of nonabiding and amanasikāra not only describes the fruition stage but also refers to meditation practice, which is evident from the first *Ornament of Manifested Wisdom* quote, that amanasikāra is virtuous, and from

Kāropa's commentary on the amanasikāra verse from the *Ornament of Manifested Wisdom*:

> The lines of this praise should be understood as presenting view, meditation, and conduct as three inseparable aspects. Freedom from duality, which is conceptual analysis, is the conduct. Not to abide in bliss or emptiness, the freedom from the duality, which is attachment, is the body of great bliss. It is the view. Amanasikāra and being without recollection in terms of the sequence of preparation, main part, and the conclusion is meditation. Not to separate through the imagination of three distinct cognitive aspects means to be without a cognitive object. Making oneself familiar with them (view, etc.) means to pay homage. This should be understood as mahāmudrā.[215]

In other words, the equating of mahāmudrā with nonabiding and amanasikāra does not only refer to buddhahood. It leaves the possibility open that mahāmudrā can be found through amanasikāra practice as described in the *Magic Formula for Entering the Nonconceptual*. In it, the four sets of hindering characteristic signs are abandoned through amanasikāra.[216] In verse 36 of the *Presentation of Empowerment*, which Sahajavajra adduces to relate both his pith instructions and reality to mahāmudrā, Maitrīpa emphasizes the *Magic Formula for Entering the Nonconceptual*'s practice of not becoming tangled up in remedies, true reality, or the desire of the result. In his commentary on this verse, Rāmapāla nearly quotes directly the part of *Magic Formula for Entering the Nonconceptual* in which characteristic signs are described as being abandoned in the act of not directing one's attention to them. In his explanation of the remedy, which is the second group of characteristic signs in the *Magic Formula for Entering the Nonconceptual*, Rāmapāla includes the first set of characteristic signs, pertaining to what consists of what is opposed to liberation:

> "In the domain of the remedy," means in the domain of the group of interpretative imaginations relating to the remedies that consist of generosity, discipline, patience, diligence, meditation, and insight, inasmuch as these remedies are interpreted in terms of an own nature, quality, or essence. "They who do not abide in them," is written because they abandon these interpretative imaginations by becoming mentally disengaged. Since the group of interpretative imaginations relating to the remedy are abandoned, the group of interpretative imaginations of what is opposed [to liberation], namely, that which consists of the contaminated five skandhas of form and so forth can be considered to have been abandoned. This is because in the absence of the first group, the second perforce does not exist [either].[217]

This corresponds with the following passage from the *Magic Formula for Entering the Nonconceptual*:

> Children of a noble family! Here, the bodhisattva and great being hear the teaching relating to the nonconceptual, direct their thought to it, and completely abandon all characteristic signs of [false] imagination. They completely abandon, as the first among them, all characteristic signs of natural false imagination (*prakṛtivikalpa*), that is to say, any perceived object or perceiving subject. This characteristic sign of natural [false] imagination is here a characteristic sign of a contaminated entity, and such a contaminated entity is any of the five skandhas, that is to say, the skandhas of form, feeling, ideation, volitional and affective impulses, and

> consciousness. How does the bodhisattva abandon these characteristic signs of natural [false] imagination? What becomes manifest by becoming an appearance they abandon through not directing their attention to them?
>
> While the bodhisattva completely abandons these characteristic signs of [natural] imagination in a gradual way, the characteristic signs of the interpretative imagination relating to the remedy, which are different from these previous ones, occur—that is, become manifest—by becoming appearances. They are as follows: the characteristic signs of the interpretative imagination relating to generosity, discipline, patience, diligence, meditation, and insight, that is to say, [a form of false imagination that arises from] interpretations involving an own nature, qualities, or essence. These characteristic signs of the interpretative imagination relating to the remedy the bodhisattva also completely abandons through not directing their attention to them.[218]

Rāmapāla continues in his commentary:

> "Is not attached to true reality" means "who is not attached to, not fixed upon, the interpretative imaginations of true reality that consists of [ideas about] emptiness, suchness, and the like, since, in such cases, true reality is interpreted in terms of an own nature and so forth."

This corresponds with the following passage from the *Magic Formula for Entering the Nonconceptual*:

> While the bodhisattva completely abandons these characteristic signs of the remedy, the characteristic signs of the interpretative imagination relating to true reality that are

different from these previous ones occur—that is, become manifest—by becoming appearances. They are as follows: the characteristic signs of the interpretative imagination relating to emptiness, suchness, the extreme of reality, the ultimate, and the dharmadhātu, that is to say, signs that arise from an interpretation relating to either particulars (*svalakṣaṇa*), qualities, or essence. These characteristic signs of the interpretative imagination relating to true reality the bodhisattva also completely abandons through not directing their attention to them.

Rāmapāla continues:

> "Who does not even desire the fruit" means "for whom there is even no desire—craving—for the fruit, [a desire] characteristic of the group of interpretative imaginations of the first bodhisattva level up to the final attainment of omniscience." He finds—attains—mahāmudrā.

This corresponds with the following passage from the *Magic Formula for Entering the Nonconceptual*:

> While the bodhisattva completely abandons these characteristic signs relating to true reality, characteristic signs of the interpretative imagination relating to attainment that are different from these previous ones occur—that is, become manifest—by becoming appearances. They are as follows: the characteristic signs of the interpretative imagination relating to the attainment from the first up to the tenth level, including the characteristic signs of the interpretative imagination relating to the attainment of being able to endure the fact that phenomena do not arise; prophecy; completely pure

> buddha fields; causing sentient beings to mature; empowerment; all the way up to omniscience, that is to say, [a sign that arises] from an interpretation involving either specifically characterized phenomena, qualities, or essence. These characteristic signs of the interpretative imagination relating to attainment the bodhisattva also completely abandons through not directing their attention to them.

This establishes a close relation of Maitrīpa's Mahāmudrā with the *Magic Formula for Entering the Nonconceptual*, which rather falls into the category of Sūtra. To be sure, the abandoning of characteristic signs through amanasikāra can be understood as in this *Magic Formula for Entering the Nonconceptual*, which means that Mahāmudrā as amanasikāra does not need to be a specifically tantric practice, even though the *Presentation of Empowerment* supplies the tantric context of an empowerment based on the sequence of the four seals. But here again, it could be argued that by quoting the *Presentation of Empowerment*, Sahajavajra merely is establishing a connection between the practice of the *Magic Formula for Entering the Nonconceptual* and Mahāmudrā. In other words, a Mahāmudrā practice based on pith instructions of the pāramitā system is only on par with the mahāmudrā of the four seals, and not an advanced practice of the completion stage in the strict sense.

In his commentary on the *Ten Verses on True Reality*, Sahajavajra further points out that the vain clinging to nonduality, that is, the interpretative imagination of true reality, does not exist as anything other than its luminous nature. Abandoning the characteristic signs of these imaginations through the practice of amanasikāra is what leads to the realization of their luminous nature. This is achieved by not focusing on the supposed own nature of phenomena, through recourse to either precise analysis or the pith instructions of a guru. The abandonment through realizing luminosity is clearly described in the next portion of the *Commentary on the Ten Verses on True Reality*, corresponding to the second half of verse 7 in the root text:

> Well then, as to the phrase "completely abandoning these characteristic signs through amanasikāra"—here, amanasikāra does not mean that one does not become mentally engaged at all, as when closing one's eyes results in not seeing objects, such as a vase. What is meant by amanasikāra, rather, is—through recourse to either precise analysis or the pith instructions of the guru—not to focus on an own nature of entities. It has been said:
>
> In brief, when walking or sitting,
> Sleeping or resting in equipoise,
> I look, listen, and smell,
> Touch and experience,
> And even though I see through eyes of insight,
> Based on analysis and pith instructions
> That no phenomenon arises,
> I have not seen.
>
> What is meant by withdrawing one's attention from characteristic signs, then, is merely the thorough knowledge that phenomena are without characteristic signs. Well then, as to characteristic signs, their interpretative imagination is a verbal concept, for it has been said [in *Treasure of Higher Teaching* (*Abhidharmakośa*), verse lines I.14cd]:
>
> > A notion (*saṃjñā*) has the nature of apprehending characteristic signs.
> >
> > The Illustrious One taught that they are unborn and pure. Where? In the *Discourse on the King of Meditation*, where it has been said:

> Being cognizance,
> A notion is characterized by the apprehension of a
> characteristic sign.[219]
> But [in reality] the notion is non-apprehension,
> Since it is taught as being empty of truly existent
> characteristic signs.
>
> The own nature of a notion has not arisen,
> Nor will it ever arise in such a way.
>
> We should abandon this notion!
> The one in whom this notion occurs
> Delights in the fabrication of notions
> And is not liberated from notions.
>
> In whom did this notion arise?
> Who brought it forth?
> Who experiences the notion,
> And who stops it?
>
> No phenomenon was found by the Buddha
> For which a notion has arisen.
> Think here about this meaning,
> And there will be no notion anymore.
>
> When notions have not arisen,
> Whose notion needs to be blocked?[220]

> Likewise, even the thought that this is inconceivable and nonconceptual is something conceivable and conceptual. It is, however, not the case that there is no realization of emptiness (lit. "the lack of an own nature").[221]

The quoted verses indeed support Sahajavajra's Mahāmudrā teaching that conceptually constructed characteristic signs are unborn, pure, and inconceivable, attributes that typically define the luminous nature of mind. The only difference is that the *Discourse on the*

King of Meditation speaks of notions instead of characteristic signs, wherefore Sahajavajra also quotes the *Treasure of Higher Teachings'* definition that "a notion has the nature of apprehending characteristic signs." That means that *saṃjñā* can also refer to the perceived aspect of cognition.

Just like in Maitrīpa's *Justification of Nonceptual Realization*, the realization of the original purity of luminous emptiness is a crucial element in the process of becoming mentally disengaged. The fact that Sahajavajra quotes the *Discourse on the King of Meditation* shows that the related pith instructions do not need to be tantric. It has become clear then that the term "pith instructions of the pāramitā system" does not refer to instructions on pāramitās, but that those pith instructions belong to the pāramitā system, even though they accord with the mantra system.

To sum up what Sahajavajra explained up to this point, nothing is really abandoned, but phenomena are ascertained for what they are: under the lens of analysis, they are seen to lack an own nature, and in the samādhi of realizing true reality, they are experienced as luminosity. It should be noted that this supreme Madhyamaka of pith instructions is referred to as mahāmudrā in a not specifically tantric context; that is, initial direct experiences of emptiness as luminosity do not require tantric empowerment, but are made possible here with the help of pith instructions of the pāramitā system.

The best support for a Mahāmudrā practice outside the sequence of the four seals remains the commentary on *Ten Verses on True Reality*, verse 8, where Sahajavajra identifies a Mahāmudrā approach distinct from both the mantra system and pāramitā system. The verse in the *Ten Verses on True Reality* is as follows:

By the power of having realized this true reality,
The yogin, with eyes wide open,

> Moves everywhere like a lion,
> By any chosen means and in any chosen manner.[222]

Sahajavajra immediately adds:

> Thanks to the yoga of firmly realizing the previously taught nondual reality through the pith instructions of the genuine guru.[223]

A little later, the text elaborates on this point:

> Well then, if one asks, what is the difference in comparison to a yogin who follows the mantra system? [The answer is as follows:] because the yogin's practice is conducted without following the sequence of the four seals, and because it takes a long time to perfect complete enlightenment through the type of equanimity that lacks the experience of great bliss resulting from pride in being the deity, there are significant differences with regard to what is accomplished and that which accomplishes. On the other hand, it differs from the yogin in the pāramitā system, specifically because the suchness of indivisible union, the emptiness discerned through the instruction of a genuine guru, is firmly realized. Therefore, those who do not practice austerities but rather have perfect certainty that the reality of one taste is emptiness are like [skillful] villagers grasping a snake: even though they touch the snake, they are not bitten. Some call this the wisdom of reality or mahāmudrā.[224]

In other words, the practice of realizing Mahāmudrā based on pith instructions is clearly distinguished from both the pāramitā system and the mantra system.

Sūtra Mahāmudrā is also taught in another Indian source, Jñānakīrti's *Entering True Reality*, where advanced practitioners of śamatha (calm abiding) and vipaśyanā (deep insight) in the pāramitā system are said to be already in possession of mahāmudrā even at an initial stage.[225] Moreover, in his description of the pāramitā system, Jñānakīrti links the traditional fourfold Mahāyāna meditation with Mahāmudrā by equating the goal "Mahāyāna" in the *Discourse of the Descent into Laṅka* (*Laṅkāvatārasūtra*) with Mahāmudrā.[226] Sahajavajra and probably his master Maitrīpa were familiar with Jñānakīrti's system of classification and picked up the idea of a Mahāmudrā path outside of the sequence of the four seals and proper completion stage practice from this famous master.[227] It should also be noted that Jñānakīrti's work was translated, in cooperation with Padmākaravarman, by the translator Rinchen Zangpo (958–1055), who helped the king Yeshé Ö (947–1024) to initiate the revival of Buddhism in Tibet known as the later dissemination of the Dharma.[228]

Even though Maitrīpa's disciple Sahajavajra teaches a sūtra-based Mahāmudrā path, namely, pith instructions of the pāramitā system that accord with the mantra system, formal tantric practice based on empowerment is clearly considered superior. In his *Single Intent* commentary, the Eighth Karmapa Mikyö Dorjé reports that Gö Lotsāwa Zhönnu Pel distinguished Nāropa's Mahāmudrā of bliss and emptiness from Maitrīpa's Mahāmudrā of the true nature of mind, which depends on the former and thus is a little inferior.[229] It is not clear what Mikyö Dorjé meant by this, but the difference between the two types of Mahāmudrā could precisely be the one between Mantra and Sūtra Mahāmudrā.

CHAPTER 8

Empowerment

WITH THE PROGRESSIVE STUDY, analysis, and meditation along the gradual path of philosophical tenets, which culminates in the Madhyamaka of Nonabiding, one has the foundation for tantric empowerment, the necessary requirement for the formal practice of the creation and completion stages. Such formal practice must have been the standard procedure at the time of Maitrīpa, notwithstanding Sūtra and Essence Mahāmudrā. In his tantric explanations, Maitrīpa mainly follows a particular interpretation of the *Hevajra Tantra*, especially when it comes to the crucial sequence of the four moments and four joys, an issue we will come back to further down. At this point, it is important to note that in Tantra, Maitrīpa also sees in Yogācāra an essential stepping stone to Madhyamaka.

In the *Explaining the Seals of the Five Tathāgatas* we thus find the explanation that the five psychophysical aggregates (*skandhas*) are in reality the five tathāgatas. The first four (Vairocana, Ratnasambhava, Amitābha, and Amoghasiddhi) are sealed with Akṣobhya, to show that they are mind only. The Akṣobhya seal thus stands for the realization of Yogācāra emptiness, namely, the absence of the subject-object duality from the dependently arising mind. The term "five seals of the tathāgatas" (*pañcatathāgatamudrā*) stands for the sealing of the five skandhas by the five tathāgatas, and the sealing of these five tathāgatas by the seal of Akṣobhya. This implies that Maitrīpa distinguishes between an Akṣobhya seal as one of the five tathāgata seals and the Akṣobhya seal of the nondual mind.[230]

To further refine one's realization in Maitrīpa's system, it is necessary to move beyond Yogācāra and embrace Madhyamaka emptiness, namely, that the dependently arising mental factors also lack the independent existence of an own nature (*svabhāva*). On the tantric level, this translates into, to use Maitrīpa's words, sealing the Akṣobhya seal with the seal of Vajradhara or Vajrasattva. This final stage concludes the recognition of successively more profound levels of the skandhas' true nature—they are nondual mind and ultimately empty of an own nature.

In an appendix to the *Explaining the Seals of the Five Tathāgatas* in the *Dharma Treasure of the Drigung Kagyü*, Bumla Bar relates the seals of the tathāgatas, Akṣobhya, and Vajradhara respectively to joy, supreme joy, and coemergent joy (i.e., the first three of the four joys that must be fully recognized during the prajñā-wisdom empowerment):

> Moreover, joy relates to being sealed by the seal of the tathāgata; supreme joy to being sealed by the seal of Akṣobhya; and coemergent joy to being sealed by the seal of Vajradhara.[231]

In other words, the realization that appearances are contained in the mind is joy, the realization of the nonconceptual mind as being empty of duality is supreme joy, and the Madhyamaka realization of bliss as being free from extremes is coemergent joy.

The Vase Empowerments

For Maitrīpa, empowerment starts with the six vase empowerments, which are best explained in the *Summary of the Meaning of Empowerment*. They are:

- the water empowerment
- the crown empowerment
- the *vajra* empowerment
- the bell empowerment
- the name empowerment
- the master empowerment

During the water empowerment, the vajra master visualizes himself as Akṣobhya in order to wash away the ignorance of the disciple, who depends on Vairocana. The crown empowerment plants the seed of the protuberance on the head of the buddha the disciple will become. This and especially the third and fourth, the vajra and bell empowerments, initiate a process of recognizing the five skandhas as the five tathāgatas. This enables the visualization of the surrounding world, sentient beings, and oneself as a maṇḍala and its deities. In his *Five Aspects* (*Pañcākāra*), Maitrīpa describes the following maṇḍala:

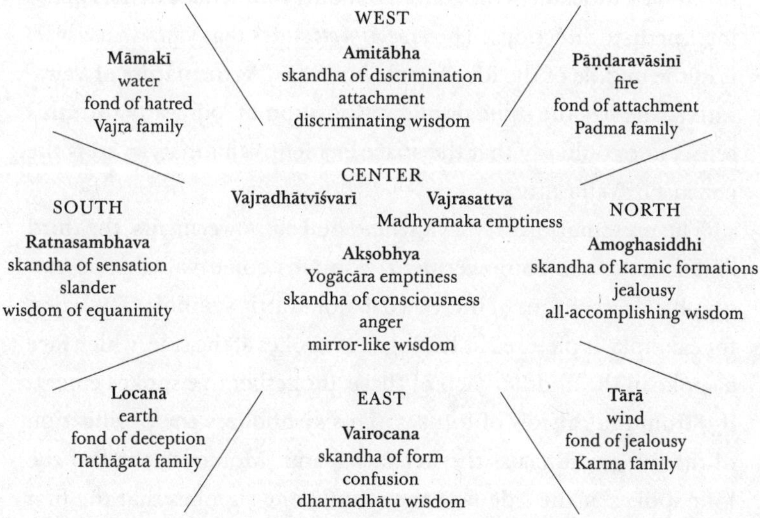

Akṣobhya, who represents Yogācāra emptiness, is in the middle. His crown is Vajrasattva, which symbolizes the sealing of everything (i.e., the five skandhas and thus the five tathāgatas) with his seal of Madhyamaka emptiness. That means that the five skandhas and thus the five tathāgatas—Vairocana in the East, Ratnasambhava in the South, Amitābha in the West, and Amoghasiddhi in the North—are ultimately sealed by Vajrasattva. The five tathāgatas stand for the transformation of the five skandhas and five spiritual defilements into the five types of wisdom. In the intermediate directions and in the middle are the five female buddhas, to whom are attributed the five elements—Vajradhātvīśvarī must be space, even though this is not explicitly spelled out in the *Five Aspects.* It should be noted that the distribution of male and female deities is asymmetric in the center, as we have there only Vajradhātvīśvarī against Akṣobhya and Vajrasattva. Either the latter are seen as two aspects of one deity, or the female deities are not considered as consorts, as in earlier dharmadhātu maṇḍalas, which have the five male deities (tathāgatas) with Vairocana in the center, but only four female deities in the intermediate directions. The *Five Aspects* states that Vajradhātvīśvarī is in the middle of the four female buddhas. As the nature of Vajrasattva, she has the same dominant position of Vajrasattva. In this sense, one could say that the space element Vajradhātvīśvarī is the consort of Vajrasattva.

The presentation of the vajra and bell empowerments, the third and fourth vase empowerment, contains some valuable iconographic descriptions of these two major tantric symbols. The vajra, for example, is pictured as having four spokes at the side, which face a spoke in the middle, each of these altogether five spokes emerging from the calyxes of lotuses. This symbolizes the purification of the five skandhas as the five tathāgatas. Moreover, the fact the four spokes at the side face the middle one signifies that the first four skandhas have the nature of the fifth, namely, mind, which means that everything is mind only. For a detailed description of these and the remaining vase empowerments, see the translation of the *Summary of the Meaning of Empowerment*. The six vase empowerments correspond to the purification of the body and the outer creation stage.

Secret, Prajñā-Wisdom Empowerments, and the Fourth

The secret empowerment purifies speech by receiving the bodhicitta (i.e., the sexual fluids) of the guru and the guru's consort. It corresponds to the profound creation stage. In his *Instructions on the Stages Handed Down by the Lineage of Gurus*, Vajrapāṇi explains:

> As to the secret empowerment of the venerable master, the bodhicitta must be taken with the tongue from his vajra. As to the secret empowerment of the venerable lady, the bodhicitta must be taken with the tongue from her lotus.[232]

Next, one needs to mark the goal of buddhahood, a glimpse of which must be first realized during the third empowerment. This depends on a correct recognition of the four moments and four joys during union with a tantric consort, who is also referred to as *karmamudrā* or *prajñā*. For this reason, the third empowerment is called *prajñājñāna*, the wisdom that arises from a *prajñā*, or prajñā-wisdom.

The four moments and four joys according to the tradition of Maitrīpa are as follows:

THE MOMENTS OF	THE FOUR JOYS
Manifold appearances	joy
Maturation	Supreme joy
Freedom from defining characteristics	co-emergent joy
Relaxation	joy of no-joy

One of the most noteworthy features of Maitrīpa's Mahāmudrā is that he presents, within the sequence of the four moments and four joys, the moment of freedom from defining characteristics (*vilakṣaṇa*) and coemergent joy in the third position.[233] He thus differs from the mainstream represented by famous scholars, such as Kamalanātha, Abhayākaragupta, Raviśrījñāna, and Vibhūticandra.[234] Maitrīpa, therefore, seems to go against his primary doctrinal source, the *Hevajra Tantra*,[235] explaining in his *Instructions on the Four Seals* (*Caturmudropadeśa*) that in treatises such as the *Hevajra Tantra,* the correct sequence has not been made explicit, in order to confuse outsiders who do not rely on a guru.[236] In his *Presentation of Empowerment*, Maitrīpa defends his interpretation of the four moments and joys at length. In particular, he shows how the recognition of the goal of coemergent joy during the moment of freedom from defining characteristics (*vilakṣaṇa*) is the only way that links tantric practice to a Mahāmudrā realization without fixed abiding in the sense of Apratiṣṭhāna Madhyamaka. In his *Presentation of Empowerment*, Maitrīpa also builds, as we have seen above, an essential bridge to the *Magic Formula for Entering the Nonconceptual*, in that Mahāmudrā is said to be found through abandoning the conceptually constructed characteristic signs of the remedy, reality, and attainment through the practice of amanasikāra.[237]

As for the fourth empowerment, in his *Summary of the Meaning of Empowerment* Maitrīpa reports a variety of competing descriptions, which reflects the fluid development from "the fourth" in the sense of continuous cultivation of what one has experienced in the third empowerment to an independent fourth empowerment.[238] For Maitrīpa, the fourth empowerment can thus be:

- the goal characterized by prajñā-wisdom;
- like the stainless autumn sky, while becoming familiar with this very prajñā-wisdom;

- prajñā-wisdom itself;
- the form of prajñā-wisdom's true nature;
- the forms of its deviation from the natural state, namely, natural arising (i.e., dependent arising);
- the pure nature of nondual continuity of indivisible union.

Maitrīpa's Prajñā-Wisdom Empowerment

Returning to the third empowerment, in the *Presentation of Empowerment*, Maitrīpa introduces this subject by explaining the meaning of the word *evaṃ*, which symbolizes the union of insight and means, and the union with an actual consort as well. He thus prostrates to the word *evaṃ*, which is the cause of the four moments and the four joys, the means to attain enlightenment. The four moments and joys can arise either from *evaṃ* as an acoustic reality (i.e., as the dharmamudrā) or, according to Kāropa (a close disciple of Maitrīpa), if this is not possible, from that for which *evaṃ* really stands, the union with a consort, which is also referred to as the source of phenomena (*dharmodayā*). In this case, the *e* in *evaṃ* stands for the mother, the *va* for the father, and the dot (i.e., the *anusvāra*) for their union.[239] When this union is practised with skillful means and in a proper way, the goal of the path comes into view, and mahāmudrā is eventually attained. In this case, Maitrīpa speaks, just as Rāmapāla does in his *Commentary on the Presentation of Empowerment*, of a correct or "good" empowerment as opposed to base and "forceful" (*haṭha*) ones.[240] We shall take this point up again below. The way the four moments and four joys arise from *evaṃ* is best summarized in Kāropa's introduction to his commentary on the *Succession of Four Seals*:

> First, the four moments occur in proper order from *evaṃ*, understood either as an acoustic phenomenon or as the real one (i.e., the letters in their actual shape).[241] From them,

> the four joys arise, and defilements are thereby abandoned together with their imprints. The resulting fruit, the manifestation of inherent mahāmudrā, is of great value. From these four joys and through the power of former aspiration and compassion, the two form-kāyas manifest as appearances familiar to sentient beings. This is of great benefit. Wherefore it is said [in the *Tantra of Devendra's Question* (*Devendraparipṛcchātantra*)]:
>
> The knower of true reality, who knows
> The two letters, which are the dharmamudrā,
> Is the one who sets the wheel of teachings in motion
> For the sake of sentient beings.
>
> Those persons who cannot comprehend such a dharmamudrā must rely on a karmamudrā. The latter is also accepted as exemplifying wisdom and "source of phenomena" (*dharmodayā*). Still, once one has renounced forceful yoga (*haṭhayoga*), a correct empowerment is taken as the exemplifying wisdom, and one practices a way that conduces to the development [of actual wisdom].[242]

This means that physical karmamudrā practice is only optional, and intended for those who cannot comprehend *evaṃ* on the level of dharmamudrā.[243]

The *Presentation of Empowerment* explains the part of empowerment based on the four seals. They are the action seal (*karmamudrā*), the dharma seal (*dharmamudrā*), the great seal (*mahāmudrā*), and the convention seal (*samayamudrā*). Karmamudrā involves the tantric yoga practice with a consort (i.e., a karmamudrā or prajñā) to gain a glimpse of the goal of coemergent joy, an intimation of which manifests briefly when the sequence of four moments and four joys are experienced on a physical level. The four joys are then experienced again on the level of dharmamudrā, which means that they are generated acoustically,[244] i.e., on the basis of teachings. Mahāmudrā impresses its seal on the other seals. This means that the wisdom that arises from a prajñā—that is prajñā-wisdom—is only a reflection of the real wisdom.

If the empowerment is to be genuine, or "good," in Maitrīpa's words, it is also necessary to realize the empty nature of this experience of prajñā-wisdom, or to use Maitrīpa's words, to seal it with the seal of Vajrasattva. Indeed, with the help of pith instructions, this is already possible on the level of karmamudrā. According to Kāṛopa, the four moments and joys can also arise directly on the level of dharmamudrā. Only if this is not possible must one rely on a karmamudrā. In any case, the emptiness of bliss is realized through pith instructions. This leads to mahāmudrā, the realization that bliss and emptiness are inseparable.[245] On this level, however, there is only the real coemergent joy and not the other three (impure) joys. Mahāmudrā mainly corresponds to the level of the result, but also includes the meditation practice of amanasikāra.[246] The four joys of the samayamudrā are experienced when the yogin manifests as the deity Heruka in union with his consort for the sake of benefiting others.

Maitrīpa not only explains the four moments and joys in terms of each seal (except for mahāmudrā), but also, in verse 37, links the first moment (that of joy) alone with the karmamudrā. The moment of maturation (that of supreme joy) then corresponds to dharmamudrā, the moment of freedom from defining characteristics (that of coemergent joy) to mahāmudrā, and the moment of relaxation (that of the joy of no-joy) to samayamudrā.

Correct empowerment and the related proper sequence of the moments (and thus the four joys) is the main topic of the first part of the *Presentation of Empowerment*, which covers more than half of the text. Maitrīpa starts by presenting his sequence of the moments, in which freedom from defining characteristics figures in the third position, and is thus opposed to the empowerment of forceful yoga (*haṭhayoga*):[247]

> There is the moment of the manifold, then the one of
> maturation.
> In the third position, however, is freedom from defining
> characteristics;
> It should be known that the moment of relaxation is after
> that,
> The sequence of forceful yoga (*haṭhayoga*) having been
> rejected.[248]

In the *Hevajra Tantra*, which is Maitrīpa's main canonical source, the four moments are defined as follows:

> The moment of the manifold is called variety,
> Since it involves embracing, kissing, and so forth.
> The moment of maturation is the reverse of the first moment,
> In that it is the enjoyment of blissful wisdom.
>
> The moment of relaxation is said to be the reflecting upon
> [the fact]
> That one has experienced bliss.
> The moment of vilakṣaṇa is something other than these three,
> Being free from both passion and absence of passion.[249]

The conventional Tibetan translation of Sanskrit *vilakṣaṇa* is *tsen drel* (*mtshan bral*, "freedom from defining characteristics"), but the Sanskrit term can also mean "other." Maitrīpa follows, like his teacher Ratnākaraśānti, a tradition that claims the moment of freedom from defining characteristics and coemergent joy are marked or recognized in the third position. As a further source for placing coemergent joy before the joy of no-joy, Shamar Chökyi Drakpa mentions the pith instructions of Maitrīpa's guru Śavaripa.[250] As already mentioned above, however, the majority of scholars put them in the fourth position. In this tradition, Sanskrit *virama* is not taken as "[the joy of] no-joy" but as "intensification of joy." The way Maitrīpa takes the four moments and four joys of genuine empowerment can be best seen from his *Instructions on the Four Seals*:

1. Starting from exterior activities [such as embracing and kissing] up to the final arousing is the joy related to the moment of the manifold.
2. The experience from that point up until [the drops of bodhicitta] have reached the tip of the jewel is the moment of maturation. This is supreme joy.
3. The Illustrious One taught: "Holding the sixteen drops twice halved."[251] Two (of what is thus present in the form of four drops) at the tip of the jewel and two on the stamen of the lotus correspond to the moment of freedom from defining characteristics, related to coemergent joy.
4. When all four drops are inside the lotus (i.e., the vagina), it is the moment of relaxation, related to the joy in the cessation of joy.[252]

Shamar Chödrak Yeshé summarizes the crucial third moment of a good empowerment in Maitrīpa's system as follows:

> When the bodhicitta[253] abides at the opening of the lord of the family (the means, *upāya*) and the tip of the beautiful lotus (the main part of the prajñā) and does not deteriorate, wisdom arises.[254]

The four moments and joys of forceful empowerment are best explained in Vajrapāṇi's *Instructions on the Stages Handed Down by the Lineage of Gurus*:

1. When one is engaged in exterior activities such as kissing and embracing, there are thoughts relating to a perceived object and a perceiving subject. This is the moment of the manifold and joy.
2. Then, through the union involving friction, one's mind becomes empty of thoughts relating to external objects. Then the inner perceiving consciousness is the moment of maturation and supreme joy.
3. As bodhicitta goes into the city of the jewel, the mind becomes empty of a perceived object and a perceiving subject. This perfect state is the moment of interruption (*vimarda*) and intensification (*virama*).[255]
4. Then, through the releasing of the bodhicitta, there are again conceptual thoughts relating to a perceived object and a perceiving subject. This is the moment of vilakṣaṇa and coemergent joy.[256]

This forceful empowerment differs from the Kālacakra-based empowerment of Nāropa, which Shamar Chökyi Drakpa also classifies as "forceful." In it the semen is not released but drawn up again.[257] In any case, for Maitrīpa, a forceful empowerment does not only have the sequence of moments wrong, but also the realization of them. Maitrīpa thus claims in the *Instructions on the Four Seals* that in forceful yoga, experience also lacks the seal of Akṣobhya, which stands for realizing the Yogācāra emptiness of duality.[258] In other words, during the third moment (freedom from defining characteristics) of a genuine empowerment, Akṣobhya must be sealed by

Vajrasattva. This is indicative of experience beyond duality, which is aware of its empty nature.

In the following two verses of the *Presentation of Empowerment*, Maitrīpa further argues for his sequence of the four moments and joys, namely, that the moment of freedom from defining characteristics (*vilakṣaṇa*) and coemergent joy must be in the third position:

> If relaxation involves reflecting [on one's having experienced bliss],
> How can it be taken to be in the third position,
> Given that at this time there is no reflecting,
> [And hence at this stage] awareness is without defining characteristics?
>
> Come on. It is therefore appropriate that the moment of freedom
> From defining characteristics be recognized in the third position!
> This can be established on the basis of one's own experience,
> While the meaning of scriptures, too, is suitable here.[259]

In the fourth position, vilakṣaṇa would be conceptual because during relaxation, reflection takes place upon having experienced bliss. Rāmapāla begins his commentary on the *Presentation of Empowerment*, verse 3, by quoting a sentence from a tantra, which is also quoted in the *Sequence of the Four Seals*, but no copy of which has yet surfaced:

> Between supreme joy and the joy of no-joy, behold the goal and stabilize it![260]

The goal is here, of course, the coemergent, wherefore coemergent joy and the corresponding moment of freedom from defining characteristics are meant to be recognized between supreme joy and the joy of no-joy. Those who prefer the coemergent in the fourth position would be quick to refer to passages in the *Hevajra Tantra,* such as:

> The beginning of the joy of no-joy (*viramādiḥ*) is next after supreme joy.
> Heruka is both empty and non-empty.[261]

Or:

> They should note at the beginning of the joy of no-joy (*viramādau*),
> It is free from the three joys.[262]

The first verse suggests that the joy of no-joy is in the third position directly after supreme joy, but Rāmapāla takes the compound *viramādi* not as the "beginning of the joy of no-joy," but as that which is both "joy of no-joy," and "beginning" (i.e., the coemergent joy).[263] In other words, that which is both joy of no-joy and coemergent joy is in the third position after supreme joy. During the fourth moment, which is relaxation, the joy of no-joy is still the coemergent joy, but then it is only a memory and not completely free from defining characteristics.[264]

Maitrīpa's main point, however, is that the moment of relaxation involves reflecting upon having experienced bliss, which is something conceptual and thus happens in the last position. The third position, during which the goal of buddhahood is marked, requires a nonconceptual state of mind. Maitrīpa's definition of a base empowerment is as follows:

> They whose moment of the manifold lies in kissing and
> embracing,
> Whose moment of maturation, as it is called, lies in friction,
> And whose moment of freedom from defining characteristics
> lies in the awareness in the jewel
> Have the correct knowledge of a base empowerment.[265]

Shamar Chökyi Drakpa explains the third moment of a base empowerment as follows:

> In a process that resembles the third empowerment, the element (i.e., the drop of bodhicitta) starts to vanish, and one recognizes that it is about to be released. In order to stop this, coemergent joy is placed in the third and virama in the fourth position. Still, the virama of this base empowerment is not taken as the cessation of attachment. This is because it is here the wisdom arisen at the end of stabilizing the coemergent of equal taste, [an experience based] on the white and red elements in the middle of the vajra and lotus. Even the venerable Nāropa takes such practice as the coemergent.[266]

It should be noted, however, that for Nāropa (whose empowerment is not called base, but forceful), this coemergent joy is still preliminary in the sense that it is followed by the ascending bodhicitta, which turns into Kālacakra upon reaching the crown of the head.[267]

The moments and joys of a base empowerment in *Presentation of Empowerment*, verse 5, are also explained in Maitrīpa's *Instructions on the Four Seals*:

> 1. Outer activities, starting with kissing and embracing, constitute the moment of the manifold. This is joy.

2. The union involving friction is the moment of maturation. It is supreme joy.
3. The experience of the drop in the jewel is the moment of freedom from defining characteristics. It is coemergent joy.
4. Releasing the drops into the lotus is the moment of relaxation. It is the joy of no-joy.

This position is not different from those of non-Buddhists. Why is that? This is because they cling to the experience [of the drop in the jewel during the third moment]. Even though they have got the sequence right, they are not privy to the meaning.[268]

In other words, Maitrīpa's understanding of a correct empowerment comes dangerously close to the non-Buddhist tantric systems. A little further down in the *Instructions on the Four Seals*, we are thus informed that a base empowerment lacks the seal of Vajrasattva and the reassurance that one is Vajradhara.[269] The difference between correct and base empowerments, then, is the recognition of the empty nature of the blissful experience during the third moment. It could be concluded that even though a base empowerment may be sealed with the seal of Akṣobhya, which corresponds to the Buddhist mind-only tenets of Sākāra and Nirākāra, this in itself is not enough during this crucial third moment. For if it is not sealed with the seal of Vajrasattva during the third moment, it is not possible to set the goal correctly, and the result will not differ from that of the non-Buddhist tantras. This would also explain why Maitrīpa summarizes, in verses 6–18, various non-Buddhist traditions of empowerment. Within this group, verse 12 shows the accordance with Bhāskara, and verses 13–18 with the Bhagavat Siddhānta.

In the *Jewel Garland of True Reality*, Maitrīpa detects a similarity in the path of the pratyekabuddhas and Bhāskara, and also by the Sākāravāda and the Bhagavat Siddhānta. Moreover, verse 18, which is from the *Bhagavadgītā*,[270] demonstrates that there, too, is a distinction between a truly existent self (ātman) and a nonexistent phenomenal or saṃsāric world.[271] In other words, we have in the *Gītā* something similar to the teaching of a buddhanature, which is empty of the unreal adventitious stains. What Maitrīpa is up to, here, is to point out that non-Buddhists even operate with concepts of emptiness, and that it is only a correctly realized Madhyamaka emptiness that saves the day.

Having demonstrated such similarity between base empowerment and the other non-Buddhist systems, Maitrīpa seizes on the weak point of such base empowerments, namely, the notion that an Akṣobhya-mind, which is empty of a perceived and perceiver (verse 19), does truly exist. One of the main differences between the Buddhist and non-Buddhist tantras revolves around the correct ascertainment of emptiness. This, of course, must be in line with Madhyamaka (the variety of it known as Apratiṣṭhāna being at the core of Maitrīpa's buddhology). Even the lower tenets of Yogācāra must be presented in such a way that their temporary realizations can be further refined in accordance with Madhyamaka. Vedānta may be similar to Yogācāra, but unlike the latter, the former is not brought into line with Madhyamaka. In Tantra, deities (or rather their seals) represent the true nature of mind as established in the various tenets of Mahāyāna. As we have seen above, Maitrīpa explains that the first four skandhas are sealed with the seal of Akṣobhya in order to realize that they are mind only (*cittamātra*). But a further seal, the seal of Vajrasattva, is needed in order to keep the wisdom that is empty of a perceived and a perceiver from really existing as an entity. A physical experience induced by the movement or position of drops in the body alone is not enough for a correct assessment of emptiness. The seal of Akṣobhya as such is not refuted here, but only an Akṣobhya realization that is not or cannot be sealed with the seal of Vajrasattva. It would simply result in the wrong recognition of the third moment of a base empowerment.

In *Presentation of Empowerment*, verse 21, Maitrīpa insists that true reality as described in Buddhist tenets must be realized on the basis of pith instructions and not on the basis of the four moments and joys alone. Still, the Akṣobhya seal is taught in a preliminary measure, as a form of reassurance that all skandhas are mind only, namely, that one's skandhas are the tathāgatas who are sealed with Akṣobhya.[272] According to the Tibetan translation of the *Commentary on the Presentation of Empowerment*, Rāmapāla quotes in support of this the famous passage on fourfold meditation from the *Discourse of the Descent into Laṅka*:

> Once one has come to rely on [the notion of] mind only,
> External objects should not be imagined;
> Based on the apprehension of suchness,
> One should pass beyond mind only.
>
> Having passed beyond mind only,
> One should pass beyond a state that is without appearances.
> A yogin who is established in a state without appearances
> Sees the Mahāyāna.[273]

The point here, again, is that lower Yogācāra tenets can be taken as first steps to Madhyamaka. In other words, there is nothing wrong with a passing reassurance that one is Vairocana and the others, which are sealed with the seal of Akṣobhya, as long as the latter can be sealed in turn with the seal of Vajrasattva.

Consequently, in *Presentation of Empowerment*, verse 21, Maitrīpa rejects what is only based on Yogācāra types of recognition of true reality during the crucial third moment. Moreover, a correct understanding depends on the pith instructions of the guru, and not on a form of recognition induced by the drop of bodhicitta in various locations inside or between the sexual organs. True reality cannot be "held" to be such:

> True reality cannot be held to be inside the vajra or at its tip,
> Or to have fallen into the *kapāla*,[274]
> Or to be in the space in between. Realization of true reality comes
> From the mouth of the guru.[275]

As to recognizing true reality from the mouth of the guru, Maitrīpa refers in his *Instructions on the Four Seals* to *Chanting the Names of Mañjusrī* (*Mañjuśrīnāmasaṃgīti*)[276] and a verse in Apabhraṃśa, which is also quoted in Rāmapāla's commentary and Vajrapāṇi's *Instructions on the Stages Handed Down by the Lineage of Gurus*. The main point of a genuine empowerment is, again, that the nonconceptual Akṣobhya-type experience of the third moment is to be sealed with the seal of Vajrasattva on the basis of pith instructions.[277]

In the last three verses on karmamudrā, Maitrīpa finally presents his definition of the four moments and joys on the basis of a particular interpretation of *Hevajra Tantra* II.3.7–8. This mainly involves following pith instructions and accepting that the moment of freedom from defining characteristics belongs in the third position, even though it is mentioned last. The arguments for this sequence have already been dealt with above and are not repeated here.

Verses 23–25 discuss the four moments and four joys against the background of the *Hevajra Tantra* verse line II.3.7a and the verse II.3.11. In this context, it is essential to note that the order of the four joys (and implicitly the order of the four seals) can also be determined by the order of the four empowerments. The four joys of the karmamudrā must be counted as a single joy (namely, the first joy) when the four empowerments are paired with the four joys. In the *Hevajra Tantra*, the foremost scriptural authority for Maitrīpa, it is stated:

> Master, secret, prajñā,
> And the fourth is that again, the same way—
> The sequence of the joys should be known
> According to the order of the four empowerments.[278]

In other words, the third joy must be the coemergent one. Otherwise, it would not relate to mahāmudrā, which is the third seal.

In *Presentation of Empowerment*, verse 24, Maitrīpa addresses the problem of what the master empowerment has to do with karmamudrā. In his *Summary of the Meaning of Empowerment*, he presents the master empowerment as the sixth vase empowerment. In the subsequent verse in the *Hevajra Tantra*, too, one might be led to think that karmamudrā is the fourth and not the first empowerment:

> The master empowerment is transmitted through the
> purificatory act of a smile;
> The secret empowerment, within that of a gaze;
> The prajñā empowerment, within that of an embrace;
> And the fourth, within that of the pair's union.[279]

But a little further down, in *Hevajra Tantra* II.3.13, there is another type of master empowerment that perfectly satisfies the required relation between a master empowerment and karmamudrā:[280]

> With the embracing of a sixteen-year-old
> Consort (prajñā) in one's arms
> And with the uniting of bell and vajra,[281]
> The master empowerment is held to have taken place.[282]

Rāmapāla, referring to this verse, explains in his commentary on *Presentation of Empowerment*, verse 23, that on the level of the outer creation stage, the master empowerment is given in the common context of the vase empowerments, whereas on the level of the perfect completion stage, it is linked to the level of karmamudrā. This is also stated in the following explanation of a genuine empowerment in Vajrapāṇi's *Instructions on the Stages Handed Down by the Lineage of Gurus*:

> The master empowerment is joy. It must be understood that it results from the union of penis and vagina. Well, is not then the explanation of the water empowerment and so forth as the master empowerment to no purpose? No. This latter master empowerment is the outer creation stage, not the completion stage.[283]

In the last verse on karmamudrā, *Presentation of Empowerment*, verse 25, Maitrīpa finally presents his sequence of the four moments and joys. Unfortunately, this conclusion merely contains the advice to gain an understanding of the third moment and joy with the aid of the guru.

The Four Seals

After the detailed presentation of karmamudrā, Maitrīpa first introduces the sequence of the four seals in the context of their causal connection, and Rāmapāla makes it clear that each seal is a cause of the following one.[284] The exemplifying wisdom first arises from a karmamudrā, for a short moment when the sequence of the four joys is experienced on the physical level. Then the four joys are experienced again on the level of dharmamudrā (see below). This leads to the realization of mahāmudrā and the manifestation of the form kāyas (*samayamudrā*). In his *Instructions on the Four Seals*, Maitrīpa understands karmamudrā as having the nature of all four empowerments:

> The karmamudrā has the nature of empowerment. It consists of the four empowerments referred to as vase, secret, prajñā-wisdom, and the fourth empowerment. The vase empowerment goes up to the master empowerment. It purifies the body. During the secret empowerment, bodhicitta, which has arisen from means and insight, is bestowed. It purifies speech. As to the wisdom that arises from a consort (prajñā-wisdom), there are three types: forceful, base, and genuine ones. . . .[285] These constitute the empowerment with prajñā-wisdom and purify the mind. The fourth empowerment has the nature of the type of wisdom that arises from a prajñā, thus is not different from the three [impure] joys, and is united into a pair with what has the form of dependent arising (i.e., prajñā-wisdom). This is the fourth. These four empowerments constitute the karmamudrā. [In his *Succession of the Four Seals*,][286] the venerable master Nāgārjuna explained that through them a fruit similar [to the real one] is produced.[287]

In the *Succession of the Four Seals*, the wisdom that arises from a prajñā is described as an imitation of an image of the real coemergent:

> All that appears as coemergent is called coemergent because it duplicates the image of the real coemergent. This image of the coemergent leads to the realization of a type of wisdom that is similar to the coemergent. The coemergent is thus [only in this limited sense] the prajñā-wisdom. Therefore, there is no arising of the coemergent in the prajñā-wisdom.

> For inasmuch as the true nature of all phenomena, namely, what is called the coemergent, is the specific characteristic of the uncontrived, a fruit similar [to the real coemergent] is produced by relying on a karmamudrā.[288]

The idea is, that while the coemergent nature can (and should) be realized any time during all kinds of activity, the one performed between partners during union provides an excellent chance to recognize the coemergent nature, or at least an imitation of it, for the first time. A little further down in the *Succession of the Four Seals* we find an interesting discussion of the causal relation between the karmamudrā and the seals following it:

> How can the uncontrived wisdom called coemergent arise for those who do not know the [teachings of] the dharmamudrā, that is, only through the contrived practice of uniting with a karmamudrā? Only from a cause of a specific kind does a fruit of this same specific kind arise, and not from another kind. Just as the sprout of a *śālī* tree and not a *kodrava* plant arises from a śālī seed, the uncontrived coemergent arises from the presence of the uncontrived dharmamudrā. Therefore, it is only the dharmamudrā that is the cause of mahāmudrā (to figuratively apply a distinction [between a cause and an effect] to what in fact admits of no such) distinction.[289]

In other words, karmamudrā cannot be the direct cause of mahāmudrā. It only enables a nondual Akṣobhya-type experience, which still needs to be sealed with the seal of Vajrasattva on the basis of pith instructions. These instructions represent an element of dharmamudrā, with which karmamudrā must be combined, and it is only this uncontrived element of dharmamudra that leads to mahāmudrā. In reality, the latter two seals are indivisible, the tiny part of mahāmudrā that shines through based on pith instructions being called dharmamudrā. Shamar Chökyi Drakpa, too, observed that it is the dharmamudrā that serves as a cause of mahāmudrā, and not the karmamudrā.[290] It is not clear, though, when these pith instructions are given. However, if they are necessary for correct recognition of the goal during the third moment, they must precede it.

It should be remembered here that Kāropa sees in *evaṃ*, the symbol of means and insight in union, first of all the acoustic reality of the dharmamudrā, and explains that only those persons who cannot comprehend such a dharmamudrā rely on *evaṃ* in the form of a karmamudrā.[291] From that, one could follow that a karmamudrā is optional and in no way an indispensable initiator of the sequence of seals.

In Maitrīpa's *Instructions on the Four Seals* we find, concerning the dharmamudrā:

> The dharmamudrā includes all phenomena (*dharma*) of sights and sounds, and the true nature of manifold appearances. It is free from the [momentary] coemergent of a karmamudrā....[292] Therefore, that is, given that uncontrived mahāmudrā arises from this dharmamudrā, whose nature is that of an uncontrived entity, the dharmamudrā is called the fruit of maturation.[293]

In his commentary, Rāmapāla explains dharmamudrā in terms of the purification of phenomena through the fivefold enlightenment.[294] This means that the dharmamudrā is here related to a central practice of the outer creation phase, namely, the purification of phenomena through the fivefold enlightenment. This is noteworthy since Rāmapāla says in his commentary on *Presentation of*

Empowerment, verse 24, that of the four seals, the karmamudrā is to be taken as the master empowerment, corresponding with the perfect completion stage. In other words, the way dharmamudrā is presented here suggests not so much a progressive succession after starting with karmamudrā empowerment as rather the possibility of an alternative path that begins with the outer creation phase, or the causal samayamudrā (and so virtually without a karmamudrā).

Mahāmudrā in the *Instructions on the Four Seals* is expounded as follows:

> Mahāmudrā stands for the union of all phenomena into a pair with their own true nature of nonarising. It is free from any thought relating to a perceived object and a perceiving subject—the hindrances of defilements, knowable objects, and so forth having been abandoned. One experiences it as it truly is according to its specific characteristics. It is called stainless fruit. As for its nature, it does not have a form, like all phenomena everywhere, and is all-pervading, unchangeable, and ever present. Mahāmudrā is, therefore, perfect enlightenment in a single moment, and not something that can be broken down into four moments and four joys.[295] . . . When it comes to reality as it truly is, it needs to be learned from the mouth of the guru when they set the wheel of the Dharma in motion.[296]

"Enlightenment in a single moment" does not mean here that mahāmudrā is experienced for a single moment only. It instead refers to an instantaneous realization, because once true reality is experienced as it is, this realization remains.[297]

Concerning the samayamudrā, we find in the *Instructions on the Four Seals* the following:

> The samayamudrā is a fruition maṇḍala of deities that symbolize true reality. The male deity symbolizes means, the female deity insight, and their union nonduality. It, therefore, represents a convention (*samaya*).[298] . . . Since this fruition maṇḍala of deities serves the purpose of sentient beings, it is called a fruit made by people for the sake of others.[299]

The four joys are not only explained on the level of karmamudrā, but also on the levels of dharmamudrā, and samayamudrā. To be sure, there are no four joys, but only coemergent joy, with regard to mahāmudrā. Apart from this, Maitrīpa also relates the first joy alone to the karmamudrā, supreme joy to the dharmamudrā, coemergent joy to mahāmudrā, and the joy of no-joy to the samayamudrā.

In his *Presentation of Empowerment*, Maitrīpa defines the four joys on the level of the dharmamudrā as follows:

> The manifold is realized through the karmamudrā;
> Maturation is the nature of the world.
> Steadfastness in that is freedom from defining
> characteristics;
> And relaxation is the gazing at the world.[300]

While the experience of the four joys was induced physically during the practice of karmamudrā, they arise from words on the level of dharmamudrā. The respective instructions on this level can be gathered from Maitrīpa's *Instructions on the Four Seals*:

> 1. The concept of manifold appearances arises.[301]
> 2. The concept of manifold appearances ceases, and one abides in their coemergent nature
> 3. One realizes that the manifold appearances and the coemergent nature are not two [different things].

4. One does not entertain concepts of either the manifold appearances or the coemergent nature.

These four are respectively joy, supreme joy, coemergent joy, and the joy of no-joy on the level of the dharmamudrā.[302]

The physically induced joy during the moment of manifold activity, such as embracing and kissing,[303] thus corresponds to joy experienced during the recognition that the manifold world are appearances in mind. Their disappearance and one's abiding in the coemergent nature leads to supreme joy, which has first been experienced during the physical level of maturation when bodhicitta reached the tip of the vajra.[304] The coemergent joy—which is experienced on the level of physical karmamudrā during the peak of intercourse at the moment of freedom from defining characteristics[305]—becomes on the dharmamudrā level the realization that the manifold forms are not different from the coemergent nature. The moment of relaxation becomes a state free from the concepts of either the manifold or the coemergent.

In his eight verses on Mahāmudrā, Maitrīpa first equates the latter with nonabiding and explains it in terms of his favored Apratiṣṭhāna Madhyamaka and the practice of amanasikāra. The way Mahāmudrā is presented is entirely in line with the Madhyamaka presentation in the *Jewel Garland of True Reality* and could qualify as a description of Sahajavajra's Sūtra Mahāmudrā. The first Mahāmudrā verse is as follows:

Not to abide in anything
Is known as mahāmudrā.
As self-awareness (i.e., mahāmudrā) is stainless,
The moments of enjoying manifold appearances and so forth do not arise.[306]

Rāmapāla explains "Not to abide in anything" as meaning *amanasikāra*, a practice described as wholesome in the *Ornament of Manifested Wisdom*. Rāmapāla also quotes from this sūtra a verse praising the Buddha as being without recollection and so forth:

> Homage to you, who is without imagined thoughts,
> Whose intellect is not based on anything,
> Who is without recollection, whose realization is
> nonconceptual,
> And who is devoid of all cognitive object.[307]

Rāmapāla concludes that the practice of amanasikāra yields the result of Mahāmudrā through the kindness of the guru:

> ...One should not think that this cannot be practiced because thanks to the kindness of one's venerable guru, mahāmudrā, which has the defining characteristic of being endowed with all supreme qualities, can certainly be made directly manifest. Does mahāmudrā not have the nature of the four moments then? It is stated: "Because self-awareness (i.e., mahāmudrā) is stainless." Being stainless, the three [impure] moments of the manifold and so forth, including their stains, do not occur in it. Therefore, the three [impure] joys do not arise in it either.[308]

Rāmapāla explains here an amanasikāra-based Mahāmudrā beyond the three impure moments. Even though the "pure moment" (i.e., the third moment) and coemergent joy are related to Mahāmudrā in the context of referring the four joys to the four seals, it is beyond the four moments and joys. This is clear from the above quoted *Instructions on the Four Seals*, where Maitrīpa explains with reference to Mahāmudrā as coemergent joy that the latter is perfect enlightenment in a single moment, which cannot be broken down into four moments. As already mentioned above, "enlightenment in a single moment" does not mean here that Mahāmudrā is experienced for a single moment only, but that it is attained instantaneously. Maitrīpa also explains here that the hindrances of defilements and knowable objects are abandoned, and this can hardly relate to a level when still engaged in karmamudrā practice. Moreover, it cannot be the coemergent joy of karmamudrā practice because the closely related *Succession of the Four Seals* takes the wisdom that arises from a prajñā as an "image of the real coemergent."[309] In his *Manifestation of Great Bliss* (*Mahāsukhaprakāśa*),[310] Maitrīpa must be referring to something similar when he notes that the "pure apparent truth should be known to be something in which there is a false manifestation of bliss."

The question thus arises, whether this part of the *Presentation of Empowerment*, or even the preceding verses on dharmamudrā, still describe the exclusively karmamudrā-based third empowerment (i.e., prajñā-wisdom empowerment) or already what Vajrapāṇi calls, in his *Instructions on the Stages Handed Down by the Lineage of Gurus*, the supreme dharmamudrā empowerment on the complete perfection stage and the supreme most mahāmudrā empowerment on the natural completion stage[311] respectively:

> There are two creation stages, an outer one and an inner, profound one. Of the completion stage, there are three divisions: the completion stage proper, the perfect completion stage, and the natural completion stage. Likewise, there are two types of empowerment: artificial, worldly empowerment, and natural, supramundane empowerment. Of the artificial type, there are three subtypes: the master empowerment, the secret empowerment, and the empowerment of prajñā-wisdom. Of the natural type, there are two: the

dharmamudrā and mahāmudrā, which together constitute the fourth. This is as stated [in *Summary of the Meaning of Empowerment*, verse 3]:

The first is the vase empowerment;
And the second, the excellent secret empowerment;
The third is the prajñā-wisdom empowerment;
And the fourth one is just like that.

The master empowerment purifies the body; the secret empowerment, speech; prajñā-wisdom empowerment, the mind; and the fourth is a pith instruction, the seed of bodhicitta. Empowerments can be further categorized as supreme, average, or inferior ones. Inferior empowerment corresponds to the outer creation stage (that is, the [causal] samayamudrā), the master empowerment, and the creation stage, that is, deity yoga. Average empowerment is the karmamudrā, of which there are two types: the reassurance that one is a tathāgata and the reassurance that one is a Vajradhara. The secret empowerment and the reassurance that one is a tathāgata constitute the profound creation stage. The reassurance that one is a Vajradhara represents the completion stage proper. Supreme empowerment is the perfect completion stage, that is, the dharmamudrā. The supreme most empowerment is the natural completion stage, that is, mahāmudrā.[312]

Maitrīpa's Direct Approach

The supreme most mahāmudrā empowerment could be also a complete empowerment of its own, independent of the first empowerments. This is at least what we can gather from the *Twenty Verses on True Reality*, where Maitrīpa distinguishes inferior practitioners relying on karmamudrā and samayamudrā from those with sharp faculties approaching mahāmudrā directly:

> Those with inferior capacities have perfectly cultivated the circle,
> With the help of the karma- and samaya-mudrās.
> With a mind directed to the external in the matter of pure reality,
> They meditate on enlightenment.
>
> In union with a *jñānamudrā*,[313]
> With Mañjuvajra or the like as chief deity,
> All this being neither a true nor a false appearance—
> This is the practice of yogins with average faculties.
>
> To those unable to know
> The level of self-empowerment as it really is,
> The path is taught in gradual steps
> Toward the attaining of enlightenment.
>
> Given your affection for deities,
> How is there not a mental imprint?
> Even if this mental imprint is pure,
> It will still be like all other imprints.
>
> The yogin who has seen true reality, however,
> Is wholly devoted to mahāmudrā;
> His faculties being unsurpassable,
> He abides in [the realization of] the nature of all entities.[314]

In other words, Maitrīpa considers immediate access to the goal of buddhahood possible, either through pointing-out instructions or the kind of direct mind-to-mind transmission Maitrīpa received from Śavaripa. In his *Explaining the Recognition of the Three Kāyas* (*Sku gsum ngo sprod rnam bshad*), the Eighth Karmapa Mikyö Dorjé interestingly refers to Maitrīpa's *Five Aspects* in support of such an approach:[315]

> In the *Five Aspects* from Maitrīpa's amanasikāra cycle it is said: "[The crown of his head displays a Vajrasattva, for] he has the nature of Vajrasattva, being inseparable from emptiness and compassion. Therefore,[316] he has the nature of cause and effect and the defining characteristic of emptiness, which is endowed with all supreme aspects. Being unconditioned and having the nature of suchness, he is [also] the dharmakāya. Being a mere appearance, he is the sambhogakāya. Given that he has the nature of consciousness on the level of the imagined,[317] he is the nirmāṇakāya. Possessing the single taste of all three kāyas, he is the svābhāvikakāya.[318] This is stated [in *Twenty Verses on Mahāyāna*, verse 19]: 'The unconditioned mind is the dharmakāya; realization is the defining characteristics of the sambhogakāya. Then there is that: a variety has been emanated (i.e., the nirmāṇakāya). The natural one (i.e., the nijakāya) is the nature of all three.'"
>
> In these excellent explanations, it has been taught that the three kāyas from the coemergent luminosity of one's mind are directly pointed out, which means that it is not as if they are taken as the path and practiced.[319]

What we have here is a disclosure model of reality, the Vajrasattva maṇḍala not being cultivated in the usual creation stage manner but directly pointed out. In other words, one has, in the eyes of

Mikyö Dorjé, a direct access to the buddha kāyas. Mikyö Dorjé further explains that since such pointing-out introductions are common with sūtra and tantra, they differ from the mahāmudrā of the completion stage of the Unsurpassable Yoga Tantra. The related view and meditation of this practice are then explained to be based mainly on Maitrīpa's amanasikāra cycle:

> Likewise, mere mahāmudrā like that is not posited as the mahāmudrā of the completion stage of the Unsurpassable Mantrayāna. The way of this view and meditation cannot be compared to the practice of what is common in sūtra and tantra, because the great master Maitrīpa emphasized the amanasikāra cycle of not becoming mentally engaged, nonarising, and transcending the mind, while he abided well by these instructions.[320]

CHAPTER 9

Mahāmudrā Practice

Creation and Completion Stages

In Maitrīpa's system, the twofold division of tantric practice into the creation (*utpattikrama*) and completion stages (*utpannakrama*) of the *Hevajra Tantra*[321] (a Yoginī Tantra) undergoes further division to relate the system of the four seals in the Yoginī Tantras to the five stages of the Yoga Tantras (i.e., the *Ārya* tradition of the *Tantra of the Sum Total of Mysteries*). The creation stage thus fans out into an outer and an inner one, and the completion stage into a simple completion stage, a perfect completion stage (*pariniṣpannakrama*), and a natural completion stage (*svābhāvikakrama*).[322] From Rāmapāla's commentary on *Presentation of Empowerment*, verse 38,[323] we get the following:

YOGINĪ TANTRA (MAITRĪPA)	ĀRYA SCHOOL (MAGADHI TRADITION)	ĀRYA SCHOOL (KASHMIRI TRADITION)
outer creation stage	sphere stage (*piṇḍīkrama*)	vajra recitation stage (*vajrajāpakrama*)
inner creation stage	vajra recitation stage (*vajrajāpakakrama*)	universally pure stage (*sarvaśuddhiviśud-dhikrama*)
completion stage	stage of self-empowerment (*svādhiṣṭhānakrama*)	stage of self-empowerment (*svādhiṣṭhānakrama*)

YOGINĪ TANTRA (MAITRĪPA)	ĀRYA SCHOOL (MAGADHI TRADITION)	ĀRYA SCHOOL (KASHMIRI TRADITION)
perfect completion stage	stage of perfect enlightenment (*abhisambodhikrama*)	supreme secret bliss of enlightenment stage (*paramarahasya-sukhābhisaṁbodhikrama*)
natural completion stage	stage of indivisible union (*yuganaddhakrama*)	stage of indivisible union (*yuganaddhakrama*)

The term "sphere stage" for the outer creation stage is reminiscent of Nāgārjuna's *Practice of the Sphere Stage* (*Piṇḍīkramasādhana*), which describes the rites and visualizations of the maṇḍalas and deities involved in the creation stage of the *Tantra of the Sum Total of Mysteries*.[324] In the same commentary on verse 38, Rāmapāla also calls the first stage "having-the-form-of-*mantra*" (*mantramūrti*) and the second, mind-objective (*cittannidhyapti*), which also goes under the name "universally pure stage" (*sarvaśuddhiviśuddhikrama*).[325] In his *Brightening Lamp* (*Pradīpoddyotana*), Candrakīrti describes the mind-objective stage as the one where the ordinary five sense faculties and their objective realms have dissolved.[326] In another series, vajra recitation is also known as the isolation of speech (*vākviveka*), the second stage ("mind-objective") as isolation of mind (*cittaviveka*), self-empowerment as the illusory body (*māyādeha*), and enlightenment as luminosity (*prabhāsvaratā*).[327]

The two systems found in Rāmapāla's commentary correspond to the Magadhi and Kashmiri traditions of the five stages. The Magadhi tradition, represented by Abhayākaragupta, Muniśrībhadra, and others, has the extra "sphere stage" (*piṇḍīkrama*) preceding the vajra recitation stage at the expense of the universally pure stage.[328] The Kashmiri tradition represented by masters such as Lakṣmī and Nāgabodhi accords with Nāgārjuna's *Five Stages* (*Pañcakrama*).[329]

This leads us to the question of where the beginning of Maitrīpa's four seals is located in the system of the five stages. In his commentary on *Presentation of Empowerment*, verse 23, Rāmapāla claims that karmamudrā should be regarded as the master empowerment, corresponding to the perfect completion stage. Still, in his equation of the five stages with the four seals, he takes karmamudrā to correspond to the first two stages of the *Five Stages*. This means that the sequence of the four seals starts with vitality control (*prāṇāyāma*) through the manipulation of the vital winds (i.e., vajra recitation or the isolation of speech). While for Āryadeva, this is already part of the completion stage, for Rāmapāla, it is still the profound creation stage. In his *Instructions on the Stages Handed Down by the Lineage of Gurus*, Vajrapāṇi, too, distinguishes two types of karmamudrā, those leading to the reassurance that one is a tathāgata and the reassurance that one is a Vajradhara. For Vajrapāṇi, the secret empowerment and the former reassurance constitute the profound creation stage, while the latter reassurance forms the completion stage.[330]

Maitrīpa's *Manifestation of the Goddess Essencelessness* (*Nairātmyāprakāśa*)

The way Maitrīpa conceives of tantric practice in these five stages can be best learned from his *Manifestation of the Goddess Essencelessness*, which is a short practice (*sādhana*) of the Goddess Essencelessness (Nairātmyā), the female consort of Hevajra. Here one starts by visualizing the five aspects of Nairātmyā, which correspond to the five buddha families in the standard maṇḍala. Next comes a karmamudrā-type practice, in order to generate bodhicitta, whose nature is the fifteen yoginīs of Nairātmyā.[331] As the goal of coemergent joy, which is marked in the third position within the four moments and joys, bodhicitta has the nature of great bliss. This leads to the first completion stage, in which the maṇḍala emerges instantaneously without creating it from seed syllables, and so forth, as is done during the outer creation stage. Next comes the perfect completion stage, on which one's body is realized as having the nature of Nairātmyā's circle. The fifteen yoginīs then are the thirty-two channels running from the place of great bliss. The final completion stage, which is called natural, is the direct manifestation of bodhicitta, the inseparable union of emptiness and compassion. In the *Manifestation of the Goddess Essencelessness*, Maitrīpa describes his five stages as follows:

> Possessing the pride of being Nairātmyā, one is identical with her. Here, in order to perform the six-branch yoga, she must be cultivated as appearing in the colors black, red, yellow, green, blue, and white, in that order.[332] As the vividness of meditation increases, she first appears as the full moon covered by clouds. Then, with even greater vividness, she appears as an illusion. Then, with even more vividness, she manifests as if in a dream. Immediately after that, with the full maturation of vividness, the Mahāmudrā yogin succeeds [in reaching the goal of this practice], attaining a state in which dreams and the waking state are not different. This is the creation stage.
>
> Alternatively, the bodhicitta that arises from the union of the penis and the vagina and has the nature of great bliss is located between the supreme joy and the joy of no-joy (i.e., coemergent joy). [Inasmuch as] it has the nature of the fifteen [moon] parts, this bodhicitta should be instantly seen as having the nature of the fifteen yoginīs, who appear with the previously mentioned colors and attributes. This is because bodhicitta is the nature of the five skandhas, four elements, six objects, body, speech, and mind. This is the profound creation stage.[333]

> The circle of the maṇḍala, whose nature is the fifteen yoginīs, must be perceived instantly without even seeing a seed. This is the completion stage.
>
> Then there is the complete perfection stage. In the vajra body, which is undoubtedly empowered by wisdom, thirty-two channels run from the place of great bliss. They are the fifteen yoginīs in the sense that the very vajra body has the nature of Nairātmyā's circle....
>
> The natural completion stage is the act of making the bodhicitta, which flows as the effortless inseparable union [of compassion and emptiness], directly manifest.[334]

It is important to note here that Maitrīpa explains the ordinary creation stage as an optional practice and not a requirement for the subsequent stages. The word "alternatively" at the beginning of the second paragraph above implies that the yogin can start directly at the profound creation stage, and by implication, possibly even at a perfection stage. Now, if it is possible to begin with profound creation stage or karmamudrā practice, then an empowerment and related practice could also start on this level, or at one that is even more advanced. In other words, an empowerment could merely consist of its most central element, an immediate mind-to-mind transmission, during which a qualified master introduces an open disciple to the true nature of mind. Afterward, the practice is to simply cultivate that experience. This, after all, would be what Gö Lotsāwa Zhönnu Pel and Tukwan Lobzang Chökyi Nyima mean by a tradition "not based on deity yoga and without the sequence of the four seals."[335]

In this context, it should also be noted that Maitrīpa stands in a tradition that goes back to Saraha, who propagated in the majority of his dohās immediate access to the enlightened qualities of the guru beyond the methods of tantras and mantras:

When one's own mind is completely purified,
The [enlightened] quality of the guru enters one's heart.
In this way, Saraha realized the state of the sage (i.e., his guru) through not becoming mentally engaged.
I have not seen a single tantra, a single mantra.[336]

Mahāmudrā Practice and the Maitreya Works

As we have seen above, Rāmapāla relates Maitrīpa's Mahāmudrā to nonabiding and not becoming mentally engaged, to be understood along the lines of the *Magic Formula for Entering the Nonconceptual.* This also establishes a relation to the *Distinguishing the Phenomenal World of Mental Representation from the True Nature of Phenomena*, because here as well nonconceptual wisdom is cultivated by abandoning the same set of characteristic signs as in the *Magic Formula for Entering the Nonconceptual.*[337] However, the *Distinguishing the Phenomenal World of Mental Representation from the True Nature of Phenomena* does not explain that the characteristic signs are abandoned through mental nonengagement, and Maitreya explicitly states that nonconceptual wisdom is not merely mental nonengagement.[338] If we also understand amanasikāra to mean self-empowerment within luminosity as explained in Maitrīpa's *Justification of Nonconceptual Realization*, we have here a cognizant element of nonconceptual realization, which accords with the *Distinguishing the Phenomenal World of Mental Representation from the True Nature of Phenomena*'s nonconceptual wisdom. In the absence of conceptual engagement in terms of a perceived and perceiver, mind's luminosity or cognizant aspect turns into a direct realization of its own true nature. In other words, the simple capacity of any cognition to experience itself in the most basic sense deepens into the direct realization of nonconceptual wisdom, which has the capacity to experience its own nature (emptiness) while simultaneously experiencing its lucidity as inseparable from this nature.[339]

In the *Distinguishing the Phenomenal World of Mental Representation from the True Nature of Phenomena*, a Maitreya text Maitrīpa allegedly rediscovered,[340] the process of abandoning the set of four characteristic signs is accompanied by a four-stage practice (*prayoga*) that not only deconstructs the duality of a perceived object and perceiving subject but also enables a realization of nonduality. This state is characterized in the *Distinguishing the Phenomenal World of Mental Representation from the True Nature of Phenomena* as the luminosity of fundamental transformation.[341] The relevant passage (the root text is in bold) together with Vasubandhu's commentary reads as follows:

> **Correct practice (*prayoga*) is comprehended under four points, namely, because of the practice of apprehending** means: because one apprehends everything as cognition-only (*vijñaptimātra*); **the practice of not apprehending** means: because one does not apprehend objects of reference; **the practice of not apprehending apprehending** means: because in the absence of an object, mere cognition (*vijñaptimātra*) is not apprehended, because cognition (*vijñapti*) is not possible in the absence of an object of cognition; **the practice of apprehending by not apprehending** means: because nonduality is apprehended by not apprehending duality.[342]

If nonduality was the mere absence of duality, nothing could be apprehended, and therefore, as we have seen above, a cognizant aspect of amanasikāra, luminous self-empowerment comes into play. In the *Distinguishing the Phenomenal World of Mental Representation from the True Nature of Phenomena*, that nonduality is also constituted by something positive is clear from how Vasubandhu describes the final state of fundamental transformation, to which the fourth practice leads. In the last part of his commentary on the

Distinguishing the Phenomenal World of Mental Representation from the True Nature of Phenomena, he states:

> Likewise, in the case of the fundamental transformation, it is not that natural luminosity did not exist before; it is only that it did not appear due to the manifestation of adventitious hindrances. . . .[343]

The proximity of this Maitreya text to the *Justification of Nonconceptual Realization* must be also seen against the background of Maitrīpa's rediscovery of the *Distinguishing the Phenomenal World of Mental Representation from the True Nature of Phenomena* and *Sublime Continuum*. In the *Pith Instructions on the Sublime Continuum*[344] it is stated, in a slight variety of the story, that Maitrīpa received pith instructions on these two texts from the future buddha Maitreya in a dream, instead of receiving them themselves.[345] This account better corresponds with the fact that the *Distinguishing the Phenomenal World of Mental Representation from the True Nature of Phenomena* and *Sublime Continuum* were known by Maitrīpa's teacher at Vikramaśīla Jñānaśrīmitra (ca. 980–1040).[346] In any case, Maitrīpa's close relation to the Maitreya works has a discernible impact on his Mahāmudrā practice.

Both texts, the *Pith Instructions on the Sublime Continuum* and the *Guiding Explanation on the Basis of the Distinguishing the Phenomenal World of Mental Representation from the True Nature of Phenomena* (*Chos nyid kyi khrid*) contain transmission lists, which specify that the pith instructions Maitrīpa received from Maitreya were transmitted to the Kashmiri Paṇḍita Sajjana and Tsen Khawoché (b. 1021). Tsen Khawoché, a disciple of Drapa Ngonshé, requested Sajjana to bestow on him the Maitreya works along with their pith instructions, since he wanted to make these works his "practice of preparing for death" (*'chi chos*). Sajjana taught all five works of

Maitreya, with Lotsāwa Zu Gawé Dorjé acting as the translator.[347] Besides, Sajjana gave special pith instructions on the *Sublime Continuum*.[348] These two masters, Sajjana and Tsen Khawoché, thus started the Tsen tradition of the Maitreya works that sometimes also referred to as the meditation tradition (*sgom lugs*). The corresponding analytical tradition (*mtshan nyid lugs*) of the Maitreya works goes back to teachings Ngog Loden Shérab (1059–1109) received from Sajjana. The analytical and meditation traditions of the Maitreya works nicely reflect Maitrīpa's blend of Mahāmudrā and Madhyamaka, the combination of direct and analytical approaches that crucially constitutes the underlying structure of Maitrīpa's texts.

The *Guiding Explanation on the Basis of the Distinguishing the Phenomenal World of Mental Representation from the True Nature of Phenomena*, another instruction transmitted through Maitrīpa, includes an interesting distinction of the usual four stages of meditation from an instantaeous approach not found as such in the *Distinguishing the Phenomenal World of Mental Representation from the True Nature of Phenomena*:

> There are two ways of meditating on the nature of phenomena (*dharmatā*). When meditating gradually, one meditates that anything that appears is one's mind, like in a dream. Then one meditates that external things do not exist in their own right as material objects in a dream. Then one meditates that consciousness without a corresponding external thing does not exist in its own right either, just as the consciousness of a nonexisting vase does not exist. Since neither of the two exists, one finally meditates that consciousness never existed in the first place, not [truly] existing just like the sky. When meditating instantaneously that both object and subject do not exist, one abides without the movement

> of thoughts in the true nature of phenomena beyond mind.
> This is because one's confused thoughts are not real.[349]

What Maitrīpa was thus told by Maitreya is very similar to Vajrapāṇi's explanation of the four signs of Mahāmudrā meditation (see chapter 10) and Gö Lotsāwa Zhönnu Pel's reading of the four Mahāmudrā yogas into the four steps of meditation in the *Distinguishing the Phenomenal World of Mental Representation from the True Nature of Phenomena*.[350] With reference to Lama Zhang Tsalpa Tsöndrü (1123–1193), Zhönnu Pel also maintains that Mahāmudrā is attained in one moment, and confused persons conceive it in terms of levels and paths.[351] In the meditation tradition of the Maitreya works, we thus have, besides the gradual path of the four steps of meditation (*prayoga*), the possibility of immediate access to ultimate reality (i.e., *dharmatā*). It is not clear whether this was intended by Maitrīpa himself, but it is clearly spelled out in Vajrapāṇi's commentary on Maitrīpa's *Jewel Garland of True Reality*.

In the *Pith Instructions on the Sublime Continuum* that Maitrīpa received from Maitreya, the main topics of the *Sublime Continuum* are presented in terms of pointing-out instructions on the true nature of mind. In a dream, Maitreya introduces Maitrīpa to the relationship between the naturally pure mind and the saṃsāra of thoughts (that arise from the pure mind) by instructing him to cut loose his fear and attachment and jump into a fire. Maitreya then asked Maitrīpa where to locate his person and fear. Since this was only a dream, Maitrīpa became aware that these appearances had no basis. Maitreya then told him that the dream was naturally pure, whereupon he re-emerged together with all the appearances of his former self before he had jumped into the fire. Maitrīpa thus understood that similarly, all phenomena arise from the naturally pure mind, and because of this, he realized the remaining three of the four inconceivable points of the *Sublime Continuum*.[352]

CHAPTER 10

The Four Signs of Mahāmudrā Meditation

THE OLD FOURFOLD Yogācāra practice, by which the four sets of characteristic signs are abandoned, in the *Distinguishing the Phenomenal World of Mental Representation from the True Nature of Phenomena*, reappears in a slightly modified form as the four signs of Mahāmudrā meditation. They cannot be directly attributed to Maitrīpa, but the Karma Kagyü master Karma Trinlépa (1456–1539) repeatedly comments on the *Dohākoṣa* of Saraha (in whose tradition Maitrīpa stands) in terms of the four signs or symbols (*brda*) in ḍākinī language.[353] They are mindfulness, beyond mindfulness, non-arising, and transcending the intellect,[354] which stand for a four-step Mahāmudrā meditation. With mindfulness, one realizes that external objects are but the vibrant radiance of one's mind. This triggers a process of deconstructing all perceived objects so that there is nothing left to focus on. This is what is referred to as "beyond mindfulness," a state in which a perceiving subject does not make sense anymore, the other half constituting duality—what it perceives—having disappeared. The remaining nondual mind is then realized as nonarisen (the third sign), or in other words, as being empty of an own nature. This Yogācāra-Madhyamaka collapsing of our common experience makes room for the soterial relevant emergence of coemergent bliss or wisdom, which "transcends the intellect." These four signs are already found in the *Heart Sūtra* commentary of Maitrīpa's heart disciple Vajrapāṇi:

> The four dharmas (i.e., the four signs or practices) pertaining to the identical essence of the nature of mind and the nature of phenomena are mindfulness, beyond mindfulness, nonarising, and transcending the intellect. They are heard at one and the same time in two ways—profound and manifest. The profound is beyond studying, reflecting, and meditating. It is an expression that denotes instantaneous abiding in an equipoise that is not essentially different from the dharmadhātu of all the buddhas of the three times and all sentient beings of the three realms.[355]

The four signs are also found in another *Dohākoṣa* commentary, the *Commentary on a Treasure of Dohās, Songs of Essential Meaning* (*Dohākoṣasārārthagītāṭikā*) of Advaya Avadhūtipa (ca. eleventh to thirteenth century). The commentary was probably not by Maitrīpa, but written in his spirit:

> To encounter any appearance is "mindfulness." To encounter its emptiness is "beyond mindfulness." To encounter "nonarising" is nonarisen reality.[356]

Of interest is also the following passage from the same *Dohākoṣa* commentary:

> At the time one is still ignorant—neither knowing, nor realizing, nor perceiving—the genuine guru's teaching in terms of the signs and means is as follows: Abandoning mindfulness is generosity, experiencing the state beyond mindfulness is

> discipline, enduring nonarising is acceptance, and the meditative concentration of inseparable, uninterrupted diligence is insight transcending the intellect.[357]

It is particularly noteworthy that while still ignorant and not knowing, one even abandons mindfulness in an act of generosity. This excludes the possibility of restricting "beyond mindfulness" and the rest to an advanced level of the path. In the *Commentary on a Treasure of Dohās, Songs of Essential Meaning* we also find an explanation of the first three of the four signs concerning appearances, found again in different variations in Karma Trinlépa's commentary:

> To encounter any appearance is "mindfulness." To encounter its emptiness is "beyond mindfulness."' To encounter "nonarising" is nonarisen reality.[358]

Of particular interest is Karma Trinlépa's interpretation of Saraha's dohā for the tantric feast of the "assembly circle"[359] in terms of the four signs on the secret level. Saraha's *Dohākoṣa*, verse 25, is as follows:

> Eating, drinking, enjoying intercourse,
> And always filling the *cakra*s, again and again—
> Through such a teaching, one attains the other world (i.e., mahāmudrā).
> The master stamps on the heads of those in the ignorant world and moves on.[360]

Karma Trinlépa's outer and inner explanation elaborates the *gaṇacakra* feast in a way that reveals tantric details, which are typically kept secret. The exoteric (or "sūtric") yet "secret" commentary correlates the four main activities of the feast—eating and drinking the samaya substancies, intercourse, and cakra practice ("filling the cakras") with the four signs of Mahāmudrā meditation:

> As for the secret explanation, through the pith instructions on "mindfulness," one recognizes the manifold appearances as mind and eats them. Through the pith instructions on "beyond mindfulness," one knows this very mind as empty and drinks it. Through the pith instructions on "nonarising," both appearance and mind meet in the single taste [of everything] and are thus realized as being united in indivisible union. Through the pith instructions on "transcending the intellect," one embraces self-awareness as coemergent joy. Through the pith instruction on practicing ineffable reality, one fills one's mental continuum continuously with wisdom again and again in an effort that is unceasing as a turning wheel.[361] By practicing such teaching, one passes beyond this world.[362]

In other words, eating and drinking the samaya substances equates with mindfulness and beyond mindfulness. This means that with "mindfulness," one eats the manifold appearances by recognizing them as not being different from mind. "Beyond mindfulness" refers to drinking the mind by realizing its emptiness. "Nonarising" is then related to intercourse, understood in the sense of the indivisible union of appearances and mind. This must be taken against the background that appearances and mind are identical in terms of their nonarising or emptiness. In the formal tantric practice of the outer and inner explanations, the cakras are filled through controlling the winds in the energy channels. This helps to recognize and sustain the four joys. The pith instructions called "transcending the intellect" lead to embracing self-awareness as coemergent joy, the most supreme of the four joys. Karma Trinlépa further elaborates the four gaṇacakra phases of eating, drinking, intercourse, and filling the cakras in another explanation of verse 25 of the *Dohākoṣa*:

> As for the explanation in terms of true reality, the Mahāmudrā yogins take as their food appearances emerging in unobstructed vibrant radiance. They make as their drink emptiness—their dissolving into the nonarising original state. Both appearance and emptiness are united in indivisible union. Putting this into practice, the effortless joy of self-awareness becomes directly manifest. If one practices repeating such a sequence, continuously filling the cakras of knowable objects (all phenomenal existence) with coemergent wisdom, one reaches the other world through this Dharma of indivisible union. . . .[363]

This departure from the physical elements of gaṇacakra to a mere mental level of eating appearances and drinking the mind finds its parallels in the tantric Nāgārjuna's *Succession of the Four Seals* and the works of Maitrīpa, such as the *Presentation of Empowerment* and *Instructions on the Four Seals*. As we have seen above, these texts teach the sequence of four seals (karmamudrā, dharmamudrā, mahāmudrā, and samayamudrā), which lies at the center of the completion stage practice in the Yoginī Tantras. Karmamudrā practice involves an initial recognition of the four joys at four distinct moments on a physical level, similar to what happens during a gaṇacakra feast. The four joys are then experienced again on the level of dharmamudrā, which is based on speech,[364] and the respective instructions are similar to Karma Trinlépa's pith instructions quoted above.

Maitrīpa's teaching, in this case his particular twofold understanding of amanasikāra, also shines through in Karma Trinlépa's commentary on *Dohākoṣa*, verse 90:[365]

> As for the secret explanation, the means to accomplish the supreme siddhi is fourfold and indicated by the letters [*e vaṃ ma yā*]: mindfulness, beyond mindfulness, nonarising, and transcending the intellect. First, by way of special instructions, I teach "mindfulness," which means cutting [ordinary conceptual] mind from its root. Then, second, drinking the juice of "beyond mindfulness," that is, of resting in the sphere of mental nonengagement (*a-manasikāra*), one forgets to cling to the notion "mine." Then, third, through special instructions on "nonarising," which make one understand the meaning of the single syllable for "nonarising," [the privative] *a*, one realizes that the nature of mind has never arisen. Then, fourth, through the special instructions on "transcending the intellect," which allow passing over to the ultimate, one no longer knows even the words or signs for "nonarising." This is liberation beyond expression in words or thoughts.[366]

For Maitrīpa, beyond mindfulness is linked with nonarising through the wide semantic range he attributes to his central term amanasikāra. As we have seen above, it not only means "mental nonengagement," but also mental engagement with the privative *a* of amanasikāra, which stands for *anutpāda* ("nonarising") or emptiness. The final analysis of the letter *a* as luminosity and *manasikāra* as self-empowerment is then the fourth sign, which is at times taken as self-awareness or coemergent joy.

To sum up, leaving initial mindfulness behind, the remaining three signs—beyond mindfulness, nonarising, and transcending the intellect—stand for a practice beyond the usual duality of a perceived and perceiver. Again, once one has established through mindfulness that all external appearances are mind only, one eventually realizes that there is nothing to concentrate on. At this point, the final three signs, which in the eyes of Padampa Sangyé are Saraha's three signs alone, describe the progressive realization of nonduality, Madhyamaka emptiness, and finally, the soteriologically relevant emergence of coemergent bliss or wisdom. The four signs are thus based on and closely related to Yogācāra texts, such as the *Distinguishing the Phenomenal World of Mental Representation from the True Nature of Phenomena* .

The example of Maitreya pointing out Maitrīpa's naturally pure mind shows that the thick net of conceptually created duality that usually prevents immediate access to the true nature of mind below the first bodhisattva level can also be cut through by unconventional techniques. Going by Maitrīpa's disciple Sahajavajra, this does not necessarily involve formal tantric empowerment and practice.

Conclusion

The life of Maitrīpa fully reflects his century, when Indian Buddhism went through dramatic changes through fully integrating the latest forms of highest yoga tantras. Having been trained under famous teachers, such as Nāropa and Ratnākaraśānti, and exposed to the Siddha milieu of infamous Śavaripa, Maitrīpa produced a fascinating oeuvre that combines a challenging Yogācāra-Madhyamaka philosophy of non-foundationalism with the *Hevajra Tantra*. Maitrīpa thus compares buddhahood to the truly nondual bliss and emptiness of coemergent joy. Thanks to special pith instructions, coemergent joy can be experienced for the first time during the peak of physical union with a karmamudrā during empowerment. Two of the four drops descending from the crown of the head are then released from the tip of the vajra. This lines Maitrīpa up with his early teacher Ratnākaraśānti and puts him in opposition to Nāropa, whose tantric practice is closely related to the *Kālacakra Tantra*, as it involves completely retaining the descending drop and drawing it up again. Maitrīpa accepts this as Buddhist but classifies it as forceful (*haṭha*) yoga, which he did not follow. No traces of Kālacakra's influence can be observed in Maitrīpa's works. His disciple Sahajavajra, however, describes empowerment in the *Compendium of Tenets* in accordance with the *Summary of Empowerment* (*Sekoddeśa*), the only surviving part of the original *Kālacakra Tantra*.

Among the Buddhist tantric scholars of the eleventh and twelfth centuries, opposing systems of empowerment were one of the most discussed issues. The topic gets even more critical in the Kagyü schools, as Maitrīpa and Nāropa are both considered essential teachers of Marpa Lotsāwa. The Fourth Shamarpa, Chödrak Yeshé, thus found it necessary to explain in a long comparative study how Maitrīpa's and Nāropa's empowerments can be brought in line. Interestingly, Chödrak Yeshé sides with Maitrīpa, accepting the competing Kālacakra-based system merely in an inclusive way as provisional teaching to further beginners in the generation stage. Maitrīpa's and Rāmapāla's interpretation of the *Hevajra Tantra*, which involves changing the sequence of the third and fourth joys, putting coemergent joy in the third position, proves to be useful for Chödrak Yeshé's strategy to demonstrate the common intentional ground that Maitrīpa and Nāropa share.[367]

Even in the field of philosophy, Maitrīpa did not move so far away from his Yogācāra teacher, Ratnākaraśānti. Indeed, Yogācāra did not remain at the peak of his buddhology. Still, for Maitrīpa, the Yogācāra tenets and the realization of Yogācāra emptiness remain an essential step to the non-foundational Madhyamaka of Nonabiding. Moreover, Yogācāra terminology, such as self-awareness, plays a vital role in providing experiential terms to describe Maitrīpa's direct Mahāmudrā realization of a true reality that is otherwise taken as ineffable. It is in this sense that Maitrīpa claims that a Madhyamaka based on self-awareness is superior. One could say that the paradox of trying to describe the ineffable lies at the heart of Buddhist doctrine, as the Buddha first thought it impossible to express his enlightenment in words, but ended up spending the rest of his roughly forty-five years trying to communicate what cannot be said.

Teachings

Maitrīpa's Collection of Texts on Nonconceptual Realization (Amanasikāra)

CHAPTER 11

A Summary of the Amanasikāra Texts

THIS SUMMARY introduces the translation part of the book starting with a brief overview to facilitate the amanasikāra texts.[368] On top of the twenty-four texts found in Haraprasad Shastri's *Collected Works of Advayavajra* (*Advayavajrasaṃgraha*),[369] I include here also, as in the 2015 publication, the *Pith Instruction on True Reality Called a Tresasure of Dohās* and the *Pith Instruction on Settling the Mind Without Becoming Engaged in the Thought Processes of Projecting and Gathering—A Genuine Secret*, both of which are part of the Seventh Karmapa Chödrak Gyatso's amanasikāra cycle. In Chödrak Gyatso's collection of Indian Mahāmudrā works, the *Succession of the Four Seals* forms part not of the amanasikāra cycle but of the cycle of the six works on essential meaning. Even though its authorship remains controversial, I include it also here on the basis of the Indian manuscripts.[370] It may not be by Maitrīpa, but its combination of tantric Mahāmudrā with the amanasikāra practice of the sūtras provides the amanasikāra cycle with a perfect doctrinal basis. It should be further noted that the compilers of the Tengyur did not recognize that two texts of the Tibetan cycle[371] were translations of the same Indian text *The Five Verses on Transcendant Love* (*Premapañcaka*). On a final note, I did not translate the *Abbreviated Manual of Empowerment*,[372] which is found in both Butön's *Catalogue of Instructions* (*gsan yig*) and the *Indian Mahāmudrā Works* and attributed to Maitrīpa. Several passages are similar to the *Summary of the Meaning of Empowerment*, but written in a way that differs from what we expect of a typical translation from a written Sanskrit text. Thus, the *Abbreviated Manual of Empowerment* probably never existed as a Sanskrit text.[373]

1. The Destruction of Wrong Views (*Kudṛṣṭinirghātana*)

The *Destruction of Wrong Views* situates Maitrīpa's blend of Mahāmudrā and Madhyamaka within the more general Mahāyāna context of the six perfections (*pāramitā*). It then elaborates in detail the daily routine of a good adept, such as taking refuge, observing the vows of not killing and so forth, avoiding the ten unwholesome deeds, washing one's face with clean water, recalling the three jewels, mantra recitations, and meditation. The meditation includes the visualization, worship, and praise of a maṇḍala of the five buddha families with Akṣobhya in the center. With these many details, Maitrīpa shows the necessity of conventional Dharma practice. The quintessence of the *Destruction of Wrong Views* is that even though the first five perfections of generosity, discipline, patience, diligence, and meditation (i.e., "initial activity") are performed automatically by those who are realized, they need to be intentionally performed by those who are still learning. In other words, if initial activity does not unfold without effort, one is obviously still in need of learning on the path of accumulating merit and wisdom. The sixth perfection (i.e., the perfection of insight, *prajñāpāramitā*) is inseparably linked with the first five perfections. This union results in an advanced practice of initial activity, such as being generous (*dāna*) by even offering one's body. This is how Maitrīpa defines the tantric concept of "mad conduct"—that is, conduct in which the adept appears to be mad in order to test his own freedom from worldly concerns.

2. The *Commentary on the [Initial] Statement of* The Destruction of Wrong Views (*Kudṛṣṭinirghātavākyaṭippinikā*)

The relatively short commentary on the *The Destruction of Wrong Views* adds only a few points of clarification. For example, it subdivides the state of no more learning into the state of fruition and the state of working for others. Furthermore, it elaborates on three aspects of initial activity, i.e., proper intention, the practice of conviction, and having gained power over the following five concerns: defilements, appearances, karma, means, and causing sentient beings to ripen. The practice of conviction is here explained in terms of ten perfections: generosity, discipline, patience, diligence, meditation, insight, skill in means, aspiration, strength, and wisdom; and the attainment of bodhisattva levels in terms of seven perfections: generosity, discipline, patience, diligence, meditation, insight, and skill in means.

3. The Major Offenses (*Mūlāpattayaḥ*) and 4. The Gross Offenses (*Sthūlāpattayaḥ*)

The next two texts, which list major and gross offenses, are missing in the Tibetan Tengyur, but are suited to the context of formal tantric practice, such as keeping one's commitments (*samaya*). Not doing so is considered a gross offence. In case of having committed any of the major or gross offenses, one should perform *pūjā* and keep the enlightened attitude (in the case of major offenses) or worship one's teacher and confess openly (in the case of gross offenses).

5. A Jewel Garland of True Reality (*Tattvaratnāvalī*)

The *Jewel Garland of True Reality* is one of Maitrīpa's most important texts, as it systematically presents the four philosophical tenets: Vaibhāṣika, Sautrāntika, Yogācāra, and Madhyamaka. This is followed by the famous verse from the *Lamp Illumination of the Three Systems* (*Nayatrayapradīpa*), which states the reasons for the mantra system (*mantranaya*) being superior. For further information about this method, Maitrīpa refers the reader to his *Presentation of Empowerment*. This comment is interesting, since it builds a bridge between the non-tantric method of perfections and the *Presentation of Empowerment*'s explanation of the four seals,[374] skipping the six vase empowerments and implicitly any creation stage practice. It should be noticed that in his *Compendium of Tenets* (*Sthitisamāsa*), Sahajavajra[375] follows the lead of his master's *Jewel Garland of True Reality* and presents the four seals and thus completion stage practice immediately after the four tenets.[376] In his *Instructions on the Stages Handed Down by the Lineage of Gurus*,[377] Vajrapāṇi, though, includes between the four tenets and the four seal-based empowerments the six vase empowerments. The *Jewel Garland of True Reality* follows the common division into three vehicles (Śrāvakayāna, Pratyekabuddhayāna, and Mahāyāna) and includes Tantra in Mahāyāna, dividing the latter into the pāramitā system and the mantra system. Noteworthy also is the inclusion of Sautrāntika within the pāramitā system, and the statement that the mantra system can be practiced only on the basis of the tenets of Yogācāra and/or Madhyamaka. At the peak of Madhyamaka, and thus all tenets, is Maitrīpa's favored Apratiṣṭhāna ("nonabiding"), which, according to Rāmapāla's commentary on the *Presentation of Empowerment*, must be taken as amanasikāra, which means that one must refrain from any superimposition in order to realize true reality, which does not provide any "basis to stand on" (*apratiṣṭhāna*).

6. Explaining the Seals of the Five Tathāgatas (*Pañcatathāgatamudrāvivaraṇa*)

Maitrīpa explains in this text that the five psychophysical aggregates (*skandhas*) are in reality the five tathāgatas, which means that sentient beings have the nature of the five tathāgatas. The first four (Vairocana, Ratnasambhava, Amitābha, and Amoghasiddhi) are sealed with Akṣobhya, in order to show that they are mind only. The Akṣobhya seal thus stands for the realization of Yogācāra emptiness, namely, the absence of the subject-object duality from the dependently arising mind. In order to further refine one's realization, in Maitrīpa's system, it is necessary to embrace Madhyamaka emptiness, namely, that the dependently arising mind also lacks the independent existence of an own nature (*svabhāva*). This is then symbolized by sealing the Akṣobhya seal with the seal of Vajrasattva or Vajradhara. Of great interest here is also that *Sublime Continuum* II.61b ("And the latter two, the form-kāyas")[378] is quoted in the context of explaining the Yogācāra meditation of Nirākāravāda and the resultant state attained afterward. Worth mentioning also is the statement in the prose after *Explaining the Seals of the Five Tathāgatas*, verse 13, that a Madhyamaka tenet is seen to be superior, that is, established on the basis of awareness (the Tibetan has "self-awareness"). It should be noted that Maitrīpa still calls such a self-awareness-based Madhyamaka Apratiṣṭhāna, on the grounds that self-awareness is not ascribed any privileged ontological status, but simply dependent origination like anything else.

7. A Presentation of Empowerment (*Sekanirdeśa*)

In the introduction to his *Commentary on the Presentation of Empowerment*, Rāmapāla claims that the *Presentation of Empowerment* was composed in accordance with the *Succession of the Four Seals* of (the tantric) Nāgārjuna.[379] Maitrīpa thus presents tantric empowerment on the basis of the four moments: the moments of the manifold activity of embracing, kissing and so forth; the moment of maturation, which is the enjoyment of blissful wisdom; the moment of freedom from defining characteristics; and the moment of relaxation.[380] The four moments correspond to the four joys (i.e., joy, supreme joy, coemergent joy, and the joy of no-joy). As for his sequence of the four moments and joys, Maitrīpa explains in his *Instructions on the Four Seals* that in treatises such as the *Hevajra Tantra* the correct sequence has not been made explicit, in order to confuse outsiders who do not rely on a guru.[381] Maitrīpa clearly follows, like his teacher Ratnākaraśānti, a tradition that claims the moment of freedom from defining characteristics and coemergent joy are marked or recognized in the third position. As a further source for placing coemergent joy before the joy of no-joy, the Fourth Shamarpa Chökyi Drakpa mentions the pith instructions of Maitrīpa's guru, Śavaripa.[382] However, the majority of scholars—Kamalanātha, Abhayākaragupta, Raviśrījñāna, Vibhūticandra, and others—put them in the fourth position.[383] The Sanskrit *virama* ("the [joy of] no-joy") is then understood as "intensification of joy." The moment called *vilakṣaṇa* is then not taken as "freedom from defining characteristics," but "other."

In *Presentation of Empowerment*, verse 38, the four moments (and thus the four joys) are also linked with the four mudrās, the moment of enjoying manifold appearances being related to the karmamudrā, the moment of maturation to the dharmamudrā, the moment of freedom from defining characteristics to mahāmudrā, and the moment of relaxation to the samayamudrā. The four joys are first enjoyed physically with a karmamudrā (a technical term standing for a consort). This proceeds to the phase of dharmamudrā, wherein the practitioner again realizes the four joys, but this time on the basis of teachings such that the sights and sounds of the manifold world are one's own mind. This leads to the realization of mahāmudrā. The four joys of the samayamudrā are experienced when the yogin manifests as Heruka in union with his consort for the sake of benefiting others.

The *Presentation of Empowerment* plays a central role among the amanasikāra texts, for mahāmudrā is not only presented in the tantric context of the four seals but also equated with the Madhyamaka view of nonabiding (*apratiṣṭhāna*). With reference to two quotations from the *Ornament of Manifested Wisdom*, Rāmapāla equates, in his *Commentary on the Presentation of Empowerment* on verse 29, nonabiding with amanasikāra and reassures us that, thanks to the kindness of one's guru, mahāmudrā can be directly made manifest. That amanasikāra also includes meditation practice on the path can be gathered from the first quotation from the *Ornament of Manifested Wisdom* that amanasikāra is virtuous, and from Rāmapāla's commentary on *Presentation of Empowerment*, verse 36, where mahāmudrā is said to be found through the abandonment of characteristic signs. In his commentary on verse 36, Rāmapāla nearly quotes literally from the part of the *Magic Formula for Entering the Nonconceptual* in which characteristic signs are described as being abandoned in the act of "not directing one's attention to them" (amanasikāra). All eight verses on mahāmudrā in the *Presentation of Empowerment*, verses 29–36, teach Apratiṣṭhāna Madhyamaka, three of them being identical with Apratiṣṭhāna verses in the *Jewel Garland of True Reality*. From the *Justification of Nonconceptual Realization*, we know that Maitrīpa does not understand amanasikāra only in the sense of "becoming mentally disengaged," but also understands the term in the sense of "luminous self-empowerment"—terminology that suggests a tantric framework (see below). In other words, in Mahāmudrā, the term amanasikāra also stands for a direct realization of luminosity or emptiness, wherefore I translate it in this context as "nonconceptual realization." To what extent amanasikāra practice can do without initial manasikāra (i.e., investigation), and also without the four seals, remains a controversial issue. But in his *Twenty Verses on True Reality*, Maitrīpa claims that within the mantra system advanced practitioners have a direct access to mahāmudrā, and Sahajavajra describes in his *Commentary on the Ten Verses on True Reality* a Mahāmudrā practice that operates without the usual creation and completion stage practice (see below).

8. The Succession of the Four Seals (*Caturmudrānvaya*)

The *Succession of the Four Seals* served as a basis for the *Presentation of Empowerment*, and thus represents the most important source for Maitrīpa's blend of Mahāmudrā and Madhyamaka. In the sequence of the four seals it is explained how something artificially created, such as the physical experience of the four joys (i.e., the wisdom arisen from a karmamudrā), can initiate a process that leads to buddhahood (mahāmudrā). The wisdom that arises from a karmamudrā or prajñā (i.e., the prajñā-wisdom) is only an imitation of the real wisdom, the prajñā-wisdom of the third empowerment only being an exemplifying wisdom. Only in combination with the teaching of the dharmamudrā does it become a cause for mahāmudrā. Divākaracandra, a disciple of Maitrīpa, warns us in his *Elucidation of the Wisdom from a Prajñā* (*Prajñājñānaprakāśa*) that the related practice of karmamudrā must go together with mahāmudrā. On the other hand, Divākaracandra insists that without sexual union one does not realize true reality in its manifestation of bliss.[384]

In his introduction to the *Commentary on the Presentation of Empowerment*, Rāmapāla attributes the *Succession of the Four Seals* to (the tantric) Nāgārjuna,[385] which is corroborated by the colophon to it in the Tibetan translation and the *Butön's Catalogue of Instructions*.[386] This attribution is contested, however, by Vibhūticandra in his *Work Illuminating Nectar Drops* (*Amṛtakaṇikoddyotanibandha*).

Whether taught by the tantric Nāgārjuna or not, the *Succession of the Four Seals* is of crucial importance to Maitrīpa's amanasikāra cycle, inasmuch as it combines the tantric Mahāmudrā system of the four seals with the non-tantric teachings of the *Ornament of Manifested Wisdom* and the *Ornament of Realization* (or *Sublime Continuum*), and thus with the Maitreya works. On the basis of grammatical considerations, I suggest that the *Ornament of Manifested Wisdom* quotes in the definition of mahāmudrā are insertions. Whether interpolations or not, the quotes served to link Mahāmudrā with the view of non-abiding and the practice of amanasikāra. As we have seen above, this blend of sūtras and tantras is elaborated in the *Presentation of Empowerment* and Rāmapāla's commentary on it.

9. A Summary of the Meaning of Empowerment (*Sekatātparyasaṃgraha*)

The *Summary of the Meaning of Empowerment* offers a complete explanation of the entire procedure of tantric initiation that starts in a traditional way with the six vase empowerments. The presentation of the six, in particular, contains some unexpected and most valuable iconographic descriptions of the vajra and bell. For example, the vajra is pictured as having five spokes emerging from the calyxes of lotuses, which symbolize the five tathāgatas.

10. The Five Aspects [of Vajrasattva] (*[Vajrasattva-]Pañcākāra*)

The *Five Aspects* describes the maṇḍala of the five tathāgatas, with Akṣobhya in the middle, Vairocana in the East, Ratnasambhava in the South, Amitābha in the West, and Amoghasiddhi in the North. On Akṣobhya's crown is Vajrasattva, who symbolizes the sealing of everything (i.e., the five skandhas and thus the five tathāgatas) with his seal of Madhyamaka emptiness. Interestingly, the five tathāgatas are not only related to the five skandhas, but, expanded to a group of six (including Vajrasattva), are also correlated with the six seasons, six types of taste, and groups of Sanskrit letters. In the intermediate directions are the female buddhas Locanā (southeast), Māmakī (southwest), Pāṇḍaravāsinī (northwest), and Tārā (northeast). The mistress of these four is Vajradhātvīśvarī in the middle.

11. A Discourse on Illusion (*Māyānirukti*)

In this text on tenets, Maitrīpa does not, like in similar texts of this kind, explain the role illusion plays in each of the philosophical systems. What the simile of illusion refers to is that the world lacks any own nature. The underlying view thus is Madhyamaka, probably its variety of Māyopamādvaya ("nonduality in the sense [of everything being] like an illusion").

12. A Discourse on Dream (*Svapnanirukti*)

Maitrīpa discusses here the role the dream example plays in six different philosophial positions. Two of them (Vaibhāṣika and Sautrāntika) have to be abandoned,[387] and among the remaining four (i.e., the two Yogācāra and two Madhyamaka tenets), Apratiṣṭhāna Madhyamaka is considered to be supreme.

13. An Elucidation of True Reality (*Tattvaprakāśa*)

True reality is here presented in terms of the Buddha's threefold kāya, from which cyclic existence and nirvāṇa arise. Even though the three kāyas are thus taken as a primordial ground, they are explained along the lines of Madhyamaka as nonarising, but at the same time dependently originated. In other words, we have to understand the three kāyas that underlie everything as a dynamic system of interrelatedness that occurs without any ontological foundation or building blocks that exist in terms of an "own-being" (*svabhāva*) or "other-being" (*parabhāva*), as explained in chapter fifteen of the *Main Verses of the Middle Way*.[388] Phenomena are empty of an own nature and hence only arise interdependently with other phenomena. When Maitrīpa insists that as a Mādhyamika one has to negate arising in order to stand out from Vijñānavāda, he thus means to negate arising in terms of an own nature.

14. An Elucidation of Nonabiding (*Apratiṣṭhānaprakāśa*)

Maitrīpa chose the term *apratiṣṭhāna* as a label for his strongly anti-foundationalist Madhyamaka, in which the true reality of all phenomena not only "lacks any foundation,"[389] but also, for this reason, cannot be grasped conceptually. However well-refined one's model of reality may be, the model inevitably distorts true reality by introducing wrong superimpositions or denials. In *Elucidation of Nonabiding*, verse 8, "nonabiding" (*apratiṣṭhāna*) is thus directly opposed to mental fabrication. Maitrīpa informs us that the arising of phenomena (i.e., dependent origination) even remains inconceivable for self-awareness, which, so we are warned, should not be reified as existent. Like in the text before, dependent origination is again equated with the three kāyas: the dharmakāya in terms of dependent origination's emptiness, the sambhogakāya in terms of the fact that dependent origination is mind, and the nirmāṇakāya in terms of dependent origination's multitude.

15. An Elucidation of Indivisible Union (*Yuganaddhaprakāśa*)

The title of the text is a little misleading since Maitrīpa does not use *yuganaddha* in its originally tantric context of "indivisible union" (*yuganaddha*) of the illusory body and luminosity, which stands for the level of the fruit. Rather, yuganaddha here stands for the more general Madhyamaka concept of indivisible arising and nonarising, i.e., dependent origination (or appearance) and emptiness. It is thus a thematic continuation of the *Elucidation of Nonabiding* and contains an interesting Madhyamaka analysis of causality aimed at refuting the arising of any phenomenon in terms of an own nature. Yuganaddha is then also explained as the indivisible union of emptiness and compassion or clarity. A yogin realizing this union is said to abide in great bliss.

16. The Manifestation of Great Bliss (*Mahāsukhaprakāśa*)

In this text, great bliss is taken as nonduality, which is the true nature of entities. Maitrīpa cautions against a "false manifestation of bliss," which appears in the pure apparent truth of the yogin. It goes without saying that both forms of bliss are inseparable, just as the ultimate and pure apparent truths are. It is important to note that even though great bliss is related to the ultimate, it is not reified as an entity, being nothing but dependent origination. There are a few noteworthy tantric explanations, such as taking the realization of emptiness as seed syllables from which deities arise. The blissful mind thus assumes the form of the deity, while one's consort (*prajñā*) is called emptiness. The union of bliss and emptiness symbolized by this tantric couple is taken as the goal.

17. The Twenty Verses on True Reality (*Tattvaviṃśikā*)

Prajñā is a polysemous term, two of its primary meanings being "insight" and "tantric consort." In this text, prajñā is first interpreted on the level of the four seals. Maitrīpa begins by implying—through the mention of the four moments—that true reality is realized from a prajñā as consort. The four moments are also recognized on the level of dharmamudrā, so that prajñā could also be unterstood as insight. Of particular importance is *Twenty Verses on True Reality*, verses 7–11, which indicates that only inferior practitioners rely on a karmamudrā and the samayamudrā, while a more direct approach to mahāmudrā is open to those with sharp faculties. Those of average faculties rely on the practice with a visualized consort (*jñānamudrā*). *Twenty Verses on True Reality*, verse 6, states, however, that the means of access to her (i.e., prajñā either as karmamudrā or insight) are variegated in the treatises of the mantra system, corresponding to persons of inferior, average, and superior faculties. Thus the direct Mahāmudrā approach of the advanced still falls into the category of the mantra system.

18. The Twenty Verses on Mahāyāna (*Mahāyānaviṃśikā*)

The seeing of the natural (*nija*) kāya that is contained in the three kāyas (dharma, sambhoga, and nirmāṇa) as their true nature is here taken as the appropriate practice for the attainment of enlightenment, provided that it is performed without superimposing anything. Maitrīpa then announces that this will be explained "in accordance with the mantra system," a phrase also used by Sahajavajra to characterize the pāramitā system pith instructions of the *Ten Verses on True Reality*. Since nothing specifically tantric can be found in the whole of the remaining text of the *Twenty Verses on Mahāyāna*, it could be argued, as already pointed out in some of my earlier publications, that "in accordance with the mantra system" precisely refers to this nonconceptual or direct[390] vision of the nijakāya, a special vipaśyanā practice that enables direct realization of the fruit of the path. In other words, we have here a path of fruition in the same sense that the mantra system is regarded as a path of fruition distinct from the causal pāramitā system. Yet, as Gö

Lotsāwa Zhönnu Pel claims in his *Blue Annals*, Jñānakīrti considers such a direct Mahāmudrā access possible from within the pāramitā system.[391] Moreover, Sahajavajra, in his *Commentary on the Ten Verses on True Reality* , claims that reality is directly experienced as luminosity on the basis of a vipaśyanā practice performed with direct perceptions right from the beginning. In support of this claim, Sahajavajra quotes Maitrīpa's *Twenty Verses on Mahāyāna*, verse 12.

19. The Five Verses on Penetrating Insight (*Nirvedhapañcaka*)

An unmediated vision of true reality without superimposition is the focal point of the *Five Verses on Penetrating Insight*. In the first verse, this insight is identified with the realization of the buddha within. According to the commentary in the *Dharma Treasure of the Drigung Kagyü*, Maitrīpa here teaches buddhanature. It should be noted, however, that he does not make use of the terminology found in the *Sublime Continuum*. It is also noteworthy that even though wisdom is positively described as having the nature of effortless compassion, it, for Maitrīpa like everything else, nonetheless arises in dependence. This is similar to the awareness, or self-awareness in the Tibetan translation, that, according to the *Explaining the Seals of the Five Tathāgatas*, is only dependent origination, a recognition that marks the superiority of the Madhyamaka view.

20. The Six Verses on the Middle Path (*Madhyamaṣaṭka*)

The two Yogācāra tenets are summarized in one verse each, while two verses each are dedicated to a summary of Māyopamādvaya and Apratiṣṭhāna Madhyamaka. It should be noted that the presentation of Nirākāra Yogācāra and Māyopamādvaya Madhyamaka hardly differ, in that the former upholds self-awareness without characteristic signs, while the latter maintains an awareness that is empty of entities. In Apratiṣṭhāna, clarity, which is—to go by *Explaining the Seals of the Five Tathāgatas*—a variety of awareness or self-awareness, is taught to be nondual bliss and mere dependent origination. As noted above, it is this view, that self-awareness is dependently arisen, that is held to account for the alleged superiority of Apratiṣṭhāna over Māyopamādvaya.

21. The Five Verses on Transcendent Love (*Premapañcaka*)

The five verses offer a poetic comparison of the union of dependently arising appearances and emptiness to the union of a handsome suitor and his lovely mistress. Maitrīpa also explains how the skillful guru uses the natural pleasure of the couple to generate the transcendent love of coemergence.

22. The Ten Verses on True Reality (*Tattvadaśaka*)

In his initial *namaskāra* verse, Maitrīpa venerates suchness (as true reality is referred to in the first three verses), which is not only negatively described as neither existent nor nonexistent, but also positively described as enlightenment (*bodhi*). This clearly reflects the doctrinal background of the *Sublime Continuum*, wherein suchness or the ultimate are similarly characterized.[392] While the *via negationis* of the second dharmacakra leaves no choice but to negate what true reality is not, the third dharmacakra describes it positively. For Maitrīpa, this second approach is based on a meditative concentration that realizes true reality as it is (*yathābhūtasamādhi*). In this immediate access to true reality, phenomena are experienced as being luminous. This samādhi is cultivated by arousing bodhicitta on the basis of a vipaśyanā practice that starts with direct cognitions. Beneficial concepts on the path, such as the idea that the world is beyond duality, are realized to be luminous by nature, too. In his commentary on the *Ten Verses on True Reality*, Sahajavajra calls Maitrīpa's ten verses "pāramitā system pith instructions that accord with the mantra system." In the commentary on verse 7, Sahajavajra refers to these pith instructions as Mahāmudrā. Based on that, Gö Lotsāwa Zhönnu Pel is then able to claim in his *Blue Annals*:

> In essence it is the pāramitā system, it accords with the mantra system, and its name is mahāmudrā.[393]

23. A Justification of Nonconceptual Realization (*Amanasikārādhāra*)

The first part of the title, which lends the amanasikāra cycle its name, is—as already mentioned above—somewhat misleading in that it does not simply negate mental engagement but also refers to the cultivation of realization, or self-empowerment, to use Maitrīpa's final interpretation of manasikāra. According to Maitrīpa, the initial *a-* does not only represent the simple negation of a privative *a*, but also stands for a profound Madhyamaka-type of negation, such as nonarising or emptiness, which Maitrīpa also understands positively as luminosity. The two levels of analysis—amanasikāra as (1) the negation of dualistic conceptual engagements that leads to and reinforces the belief in subject and object, and (2) luminous self-empowerment—reflect the same structure of a *via negationis* and a *via eminentiae* already encountered in the *Ten Verses on True Reality*. Such a blend of the negative Madhyamaka approach and the positive descriptions of direct Mahāmudrā experience underlies the whole structure of the amanasikāra cycle. In order to do justice to Maitrīpa's two-layered interpretation of amanasikāra, I use the translation "nonconceptual realization."

24. The Six Verses on the Coemergent (*Sahajaṣaṭka*)

In this short text on yet another important term for the ultimate, the "coemergent" (*sahaja*), we find again the basic structure of the amanasikāra cycle. True reality is first negatively described as being neither existent nor nonexistent, as there should be neither affirmation nor exclusion, when it comes to "naturally arisen phenomena." The latter phrase I take to stand for dependent origination and emptiness. The coemergent is also equated with genuine bliss without attachment, experienced in realization.

25. A Pith Instruction on Reality Called *A Treasure of Dohās* (*Dohānidhināmatattvopadeśa*)

This text is not contained in the *Collected Works of Advayavajra* and not available in its original Sanskrit. However, the Seventh Karmapa Chödrak Gyatso included it in his cycle of amanasikāra texts. It presents a summary of the four tenets as found in the *Jewel Garland of True Reality*, with Apratiṣṭhāna Madhyamaka at the summit. Contrary to the *Jewel Garland of True Reality*, though, the last part of the text contains tantric teachings, i.e., a summary of empowerment and/or completion stage practice on the basis of the four seals as explained in the *Succession of the Four Seals* and *Presentation of Empowerment*.

26. A Pith Instruction on Settling the Mind Without Becoming Engaged in the Thought Processes of Projecting and Gathering: A Genuine Secret (*Shes pa spro bsdu med par 'jog pa'i man ngag gsang ba dam pa*)

This short text is not contained in the *Collected Works of Advayavajra*, but Chödrak Gyatso includes it in his amanasikāra cycle.

Of particular interest is its endorsement of a non-gradual path: even meditation is realization once the flavor of emptiness is tasted. Moreover, the experience of true reality is direct (*thad kar*) since the yogin of nonconceptual realization (amanasikāra) has nothing to think about when it comes to emptiness. In other words, emptiness is irreducible to the abstractions of conceptual thinking.

CHAPTER 12

The Destruction of Wrong Views

Homage to the youthful Mañjuśrī!
Homage to the Buddha!

I will explain the destruction of wrong views
In the form of a prescription of initial activity.
The level of a buddha is thereby attained,
Either without effort or with effort. (1)

Here, there are two types of sentient beings: those who are still learning and those who no longer need to learn. For those, then, who are learning and thus in a causal state, there are proper intention, the practice of conviction, the practice following the attainment of bodhisattva levels, and finally, having gained power over the following [five concerns: defilements, appearances, karma, means, and causing sentient beings to ripen].[394] Perfect enlightenment is fully attained only after accumulating the two accumulations by prescription of very pure initial activity. For those who no longer need to learn, who have abandoned all notions about remedy, reality, and fruit, initial activity unfolds through the power of the impetus of former prayers, as in the case of Śākyamuni. It is uninterrupted and has the defining characteristic of fulfilling the needs of sentient beings by the effortless practice [resulting in a state called] "indivisible union" (*yuganaddha*). This is settled. It is as taught in the following:

Protector, you know neither vain imagining,
Nor thoughts, nor wavering.
Still your buddha activity unfolds
Without effort in the world. (2)

It is particularly the perfection of benefiting others
That is taken as the fruit of buddhas.
Buddhahood and the like—everything else—
Are taken as fruit on the basis of this purpose. (3)

Just like a wish-fulfilling jewel, it (i.e., the perfection of benefiting others)
Is not stirred by the fierce wind of every volition;
Still, it fulfils without exception
The wishes of all sentient beings. (4)

Having abandoned all practice of affirmation and exclusion
With regard to the fruit, reality and what is opposed [to liberation],
The wise one awakens toward supreme full enlightenment,
But even after that, he will be engaged in initial activity. (5)

Objection: The prescription of initial activity may indeed be what is acceptable for those who are learning, but how to understand the exertion of initial activity for those who no longer need to learn and have [realized perfection through] meditation on essencelessness? This initial activity, too, is only a golden chain. [Response:] True. For [it is like a golden chain] in being separated from the realization of the perfection of insight. The perfection of insight, however, is the essence of the five perfections. It is for this reason that the illustrious one said [in the *Perfection of Insight in Hundred Thousand Verses*]:

Emptiness endowed with all supreme aspects[395] is taught. (6)

Moreover, the illustrious one said: "The five perfections without the perfection of insight do not even deserve to be given the name of perfection." This is also taught in the *Discourse of the Teaching for Noble Vimalakīrti* (*Āryavimalakīrtinirdeśasūtra*):

> Means without insight is bondage;
> So is insight without means.
> Means supported by insight is liberation;
> So is insight supported by means. (7)

The identity of these two is understood thanks to the pith instruction of the genuine guru. It is established as the coemergence of means and insight, like a lamp and its light. Therefore, it is said:

> All yogins should perform
> The initial activity as taught above;
> Wisdom that is inseparable from emptiness and compassion
> Is taken to be present in the state of enlightenment.[396] (8)

Initial activity [is taken as follows]:

> The above-mentioned five perfections are known
> Under the name of "initial activity."
> The perfection of insight
> Is taken as their nature, their origin. (9)

Likewise,

> If an intelligent man practices—attentively and continuously—
> Generosity, discipline, patience,
> Diligence, meditation, and insight,
> He will be happy and also wise. (10)

Three of these perfections—generosity, discipline, and patience—
Are taken collectively as a cause of the saṃbhogakāya and nirmāṇakāya,
And two—meditation and insight—as a cause of the dharmakāya,
While diligence is a cause of both the form-kāyas and the dharmakāya. (11)

Therefore, the bodhisattva must rely on very pure initial activity. The reverse would entail the undesired consequence of nihilism. This is taught [in the following]:

Even if what is wholesome and unwholesome lack an own nature,
Wholesome actions must be performed and unwholesome ones not.
In the world of apparent truth that is like the reflection of the moon in the water,
Bliss is pleasant and suffering perpetually not. (12)

How, then, should the initial activity be carried out among those who, in a state of learning, adopt a yogic conduct that appears to be crazy and who are bent on realizing the nonconceptual? Response: By engaging in this yogic conduct through the gift of one's body. This is because it is said [in *Hevajra Tantra*]:

Having given one's body as a gift,
Yogic conduct is adopted.[397] (13)

Generosity is attained by giving even to the limit of one's body; discipline by controlling one's body, speech, and mind for the sake of sentient beings; patience by enduring the death of being sawn up in the extremely hot hell; diligence by enduring harm from the eight worldly dharmas; meditation by an effortless flow in one's own sphere in harmony with the nature of everything; and insight by means of a realization characterized by the nonperception of all phenomena.

> For those who have penetrated the single taste of everything
> without effort,
> All supreme perfections unfold without hindrance. (14)

Therefore, initial activity is certain to unfold even in the case of those who adopt yogic conduct. The words of the immature *cārvāka*s (i.e., hedonist philosophers) that there is no next world are not endorsed by us, given their complete illogicality. Here [it should be recalled] that in the *Hevajra Tantra* the buddha taught the following to a bodhisattva who, as a disciple who is still learning, manifests yogic conduct:

> First, the ritual for mending vows (*poṣadha*) must be made;
> Then, training instructions must be given.[398] (15)

"Please pay heed, venerable master! I, the lay practitioner so-and-so, take refuge in the Buddha, Dharma, and Saṅgha, until attaining the heart of enlightenment." Thus one speaks a second and even a third time. "May the venerable master behold me, the one who has thus gone for the threefold refuge. Please pay heed venerable master! I, the lay practitioner so-and-so, on the full moon of every month, from now on until the rising of the sun tomorrow, will refrain from killing any sentient being, stealing another's property, not keeping the vow of chastity, lying, having intoxicating drinks, eating at an improper time, wearing necklaces, putting on makeup, dancing, singing, entertainments, high thrones, and beds. I will abide during that time by the eightfold quality." These are the words of the ritual for mending vows.

The householder bodhisattva first takes refuge in the three jewels and then abstains from the following five deeds: killing, taking what is not given, sexual misconduct, lying, and drinking intoxicants, all of which are by nature blameworthy. Being endowed with learning and discrimination, the householder bodhisattva abandons the ten nonvirtuous acts, yet avoids inaction by performing the ten virtuous acts. They rise early in the morning, wash their face and so forth, and recall the three jewels. Saying OṂ ĀḤ HŪṂ, they protect themselves, their abode, and practice. They should then meditate, recite, and praise in accordance with their realization. They should recite the *Chanting the Names of Mañjusrī* three times. Then, reciting 108 times OṂ JAMBHALENDRĀYA SVĀHĀ they must offer 108 handfuls of water to Jambhala. Then they recite this *torma* mantra seven times:

NAMAḤ SAMANTABUDDHĀNĀṂ SARVATATHĀGATĀVALOKITE OṂ SAMBHARA SAMBHARA HŪṂ PHAṬ SVĀHĀ

With a stream of five nectars flowing from the five fingers of their stretched out hand they should see to it that one Magadha measure full of water and a torma is placed at the bottom of the door. To satisfy hungry ghosts and demons, they snap their fingers three times, and then offer the torma for bodhisattvas.

Now they must cultivate the Four Immeasurables: the love for all sentient beings like the love they would have for their only child; the compassion whose nature is the wish to save everybody from suffering and the cause of suffering, the ocean of saṃsāra; the joy that has arisen from a mind that rejoices in having taken refuge in the Three Jewels; and equanimity, which has the quality of being completely unattached.

With their mind directed toward benefiting all beings, they create a maṇḍala on a part of the ground that is empowered for the maṇḍala by pure cow dung and clean water along with the recitation of OṂ ĀḤ VAJRAREKHE HŪṂ. The maṇḍala has four sides or however many desired. In its middle, they visualize a sun disk in the center of a multicolored eight-petaled lotus. On top of this is the blue syllable HŪṂ, from which a blue Akṣobhya arises. He is dark blue and holds the earth touching mudrā. Then they visualize on the eastern petal the white syllable OṂ, from which Vairocana arises. He is white and holds the mudrā of supreme enlightenment. Then they visualize on the southern petal the yellow syllable TRĀṂ, from which Ratnasambhava arises. He is yellow and holds the mudrā of generosity. Then they visualize on the western petal the red syllable HRĪḤ, from which Amitābha arises. He is red and holds the mudrā of concentration. Then they visualize on the northern petal the green syllable KHAṂ, from which Amoghasiddhi arises. He is green and holds the mudrā of fearlessness.

Having praised them with OṂ ĀḤ VAJRAPUṢPE HŪṂ, they should offer to all who are most cherished. These five tathāgatas wear saffron robes and have crown protuberances. Their heads and faces are shaven. They sit on sun disks while Vairocana sits on a moon disk. Besides that, the remaining four tathāgatas face Akṣobhya, who, in turn, faces the practitioner. In front of these five one should recite the following verses of the triple refuge, making them as visible as his realization allows:

Homage to the Buddha, the teacher!
Homage to the Dharma, the protector!
Homage to the great Saṅgha!
To these three, unceasing homage! (16)

To the Three Jewels, my refuge,
I confess all wrongdoings.

Rejoicing in the virtue of the world,
My mind beholds the Buddha's enlightenment. (17)

Until enlightenment, I take refuge
In the Buddha, Dharma, and supreme assembly.
I generate this mind directed to enlightenment
For the sake of myself and others. (18)

I generate the supreme enlightened mind,
Inviting all sentient beings.
I practice the desired supreme practice of enlightenment,
May I become a buddha for the sake of the world! (19)

Confessing all wrongdoings
And rejoicing in all merit,
I will, as someone who fasts,
Perform the noble eightfold ritual of mending vows. (20)

Then the following is recited:

You, whose bodies are anointed with the sandalwood
fragrance of discipline,
Who are dressed in the cloth of meditation,
And who are ornamented with the flowers of the limbs of
enlightenment,
Dwell happily! (21)

Then they should dissolve the maṇḍala with the mantra OṂ VAJRAMAṆḌALA HŪṂ[399] MUḤ. Next, they should worship Mañjuśrī and the others according to the pith instructions.

This concludes the ritual of worshipping the maṇḍala.

Generosity is the cow dung mixed with water, discipline the cleansing.
Patience is the removal of small ants, endeavor the upholding of ritual duties.
Meditation is the instant creation of a one-pointed mind, insight the beauty of the drawn lines.
Having created the maṇḍala of the buddhas, they acquire the six perfections. (22)

Having performed the bodily actions with regard to the supreme house of the buddhas,
They become one whose color is golden, being free from disease.
They are distinguished from gods and men, one's brilliance being like that of the moon.
They are born into a royal family, possessing abundant wealth and gold. (23)

This concludes the verses on the benefit of the maṇḍala.

Creating the maṇḍala daily
With flowers, cow dung, and water,
And offering three times a day something to the guru,
They should honor with devotion. (24)

Satisfied due to an altruistic attitude,
They should turn away from a self-centered mind.
Happy, kind, and wise,
They will take birth in Sukhavatī. (25)

They will complete the six perfections.
Empowered by the buddhas and the like,

They who create the maṇḍala
Will be replete with limitless qualities. (26)

This conclude the verses on the full benefit.[400]

They must always recite and worship
Prajñāpāramitā in accordance with
The correct prescriptions for the maṇḍala, and so forth,
Immersed in Prajñāpāramitā's meaning. (27)

In one verse, four verses,
As a *dhāraṇī* in two verses,
Or as the six-faced Bhadracaryā,
Three times a day. (28)

In meditative concentration on the Prajñāpāramitā
In one syllable up to the version in 100,000 words—
The wise whose determination is unbroken
Should recite whatever version of Prajñāpāramitā he finds. (29)

They should worship her on a painted cloth, in books, and in the form of statues of buddhas and bodhisattvas.

This concludes the verses on the prescriptions of worshipping her on painted cloth and in books.

Now the prescriptions on fashioning a mold are explained in accordance with the *Tantra of the Arrangement of the Big Maṇḍala* (*Mahāmaṇḍalavyūhatantra*).

Homage to the samanta buddhas!

OṂ VAJRAPUṢPE SVĀHĀ—this is the mantra for grasping clay.
OṂ VAJRODBHAVĀYA SVĀHĀ—the mantra for making the image mold.
OṂ ARAJE VIRAJE SVĀHĀ—the mantra for protecting the oil.
OṂ DHARMADHĀTUGARBHE SVĀHĀ—the mantra for casting the seal.
OṂ VAJRAMUDGARĀKOṬANA SVĀHĀ—the mantra for smoothing.
OṂ DHARMARATE SVĀHĀ—the mantra for attracting.
OṂ SUPRATIṢṬHITAVAJRE SVĀHĀ—the mantra for erecting.
OṂ SARVATATHĀGATAMAṆIŚATADĪPTE JVALA JVALA DHARMADHĀTUGARBHE SVĀHĀ—the mantra for abiding.
OṂ SVABHĀVAŚUDDHE ĀHARA ĀHARA ĀGACCHĀ ĀGACCHA DHARMADHĀTUGARBHE SVĀHĀ—the mantra for dismissal.
OṂ ĀKĀŚADHĀTUGARBHE SVĀHĀ—the mantra for begging pardon.

This completes the prescription for hammering a mold.

OṂ NAMO BHAGAVATE VAIROCANAPRABHĀRĀJĀYA TATHĀGATĀYĀRHATE SAMYAKSAṂBUDDHĀYA TADYATHĀ OṂ SŪKṢME SŪKṢME SAME SAMAYE ŚĀNTE DĀNTE SAMĀROPE ANĀLAMBE TARAMBE YAŚOVATI MAHĀTEJE NIRĀKULANIRVĀṆE SARVABUDDHĀDHIṢṬHĀNADHIṢṬHITE SVĀHĀ.

Reciting this dhāraṇī twenty-one times, they must build a [miniature] *caitya* (stūpa) from a clod of earth or sand. As many atoms as there are in this clod, so many tens of millions of caityas are created. Accumulating merit as numerous as the number of atoms, they become the masters of the ten levels and quickly awaken to the supreme awakening of enlightenment. This is what the illustrious

Vairocana tathāgata said. This concludes the explanation on the dhāraṇī of great benefit.

> All phenomena arise from causes,
> Which were taught by the Tathāgata.
> The cessation of those [causes], too,
> The great Śramaṇa has taught. (30)

Consecrating the caitya with this verse, they should venerate the caitya with the following dhāraṇī:

> OṂ NAMO BHAGAVATE RATNAKETURĀJĀYA TATHĀGATĀYĀRHATE SAMYAKSAṂBUDDHĀYA TADYATHĀ OṂ RATNE RATNE MAHĀRATNE RATNAVIJAYE SVĀHĀ.

Venerating a single caitya with this dhāraṇī, ten million caityas are venerated.

This concludes the prescription of building a caitya of earth, stone, and the like.

By means of a special dedication of all that, the merit to be dedicated emerges as a special result. They should dedicate by means of the great dedication mentioned in the Prajñāpāramitā, which is as follows: The tathāgatas, arhats, and perfectly enlightened ones know by means of buddha wisdom and see by means of buddha eyes the roots of merit, ascertaining their class, category, characteristics, and nature, and by which reality they exist. In precisely this way I rejoice in the roots of merit. Just as the tathāgatas, arhats, and perfectly enlightened ones know, so I dedicate these roots of merit, which must be dedicated for the sake of unsurpassable perfect enlightenment. Again:

May I quickly become a buddha in the world
By means of these virtuous deeds.
May I then teach the Dharma for the sake of the world
And liberate sentient beings afflicted by so much suffering.
(31)

This concludes the prescription of rejoicing in and dedicating merit.

Whoever it is and whatever work one does,
One must choose a pure livelihood.
In order to be patient and pacify illness,
One must consider it to be like medicine. (32)

As for food, which is found according to a pure livelihood, recite OṂ AKĀRO MUKHAṂ SARVADHARMĀṆĀM ĀDYANUTPANNATVĀT OṂ ĀḤ HŪṂ PHAṬ SVĀHĀ. With this mantra the torma must be offered. OṂ ĀḤ SARVABUDDHABODHISATTVEBHYO VAJRANAIVEDYE HŪṂ. With this mantra edibles must be offered. OṂ HĀRĪTI MAHĀYAKṢIṆI HARA HARA SARVAPĀPĀN KṢĪṂ SVĀHĀ. Having recited this mantra, two balls of rice for Hārīti must be offered. OṂ AGRAPIṆḌĀŚIBHYAḤ SVĀHĀ—the offering of selected balls.

Then, having empowered their own eating bowl through the syllables OṂ ĀḤ HŪṂ, they should touch it with their thumb and ring finger until the bad consequences of poison and so forth are alleviated and then eat. Having then eaten to their content, the remaining food should be offered as the leftover ball reciting OṂ UTSṚṢṬAPIṆĀŚANEBHYAḤ SVĀHĀ. What is still left should be abandoned without any interest in it. This is as stated in:

One must offer the torma, the edibles,
And the supreme ball for Hārīti.

One must give the fifth part as leftover,
In order to enjoy the great fruition. (33)

Then, having sipped water [blessed by mantra] from the palm of their hand, they whose intellect has been purified and who are endowed with particular bliss should recite for the welfare and happiness of all sentient beings the following lines three times:

May the king, the donor,
And other groups of sentient beings
Always be happy
And have a long, healthy, and rich life! (34)

Then they should abide leisurely in the activities of a purified body, speech, and mind. As soon as they sit down, they should spend some time, day or night, or even during midday, together with spiritual friends talking about *jātaka*s, *nidāna*s, and *avadāna*s. Then, at sunset, they should meditate, recite mantras, sing hymns, and so forth, according to their realization and without a weary mind. Then they should offer a torma with the mantra that starts with *a*, and enter yogic sleep (*yoganidrā*).

How should the word *upāsaka* be understood?

U signifies that a lay practitioner (*upāsaka*)
Is ready (*udyukta*) to honor buddhas,
Fond (*upaśāyaka*) of tranquility (*upaśānta*),
And endowed with means (*upāya*)
To work (*upakāra*) for the sake of sentient
beings. (35)

Pā signifies that

A lay practitioner always abandons wrongdoing (*pāpa*),
As well as the companionship with evil people (*pāpiṣṭa*).
One avoids evil (*pāpa*) people
And points out evil (*pāpa*) wherever it is found. (36)

Sa signifies that

A lay practitioner is free from superimposition (*samāropa*),
Perfectly concentrated (*susamāhita*) in samādhi.
Always (*sarvadā*) endowed with supreme joy,
The wise *upāsaka* accomplishes (*sādhayed*) perfect
enlightenment (*saṃbodhi*). (37)

Ka signifies that

A lay practitioner always makes (*karoti*) an effort
And maintains compassion (*karuṇā*),
One never holds back even if something is difficult (*kaṣṭa*),
And engages (*karoti*) in helping others. (38)

Based on this, the lay practitioner is endowed with [the qualities signified by] the four letters of the word *upāsaka*.

They abandon all wrongdoing[401]
And their accumulation of merit is increased.
Because of their practice, they create merit
Even in sleep, as if they were awake. (39)

Seeing the world to be like a reflection,
It becomes pure and clear.
They must do everything without cognitive grasping,
Like a magician. (40)

Therefore, they are called "someone who does not fall back." In this way they continuously fortify the accumulation of merit, day and night, and they remain in saṃsāra, because of benefiting sentient beings, until they reach the heart of enlightenment.

Fully absorbed in the meaning of Madhyamaka,
And well settled in (i.e., effortlessly unfolding) initial activity,
The one called "Space Nature" (Gaganagarbha),
Made a firm vow to compose this text. (41)

Upon the request
Of a noble-minded brahmin
Who had come from the Vajra Seat,[402]
This "Initial Activity" was composed by me. (42)

Having requested this Space Nature here, I taught
Initial activity in the form of a liturgy in a few words only.
Once the darkness of impurity is dispelled, may the one whose defilements are removed
Be swift in training for the enlightenment of a stainless intellect. (43)

Whatever virtue[403] I have accumulated
From having taught this initial activity,
May the beginners
And the world attain excellence. (44)

The Kudṛṣṭinirghātana *is ended.*[404]

CHAPTER 13

A Commentary on the [Initial] Statement of *The Destruction of Wrong Views*

Homage to Vajradhara!

There are three states: the causal state, the state of fruition, and the state of working for the benefit of sentient beings. Those who are still learning are in the causal state. The remaining two states are the ones of the tathāgata. The causal state starts from the [generation of] bodhicitta and goes up to the sitting down on the seat of enlightenment. The state of fruition is the state in which the wisdom of perfect enlightenment has arisen, all defilements are abandoned, and all qualities attained. The state of working for the benefit of sentient beings starts from the first turning of the wheel of Dharma and lasts till the teaching disappears.

The causal state here is further divided into three states: the states of intention, practice, and having attained power. Of these, the state of intention is the wish that all sentient beings will be definitively liberated. Its four pillars are as follows: the awareness that the suffering of others must be removed, the awareness of its necessity, the awareness [of actually providing] assistance [to fellow wayfarers], and the awareness of enjoying [the Dharma with others].

These becoming the means, there is the wish [for everybody to attain] enlightenment. This is because its four causes are as follows:

The causes: the potential, a genuine spiritual friend,
Having compassion, and the abiding lack of fear of suffering;
Under these four conditions
Is bodhicitta generated. (1)

The state of intention [has also been presented] under ten points. Practice is here twofold: the ten perfections of the practice of conviction on the path of preparation; and the seven perfections associated with having attained a bodhisattva level. The ten perfections of conviction are as follows:

Generosity, discipline, patience,
Diligence, meditation, insight,
Skill in means, aspiration, strength, and wisdom:
These are the ten perfections.[405] (2)

The generosity associated with having attained a bodhisattva level is accomplished through four accomplishments, these being intention, practice, providing assistance, and what must be given. The seven perfections of this level are: generosity, discipline, patience, diligence, meditation, insight, and skill in means. These surpass the perfections practiced on the path of conviction. These two sets of perfections constitute the state of practice.

Power is fivefold: power over defilements, rebirths, karma, means, and the state of bringing sentient beings to maturation.

Initial activity must be performed entirely by those in a causal state. For those who are, as a consequence of this activity, in the state of the fruit and the state of working for the benefit of sentient beings, initial activity unfolds without effort, just as it does in the case of Śākyamuni. This can be learned in detail in the *Destruction of Wrong Views*.

*The commentary on, or the recollection (*dran pa*) of the* Destruction of Wrong Views, *composed by the paṇḍita and renunciant, the venerable Advayavajra, is ended. Translated and finalized by the learned Indian master Vajrapāṇi and the Tibetan translator Tsurtön Yeshé Jungné.*

CHAPTER 14

The Major Offenses

Having bowed to Mañjuśrī,
The nonabiding nirvāṇa,
And agreeable joy in the world,
I will explain the fourteen major offenses. (1)

In the case of disrespect for teachers,
Not following the orders of the Sugata,
Talking out of hatred about the peculiarities of one's family,
Abandoning great love, (2)

Forsaking an enlightened attitude,
Blaming the three vehicles,
Revealing secrets to common people,
Dishonoring the skandhas of the Jina, (3)

Doubting the pure Dharma,
Being passionless through lack of love,
Superimposing on phenomena what is opposed to nonduality,
Dishonoring a faithful mind, (4)

Not following one's commitments,
And when not having such a woman, belittling women of insight—
These are major offenses,
By which the commitments of a mantra practitioner are destroyed. (5)

The result of having committed them will be an absence of
accomplishments.
There will be death and a multitude of suffering.
One will suffer in hell
With various sorts of severe pain. (6)

Therefore, one should venerate
The maṇḍala, according to instructions obtained from the guru.
One must keep an enlightened attitude,
The rules of the Three Jewels, and so forth. (7)

The text on the Major Offenses *is ended.*[406]

CHAPTER 15

The Gross Offenses

In the case of using a consort (*vidyā*) only for pleasure,
Nonconformity[407] with the commitments,
Quarrelling during tantric feasts,
Disclosure of secret teachings, (1)

Perverting the genuine teaching
In the presence of the faithful,
Living for seven days
In the company of śrāvakas in large numbers, (2)

Teaching secrets to unworthy yogins,
Not being determined to practice yoga—
These are the gross offenses
By which the vows of a yogin are destroyed. (3)

In the case of having committed these offenses,
The ascetics should worship their great teacher,
Taking the approach of doing what they can
And confessing openly. (4)

The text on the Gross Offenses *is ended.*[408]

CHAPTER 16

A Jewel Garland of True Reality

HOMAGE to the venerable Vajrasattva!

Having bowed to the pair of lotuses,
The feet of Vajrasattva,
He whose brightness is like the stainless autumn moon,
We teach *A Jewel Garland of True Reality*. (1)

For those who have fallen away from genuine tradition
And whose sight is obscured,
The *Jewel Garland of True Reality*
Will perfectly illuminate true reality. (2)

Here, there are three vehicles, the Śrāvakayāna, Pratyekabuddhayāna and Mahāyāna. There are four tenets, based on the division into Vaibhāṣika, Sautrāntika, Yogācāra, and Madhyamaka. In this regard, it is according to the tenet of the Vaibhāṣikas that the Śrāvakayāna and Pratyekabuddhayāna are explained. Mahāyāna is twofold, the so-called pāramitā system and the mantra system. Here, the pāramitā system is explained according to the doctrinal positions of the Sautrāntikas, Yogācāras, and Mādhyamikas. The tradition of mantras is explained according to the doctrinal positions of the Yogācāras and Mādhyamikas. Yogācāra is twofold. It is divided into Sākāra and Nirākāra. Likewise, the Mādhyamikas are divided into two, based on the division into the "proponents of nonduality in the sense of everything being like an illusion" (Māyopamādvayavāda) and the "proponents of not abiding in any phenomena" (Sarvadharmāpratiṣṭhānavāda).

Śrāvakayāna

Of these, the vehicle of the śrāvakas is threefold, according to the division into inferior, average, and superior. The inferior and average are the Vaibhāṣikas from the West, and the superior ones are the Vaibhāṣikas from Kashmir.

Inferior Śrāvakas

Of these, the inferior śrāvakas are examined first. Having made the prior assertion that there are outer objects, such as blue or yellow things, they maintain that there is a person (*pudgala*), free from permanence and impermanence. This is their explanation, stated here:

> For the extremely (i.e., intellectually) stupid,
> Who is possessed by the demon of clinging to entities
> And who thus fears the tradition of the profound teachings,
> [The following is valid: External objects] certainly exist and
> the world consists of things that are blue and the like.[409] (3)

Persons carrying a load exist. I neither call them permanent, nor do I call them impermanent. Persons with attachment wander in saṃsāra. Therefore, in order to abandon attachment, the meditation is the cultivation of the repulsive. This cultivation of the repulsive is the examination of the body as having the nature of a collection of feces, urine, semen, blood, phlegm, mucus, intestines, joints,[410] lungs, sticky matter from the eyes,[411] kidneys,[412] spleen, liver,[413] and so forth. This is stated [in the *Bodhicaryāvatāra*]:

First of all, mentally separate
The sack-like skin [from your body],
And then with the scalpel of insight,
Separate the flesh from the skeleton! (4)

And having split open even the bones,
Look right down into the marrow!
Examine precisely your own body
To see whether there is an essence to it![414] (5)

The stain of their meditative stabilization is attachment that is preceded by the view of the permanence of the person.[415] Their view is as follows: As long as I live, I shall take refuge in the Buddha, Dharma, and Saṅgha.

I venerate the Sugata and the two elder ones.[416] (6)

Through whatever root of merit there is, I will discipline myself alone, calm myself alone, bring myself alone to complete nirvāṇa!

Average Śrāvakas

The view and explanation of the average śrāvakas are as in the previous case. They like working to a certain extent for the sake of others. Concentrating on exhaling and inhaling, they perform a form of meditation that is based on the view that a person exists but is free from permanence and impermanence. The stain of their meditative stabilization is that they become senseless through breath retention, since such retention invites lifelessness.

Superior Śrāvakas

The explanation of the superior śrāvakas, who also postulate external objects, is based on the no-self of the body. They thoroughly know the four noble truths, and their meditation is the view of emptiness with regard to the person (*pudgala*). Suffering is here the nature of the five skandhas, which must be known. The arising of this suffering is a mental construct, which must be abandoned. Cessation is deep insight, it must be actualized. The path is emptiness, it must be meditated upon. The stain of their meditation is to superimpose upon emptiness a form of continuous quiescence. With regard to their view, again, they excel other śrāvakas in benefiting others. In this matter, some claim that the inferior śrāvakas attain the awakening only of a śrāvaka, because they have a fixed potential and lack compassion.

Others say, however, that even the inferior śrāvakas among sentient beings will become perfect buddhas, as it has been said:

> All will be buddhas.
> One does not find anybody on earth who is not suitable;
> Therefore, one should not be disheartened
> In the pursuit of perfect enlightenment. (7)

They think that even those with the fixed potential of an inferior śrāvaka depend a little upon the Buddha. The average śrāvakas are future pratyekabuddhas, and the superior śrāvakas will be buddhas after four immeasurable eons.

Pratyekabuddhayāna

The explanation of the vehicle of pratyekabuddhas is precisely that of the superior śrāvakas. They have realized the emptiness of a person; the defining characteristic of the inconceivable; the naturally arisen wisdom[417] even though they have no teacher; deep insight; and calm abiding. As to deep insight, here, it is the cessation of [the operation of] the sense faculties on account of the non-apprehension of a person. Calm abiding is the control of body, speech, and mind. This is their meditation. The stains of meditative stabilization are here the blissful meditation of a mind close to being asleep, and a meditation of a mind that is fast asleep. In the former case, one enters the system of Bhāskara.[418] This mistaken meditation is stated in the following:

> One should cultivate with effort
> That mental state which manifests
> When, on the verge of sleep,
> External objects have disappeared.[419] (8)

In the latter case, one enters the system of the Vaiśeṣika. This is what the venerable Nāgārjuna said:

> Non-cognizing wisdom is established
> Through the example of sleep,
> Just as the knowledge with blocked senses is
> Maintained by the Vaiśeṣika. (9)

Even in the teachings of the Buddha, it is said:

> I happily become a jackal
> In the beautiful Jetavana Grove,
> But it is not acceptable to become like a cow,
> Attaining the liberation of a Vaiśeṣika. (10)

The view of the pratyekabuddhas resembles the previous one (i.e., that of the superior śrāvakas). They will be buddhas after four innumerable eons have passed. The compassion of both śrāvakas and pratyekabuddhas is directed toward sentient beings. Every day they focus on sentient beings, in terms of their suffering of suffering and suffering of change. The compassion created in this way is directed toward sentient beings. The teachings of the śrāvakas are based on speech, and those of the pratyekabuddhas on what is physical.[420] This is stated as:

> Even when perfect buddhas
> Have not appeared, and the śrāvakas, for their part, have gone,
> The wisdom of the pratyekabuddhas
> Unfolds, even lacking contact with a buddha. (11)

Pāramitā System Mahāyāna

Sautrāntika

Now, we will talk about the yogins in the pāramitā system. Here, the inferior tenet is that of the Sautrāntika. Their understanding of an external object is something that by its nature is an accumulation of subtle atoms, that produces cognition consisting in a [mental] form of the object. This is their analysis—that an object produces cognition consisting in a [mental] form of it. This is what Dharmakīrti taught [in *Commentary on Valid Cognition*]:

> How can a [momentary thing] be perceived when the cognition of it occurs
> At a different time? The wise say that it is perceptible.
> Those who understand reasoning take it as a cause capable of imposing
> A mental form of itself upon cognition.[421] (12)

This is their analysis—The inconceivable state of someone whose sense faculties have been turned away from the village of experiential objects is their understanding of meditation. This is stated in the following: "Moreover, this is said to happen at the time of practice, and not at the time of direct actualization." Therefore one must engage in practice. And practice is described in the following:

When practice is performed,
After the mind has been ascertained through realization,
Then I do not see the mind,
Wherever it may be or have gone.[422] (13)

Even householders should stabilize
Their mind in every moment
And meditate in a cross-legged position,
The wavering mind focused one-pointedly.[423] (14)

The stains of their meditative stabilization are like the previous ones.[424] Their view is not conceptualizing the triad of actor, action, and object, they adopt the conduct of the first five perfections in a state of perfect insight (*prajñāpāramitā*), while furthering sentient beings without hoping for a reward.

Sākāravāda Yogācāra

The average practitioners of the pāramitā system are the Yogācāras. The Sākāravijñānavādins ("those who maintain that everything is consciousness accompanied by mental forms") do not accept even subtle atoms, following as they do arguments such as the one found [in Vasubandhu's *Twenty Verses* (*Viṃśatikā*)]:

The instantaneous union of a subtle atom
With six others shows that it has six parts.[425] (15)

Thus they realize that these subtle atoms are mind only. The mind on its own bears mental forms,[426] is free from any relation of perceived object and perceiving subject, and clearly displays everything. This is also stated [in the *Discourse of the Ten Bodhisattva Levels*]: "Oh, you sons of the Victorious One! This threefold world is mind only." Likewise, Dharmakīrti says [in the *Commentary on Valid Cognition*]:

If the mind has forms of something blue or the like,
What is then the justification for an external object?[427]
If the mind does not have forms of something blue or the like,
What is then the justification for an external object?[428] (16)

Somewhere else (i.e., in the *Vajra Tent of the Ḍākiṇīs Tantra*[429]), too, it is said:

The objects of the sense faculties
Do not exist on their own outside of the mind.
It is rather the mind itself that displays
The appearances of forms and the like. (17)

Therefore, the mind itself, which contains the forms of manifold appearances, clearly displays those forms without depending on anything else (i.e., an external object). This is the explanation of the Yogācāras insofar as they are Sākāravijñānavādins.

Nirākāravāda Yogācāra

The Yogācāras who maintain that mind is devoid of truly existing mental forms (i.e., the Nirākāravādins) think, too, that this entire world is mind itself, its nature being self-awareness devoid of [truly existing mental] forms. Their explanation is taught in the following:

An external object
As imagined by immature beings is not to be found;

Agitated by mental imprints,
The mind appears as an object.[430] (18)

Insofar as something appears,
It appears as an illusion only;
In reality, the nature of mind[431] is devoid of
appearance,
Like the pure limitless sky. (19)

The dharmakāya of the great sage
Is free from mental fabrication and from appearances.
The two form kāyas have arisen from it,
And thereafter abide as illusion.[432] (20)

The meditation of the Sākāravādins is to actualize directly the mind beyond the duality of perceived and perceiver together with its manifold forms,[433] a state free from all concepts. This is taught [in *Compendium of the Essence of Wisdom* (*Jñānasārasamuccaya*),[434] verse 35]:

To whatever object of knowledge
The mind goes, it first directs its attention to it.
Toward whatever it will go after becoming stirred up,
All this, indeed, is its nature. (21)

The meditation of the Nirākāravādins is to actualize wisdom directly, without appearances—which is nondual inconceivable bliss free from mental fabrication. This is as stated in [Kambalāmbara's *Garland of Light* (*Ālokamālā*)]:

The mind's nature is taken to be clear:
Without mental forms and spotless,

And it can, in fact, never be realized
By one who is not adept.[435] (22)

When one sets something in front of oneself as an object of reference—
Even with the thought that it is mind-only—
One is not really abiding
In the realization of mind-only. (23)

But when wisdom does not apprehend
Any object of reference, then it is established in mind-only;
For in the absence of a perceived object,
There is no apprehending [on the part of a perceiving subject either].[436] (24)

With regard to the meditative stabilization of clinging to an ultimately existing, permanent consciousness that displays real mental forms—the Sākāravādins are in danger of following the tenet maintained by the proponents of Vedānta, namely Bhagavat Siddhānta,[437] which means taking the world as a transformation, and [thus] as not different from Brahman, in the form of the ultimate and permanent mind of one's own. [Such a position] is stated in the following:

Whatever is seen, however tiny it may be,
Can be understood as Brahman.
Therefore, the mind is not anything else;
It abides in Brahman alone.[438] (25)

This is the stain of the meditative stabilization of the Sākāravādins.
Likewise, with regard to the meditation of the Nirākāravādins,

too, who cultivate a permanent, self-aware consciousness that is devoid of both appearances and mental fabrication, there is the undesired consequence of following another tenet of the proponents of Vedānta, namely the textual tradition of Bhāskara. They maintain that such a permanent consciousness is Brahman, which is entirely free from all names and forms, in it the confusion of mental fabrication is completely purified, it is clear, without limit, uninterrupted and permanent. This is as stated in the following:

The empty water bubbles of the manifold appearances
Clearly manifest to me in the celestial waters of realization;
They either arise or dissolve,
Yet nothing is conceptually produced. (26)

This is the stain of the meditative stabilization of the Nirākāravādins. The view of both (i.e., the Sākāravādins and Nirākāravādins) resembles the previous one.

Māyopamādvayavāda Madhyamaka

The superior practitioners of the pāramitā system are the Mādhyamikas. Among them, there are first the Māyopamādvayavādins ("those who maintain nonduality in the sense of everything being like an illusion"). Their explanation [follows *The Compendium of the Essence of Wisdom*, verse 28]:

The Mādhyamikas know true reality
As being free from four positions, that is to say,
True reality is neither existent, nor is it not existent, nor is it a combination
Of existence and nonexistence, nor can it be that neither is the case.[439] (27)

The meaning of this is as follows: True reality is not existent, this being impossible on logical grounds. Nor does it not exist, given the power of appearance. Moreover, because of the same two defects, a combination of existence and nonexistence is not possible either. Nor can it be that neither is the case, for that would be incomprehensible. Furthermore, on the basis of another analysis different from the previous one, it is stated: "[The extreme of existence has] the undesired consequence that there is true force to matter—that the manifold world is just as it appears, namely, as a manifestation.[440] This is the explanation of the Māyopamādvayavādins.

The mental cultivation of nonduality in this sense of everything being like an illusion is their form of meditation. Attachment to nihilism is here the stain of meditation. To complete the six perfections in the conviction that nonduality in the sense of everything being like an illusion is their view.

Apratiṣṭhānavāda

The following is an examination of the proponents of not abiding in any phenomena (i.e., the Apratiṣṭhānavādins):

> The manifold world is not taken to be eternal
> Or said to be entirely annihilated either;
> Nor is it a combination of both eternal and annihilated,
> Nor can it be that neither is the case.[441] (28)
>
> The wise know the true reality of things
> As the nonabiding in anything.[442]
> Now, this is not just conceptual analysis, for a
> conceptualizing mind
> Does not know the nature of mind. (29)

All superimposition, whatever there is—
All this does not exist in any respect;
The meaning of Madhyamaka is thus the absence of superimposition;
Where is, then, the denial or establishing of anything?[443] (30)

This effortless wisdom
Is called inconceivable;
Something "inconceivable" that one has been able to conceive
Cannot truly be inconceivable.[444] (31)

The mind of theirs, by whom the world is [directly] realized as not arisen,
Is purified because of their realization.
For them, the wise, this is realized without effort:
Being their original state, the world is true.[445] (32)

This is also stated in the following:

When free from all superimpositions,
True reality appears of its own accord.
Expressions such as emptiness,
Remove superimpositions from it. (33)

To actualize without attachment this meaning that has come under analysis—whose nature is to be free from superimposition—is their form of meditation. To deny everything or become senseless [in a state of dull nothingness] are the stains of meditative stabilization. To complete the six perfections without becoming engaged in superimposition is the related view.

Here [in the pāramitā system], the compassion of those with inferior and average faculties (i.e., the Sautrāntikas and Yogācāras) has phenomena as its objects of reference. Compassion that has phenomena as its objects of reference must be understood as that which arises after all phenomena are focused on as being stirred by the wind of impermanence. But for those with superior faculties (i.e., the Mādhyamikas), compassion, for which essencelessness is the focus, is without a focus, phenomena being understood by directing one's attention toward their emptiness.

In this respect, there is a presentation of the three kāyas, taught by Maitreyanātha [in his *Ornament of Realization*]:

That by which he impartially carries out
Diverse benefits for the world,
For as long as the world exists,
Is the uninterrupted nirmāṇakāya of Śākyamuni. (34)

That body (*kāya*) of Śākyamuni,
Which consists of thirty-two marks and eighty signs,
Is regarded as the body of enjoyment (i.e., the sambhogakāya),
Because he enjoys the Mahāyāna through it. (35)

The uncontaminated qualities (*dharma*s)
Attained as purity in every aspect—
The natural body (svābhāvikakāya) of Śākyamuni
Has the defining characteristic of their nature.[446] (36)

Mantra System Mahāyāna

The mantra system is not explained by us here for the following reasons: it is very profound and a subject only for persons who have confidence in this profound tradition, and the presentation of the means of accomplishment—the four seals and the like—is extensive. This is as [stated in the *Lamp Illumination of the Three Systems*]:

> It has the same goal as the pāramitā system, but is free from confusion,
> Rich in skillful means and without difficulties.
> Moreover, it is only fit for those with sharp faculties.
> The treatises of mantra system are thus superior. (37)

A text named *Sekanirṇaya* (i.e., the *Presentation of Empowerment*) has been composed by us concerning this matter.

Mahāyāna Hermeneutics

If that which is to be practiced as the ultimate is only ascertained through Mahāyāna, why did the Illustrious One then teach the vehicles of the śrāvakas and pratyekabuddhas? It is not as one might think, for the two staircases of the Śrāvakayāna and Pratyekabuddhayāna have been provided only for the sake of realizing Mahāyāna, which is the only appropriate goal. This is taught [in the *Garland of Light*]:

> The perfect buddhas taught these means
> [In progressive order arranged] like the steps of a staircase,
> In order to introduce the beginner
> To the ultimate meaning.[447] (38)

In the *Lotus of Genuine Teaching* (*Saddharmapuṇḍarīka*), too, it is stated:

> The leaders have a single vehicle,
> A single tradition, and a single teaching.

It is due to my (i.e., the Buddha's) true skill in means
That I teach the three vehicles. (39)

Venerable Nāgārjuna, too, says [in his *Praise of the Unsurpassable* (*Niraupamyastava*)]:

Master, since there is no differentiation in the dharmadhātu,
There is no real difference between the vehicles, either.
You have taught the three vehicles
For introducing sentient beings.[448] (40)

In other treatises, too, [e.g., in the *Commentary on Valid Cognition*] it is stated:

Liberation is through the view of emptiness.[449]
The remaining forms of meditation have this view as their goal.[450] (41)

This light of the three vehicles is [our] emptiness, which is being investigated here. It should be understood in accordance with the Illustrious One. This is as [stated in the *Praise of the Unsurpassable*]:

Master! You did not teach anything,
Not even a single word,
Yet you satisfied all disciples who need to be trained
With the rain of Dharma.[451] (42)

Like a wish-fulfilling jewel, the perfection of benefiting others
Is not stirred by the fierce wind of every volition,
In this way it fulfills without exception
The wishes of all sentient beings.[452] (43)

With the dynamic of a turning wheel,
The teaching of the protector goes on,
Even without his giving any thought to it, according to the capacity
Of his disciples, as reflected in their different degrees of accumulation. (44)

As long as the ordinary mind continues,
There is no ending of the vehicles.
But once the mind is transformed,
There is neither a vehicle nor a wayfaring.[453] (45)

Stainless speech has here been strung together
Out of jewels from the genuine Dharma.
O wise ones! This jewel garland of true reality
Should be kept in your heart for the sake of your delight! (46)

I, who am fond of concise summaries
And hate weighty tomes, composed this work;
You learned ones who are fond of weighty tomes! Pardon me
That I did not speak extensively on this subject! (47)

Requested by fortunate ones, I composed with effort
This text of unsurpassable meaning.
May future sentient beings attain nearly unattainable buddhahood
Through the merit thus accumulated by me! (48)

The Jewel Garland of True Reality *is ended. This work is by a paṇḍita and renunciant, the venerable Advayavajra. Translated and finalized by the Indian paṇḍita Vajrapāṇi and the Tibetan translator monk Tsültrim Gyelwa.*

CHAPTER 17

Explaining the Seals of the Five Tathāgatas

HOMAGE to the glorious Vajrasattva!

> The five skandhas that arise in dependence are empty of the imagined.
> Empty of an own nature, they do not exist as something real.
> Not being nothingness,
> They have the nature of the one nondual mind with its manifold aspects.
> The skandhas of matter and the rest are victorious in the form of the five victorious ones. (1)

The five psychophysical aggregates are the five tathāgatas. The first four of them are sealed with Akṣobhya in order to establish that they are consciousness only. Since exterior forms are thus only mind, a perceived object does not exist, in which case the emptiness of the perceiving subject also obtains. In view of this, consciousness alone abides as an ultimately existing mere awareness per se, which is free from perceived and perceiver. This is precisely the goal of the Nirākāravādins—the wisdom of their main practice—like the stainless stretch of a midday sky in autumn. This is stated [in the following]:

That which is empty of the imagined
Has neither appearance nor form.
It is but truly existing awareness[454] and bliss;
It is also the confusion of accumulating forms after
meditation. (2)

This is also stated [in the *Sublime Continuum*]:

[Here, the first one is the dharmakāya,]
And the latter two the form kāyas.
[These latter appear on the basis of the former,
Just as visible forms appear in space.][455] (3)

As well as in the following:

The dharmakāya of the great sage
Is free from mental fabrication and appearances.
The two form kāyas arise from it,
And thereafter abide as illusion.[456] (4)

[Objection:] Since emptiness is already established by the seal of Akṣobhya, what is then the use of the canonical passage: "Akṣobhya is sealed with Vajrasattva"? To put it plainly, this second sealing serves the same purpose of establishing the emptiness of imagined forms.

[Response:] It is not so, for it is only the emptiness of the imagined that is established by the former seal (i.e., Akṣobhya's). Therefore, just as wisdom[457] is the main practice and the other (i.e., consciousness) the state attained afterward through the seal of Akṣobhya, so consciousness, too, becomes the state attained afterward through the seal of Vajrasattva, but the vajra of emptiness is now the main practice. This is also stated in the *Vajra Crown* (*Vajraśekhara*):

Emptiness is called the vajra,
Which is of a steadfast essence, not hollow,
Incombustible, and indestructible,
And whose defining characteristics are to be indivisible and impenetrable. (5)

If one was again matter and the rest during the state attained afterward
Arising from the wisdom of the main practice performed through the seal of Akṣobhya (i.e., through Yogācāra realization of emptiness),
Why, alas, is it not maintained that one would be again a hero-being (*vajrasattva*)
During the state attained afterward, arising from the practice performed through the seal of Vajrasattva (i.e., through Madhyamaka realization of emptiness)? (6)

[Objection:] But if one was a hero-being during the state attained afterward, there would be the undesired consequence of proclaiming annihilation, because the hero-being's compassion would not exist [during the next session of the main practice].[458]

[Reply: The inseparable nature of emptiness and compassion, or vajra and sattva] is maintained in the following verses:

Through vajra, emptiness is taught.
Through sattva, the state of wisdom only.
The identity of both is established
On the basis of Vajrasattva's true nature. (7)

The difference between emptiness and compassion
Is like that between a lamp and its light.

Emptiness and compassion are one,
Just as a lamp and its light are. (8)

Emptiness is not different from entities.
And there is no entity without it.
This follows from the determination of them not being without emptiness.
It is similar to the one that it is produced and impermanent. (9)

Just as the apparent truth is not annihilated[459]
When true reality is taught,
So too true reality is not apprehended
Without the apparent. (10)

And more in detail. One may wonder: Are then Akṣobhya and Vajrasattva the same? If they were, the "proponents of a nondual [mind with] manifold aspects" (Citrādvaitavāda, i.e., Sākāravāda) would be superior, since consciousness, matter, and the like are not abandoned. This is what is stated [in the following]:

For me the Sākāra system is propounded in the following terms:
Mind-only together with its manifold aspects is empty of all thought;
It is like touching grass while walking.
Others teach it as having the meaning of Madhyamaka. (11)

For the Citrādvaitavādin, mind exists ultimately, but [to claim the ultimate existence of] such a form of consciousness is not shrewd. This is for the following reason: Once sealed with the seal of Vajrasattva, it can be ruled out that a form of consciousness whose nature is that of Akṣobhya, that is, the nondual mind with its manifold aspects, which is empty of a perceived and a perceiver, really exists in terms of an entity. This is stated in the following:

> If one says that the skandha of matter and the rest, while
> empty of thought,
> Are still wisdom,[460] in virtue of Akṣobhya's seal,
> Then, in virtue of Vajrasattva's seal, it must be ruled out
> That this wisdom exists as an entity. (12)
>
> Through the realization of cognition-only
> One does not become Vajrasattva.
> Not being there from the beginning,
> Everything imagined is emptiness. (13)

Once the thorn that it (i.e., consciousness or wisdom) exists ultimately in such a way is removed, a Madhyamaka tenet is seen to be superior, one established on the basis of awareness,[461] which is continuous in its flow of effortless, indivisible union (*yuganaddha*) and characterized by not abiding in anything. This is realized through the kindness of a genuine guru. One may wonder, whether awareness[462] is established here, whether, being thus faced by the undesired consequence entailed by Māyopamādvayavāda, there is no Apratiṣṭhānavāda. This is not the case [for the reason stated in *Sixty Verses on Reasoning*:]

> That which has arisen dependently
> Has not arisen in terms of its own nature.
> How can that which has not arisen in terms of an own nature,
> Truly be called "arisen"?[463] (14)

Awareness, too, has arisen in dependence. Therefore, even awareness itself is not grounded in anything, but rather reflects the level of nonarising. This is as stated in the following:

Indeed, awareness has not arisen.
The being of real entities, too, is like that.
The sage said that the world
Has the nature of Vajrasattva. (15)

Moreover, the Tathāgata asked Mañjuśrī: "What is this inconceivable element?" Mañjuśrī replied: "The element that is inconceivable, not to be understood by the mind, not to be fathomed by the mind, and not to be realized through any volition of the mind, is what I call the inconceivable element. But again, Illustrious One, it is precisely no-mind, which is the inconceivable element. What is the reason for this? Mind is not found in no-mind. As to the element which is without mind, it is mind for through it mind is realized as it is. Again, all forms, Illustrious One, are the inconceivable element." Elsewhere (i.e., in the *Ornament of Manifested Wisdom*) it is said in this regard:

Homage to you, who is without imagined thoughts,
Whose intellect is not based on anything,
Who is without recollection, whose realization is nonconceptual,
And who is without any cognitive object. (16)

In the *Moon Light* (*Candrapradīpa*)[464] it is stated:

Whatever arises from conditions has not truly arisen,
For it does not arise in terms of own nature.
What depends on conditions is said to be empty,
And whoever knows emptiness, is not mad. (17)

In the *Discourse of the Descent into Laṅka* it is further said:

If characteristic signs still arise
After all error has been abandoned,
This will be their error,
Like the impure darkness of the eyes.[465] (18)

This is [as stated in the *Garland of Light*]:

You should not remain fixed in your everyday consciousness.
For precisely this reason the sage was afraid.
Thus his teaching repeatedly said to be essentially about
emptiness,
Differs [for various disciples].[466] (19)

And in *Hevajra Tantra* it is stated:

No object has ever arisen in terms of its own nature,
Wherefore it is neither true nor false.[467] (20)

Moreover, [we find in *Garland of Light*]:

When analyzed by a mind capable of subtle seeing,
All this, it can be determined, is the same doctrine,
Were it not for a single point that separates
Buddhists and non-Buddhists, namely, emptiness.[468] (21)

In order to avoid a form of emptiness that is equivalent to nihilism, [I said in *Presentation of Empowerment*, verse 31]:

Those who see suchness
In accordance with Madhyamaka

Are fortunate, indeed, in that they realize true reality,
Provided that they are aware of it in a direct way. (22)

In the *Vajra Tent of the Ḍākinīs* (*Ḍākinīvajrapañjara*) it is stated:

Wherever a mind of inseparably united
Emptiness and compassion is cultivated—
This indeed is the teaching of
The Buddha, Dharma, and Saṅgha.[469] (23)

Since the five skandhas that arise in dependence have the nature of the five tathāgatas, and since this nature in turn is inseparable from emptiness and compassion, it is established that the beings of the world are inseparable from emptiness and compassion. This, indeed, is uninterrupted meditation performed on the basis of the pith instructions of the genuine guru.

By following the reality of mantras
One will acquire proficiency in continuous meditation,
As continuous as the flow of a river
Or the steadiness of a flame. (24)

Likewise, the venerable Nāgārjuna says [in his *Succession of the Four Seals*]:

This is a divine palace, not the threefold world. These are not sentient beings but victorious ones.
I am the lord of the maṇḍala, not an ordinary person. These are not experiential objects—eyes, the earth, and so forth—nor are they matter and the other skandhas.

Given that they have the nature of dharmatā, these sentient
beings are the deities of the maṇḍala.
How can one, knowing as one does the manifold world to be
the circle of the maṇḍala, be confused about this?[470] (25)

Elsewhere it is stated:

Having arisen in mere dependence,
Things manifest like the city of the gandharvas.
The manifold world is not established in terms of an own
nature,
But it is not like a lotus in the sky either. (26)

Moreover, it has been said in *Hevajra Tantra*:

These phenomena are essentially nirvāṇa,
But because of delusion they have assumed the form of
saṃsāra.[471] (27)

The Explaining the Seals of the Five Tathāgatas, *composed by the great learned master Advayavajra,*[472] *is ended. Translated, corrected, and finalized by the Tibetan translator Maben Chöbar as taught by the Indian learned master Vajrapāṇi.*

CHAPTER 18

A Presentation of Empowerment

Introduction

OṂ. Homage to venerable Vajrasattva![473]

We prostrate to the word *evaṃ*,
Which is the cause of the four moments,
And in which the four joys arise, toward one's attainment of enlightenment,
In accord with the division into the four moments. (1)

Karmamudrā

There is the moment of the manifold, then the one of maturation.
In the third position, however, is freedom from defining characteristics;
It should be known that the moment of relaxation is after that,
The sequence of forceful yoga (*haṭhayoga*) having been rejected. (2)

If relaxation involves reflecting [on one's having experienced bliss],
How can it be taken to be in the third position,
Given that at this time there is no reflecting,
[And hence at this stage] awareness is without defining characteristics? (3)

Come on! it is therefore appropriate that the moment of freedom
From defining characteristics be recognized in the third position.
This can be established on the basis of one's own experience,
While the meaning of scriptures, too, is suitable here. (4)

They whose moment of the manifold lies in kissing and embracing,
Whose moment of maturation, as it is called, lies in friction,
And whose moment of freedom from defining characteristics lies in the awareness in the jewel
Have the correct knowledge of a base empowerment. (5)

If it were such awareness
In the middle of the jewel that were true reality,
Then that would be the true reality of the followers of Śiva and the Veda.
This is not what is maintained by Buddhists. (6)

This is as stated in the *Tantra Proclaiming Śiva, Requested by the Goddess* (*Devīparipṛcchāśivanirnādatantra*):

Devī, this jewel city[474]
Melts on the filament of the lotus.
In union, Rudra becomes Śiva, who is supreme.
And this exactly is Śakti, who is better than the supreme one. (7)

From the union of Śiva and Śakti,
Extraordinary bliss arises.

It is free from defining characteristics and what is defined,
And cannot be described in words. (8)

Once they are meditated on the form of Śakti (i.e., that they
are mind),
Entities are seen not to exist in reality.
Śakti is the view of emptiness,
The destroyer of all superimpositions. (9)

This is also stated in a different manner in the *Tantra of the Deity Ucchuṣma* (*Ucchuṣmatantra*):

From the union of Śiva and Śakti
There is real bliss, supreme and nondual.
It is neither Śiva nor Śakti,
But something based inside the jewel. (10)

In the *Study of Yoga* (*Yogādhyāya*), too, it is stated:

A yogin who is satiated with the nectar of wisdom
And has done what he had to do,
Does not have to do anything anymore.
If someone says there is, he does not know true reality. (11)

The proponents of Vedānta, too, say:

Bhāskara maintains a form of wisdom
That is beyond sense faculties and without sensation,
The only sensation is joy.
This is maintained in the texts of the illustrious one (i.e.,
Śaṅkarācārya). (12)

[In the *Wrathful Consciousness* (*Vijñānabhairava*), it is stated:]

Because of becoming excited through the union with Śakti,
At the end of entering her,
The bliss of experiencing Brahman-reality occurs.
It is said to be one's own [individual] bliss.[475] (13)

[Maitrīpa continues:]

Suffering does not occur in it,
Bliss is uninterrupted.
Joy is the nature of Brahman.
It is called liberation. (14)

Whatever is seen, however tiny it may be,
Should be understood as Brahman.
Therefore, the mind is not anything else,
It abides in Brahman only. (15)

The sight of the beloved is the only one worthwhile thing;
What is the use of other sights?
By such a sight is nirvāṇa attained,
Even with a mind accompanied by attachment. (16)

[In the *Great Tellings of the Descendants of Bharata* (*Mahābhārata*) it is stated:]

Abandon dharma and non-dharma!
Abandon both, true and false!
And having abandoned both of them,
Abandon also that by which one abandons them![476] (17)

This is also stated in a different manner in the *Divine Song (Bhagavadgītā)*:

> There is no existence of what does not exist,
> Nor is there nonexistence of what exists.
> The border between the two is seen
> By those who see the true reality of both.[477] (18)

[Maitrīpa continues:]

> Moreover, if an ultimately existing mind empty
> Of a perceived and so forth is called immovable,[478]
> This is invalidated by our own scriptures,
> Nor does it have the seal of Vajrasattva. (19)
>
> Why, then, is this seal of Akṣobhya
> Invariably taught by teachers?
> It was taught in a preliminary way,
> With the thought of offering reassurance that one is the tathāgatas. (20)
>
> Some decide that the middle path
> Is a Sākāra experience inside the vajra,
> Or a Nirākāra experience at its tip;
> This is not the view of our guru. (21)
>
> True reality cannot be held to be inside the vajra or at its tip,
> Or to have fallen into the kapāla,
> Or to be in the space in between. Realization of true reality comes
> From the mouth of the guru. (22)

How can [the *Hevajra Tantra*,] beginning with "The moment of the manifold is called variety,"[479]
And passages such as "inside the jewel,"
Be correct? Following the pith instructions of the genuine guru,
They are consistent. (23)

That the master empowerment and so forth are what is here intended,
Through the purifying act of a smile and so forth, is clear enough.
The corresponding verse [in the *Hevajra Tantra*][480] must be presented as creation phase
And not as referring to the nature of the completion phase. (24)

Because of manifold activities, the moment of the manifold lasts up to friction.
Because of bliss, there is maturation before[481] the jewel.
[Freedom from defining characteristics]—one needs to learn true reality from the guru.
Because of relaxation, there is the joy in the cessation of joy. (25)

The Sequence of the Four Seals

Having approached a karmamudrā,
One should meditate on the dharmamudrā.
Hereafter comes mahāmudrā,
From that the samayamudrā arises. (26)

The four joys can be maintained
With regard to each of the seals, except mahāmudrā.
This can be known through scriptures, self-awareness,
And the pith instructions of the genuine guru. (27)

Dharmamudrā

The manifold is realized through the karmamudrā;
Maturation is the nature of the world.
Steadfastness in that is freedom from defining characteristics;
And relaxation is the gazing at the world. (28)

Mahāmudrā

Not to abide in anything
Is known as mahāmudrā.
As self-awareness (i.e., mahāmudrā) is stainless,
The moments of enjoying manifold appearances and so forth
do not arise. (29)

Effortless wisdom
Can be taken as inconceivable.
Something "inconceivable" that one has been able to
conceive
Cannot truly be inconceivable.[482] (30)

Those who see suchness
In accordance with Madhyamaka
Are fortunate, in that they realize true reality,
Provided that they are aware of it in a direct way.[483] (31)

All superimposition, whatever there is—
All this does not exist in any respect;
As to the meaning of Madhyamaka, it is the absence of superimposition;
Where is, then, the denial or the establishing of anything?[484] (32)

The thought that the world is without the superimposition of knowledge
And objects of knowledge is not different from superimposition itself.
Everything is as it ever has been,
But it is not the way it was [before when there was still a conceptual] mind. (33)

The mind of them, by whom the world is directly realized as not arisen,
Is purified because of their realization.
For him, the wise, this is realized without effort:
Being their original state, the world is true.[485] (34)

The thought whose connection with nirvāṇa
Has not been uncovered[486] arises in dependence;
This very thought is nirvāṇa.
Do not create confusion, O mind! (35)

They who do not abide in the remedy,
Are not attached to true reality,
And who do not even desire the fruit,
Find mahāmudrā. (36)

Samayamudrā

Just as the four joys
Are taught on the level of the karmamudrā,
So they are on the level of the samayamudrā.
This is shown by the kindness of the vajra master. (37)

Conclusion

The karmamudrā is the manifold,
The dharmamudrā arises from maturation,
Mahāmudrā is freedom from defining characteristics,
And the samayamudrā is relaxation. (38)

Yogins who do not know mahāmudrā,
Having a karmamudrā as their only means of practice,
Are deprived of the transmitted true reality
And go to the Raurava Hell. (39)

As long as they have not touched
The dust on Lord Śavara's feet,
They do not know
The four seals and the four moments. (40)

I have presented the correct empowerment,
Free from [all elements of] forceful and base empowerments.
Whatever merit I have accomplished in doing so,
May sentient beings be happy because of it! (41)

The Presentation of Empowerment, *composed by the learned master, the victorious Maitrīpa, is ended. Translated and revised by the Indian learned master Kṛṣṇa Paṇḍita and the Tibetan translator Tsültrim Gyelwa.*[487]

CHAPTER 19

The Succession of the Four Seals

HOMAGE to Vajrasattva!

> *Evaṃ.*[488]
> Having first bowed to Vajrasattva,
> Whose nature is pure wisdom,
> I write in brief *A Succession of Seals*
> To improve my understanding. (1)

Here, [it is implied that] those whose minds are confused drift about distressed in the ocean of cyclic existence, because they are confused about the succession of seals. It is in order that they may easily realize the meaning of the four seals that the means of swiftly accomplishing great bliss is presented in accordance with the tantras. The four seals are the karmamudrā, dharmamudrā, mahāmudrā, and samayamudrā.

Among these, first the nature of the karmamudrā shall be analyzed. Action (*karma*) is intention as it relates to body, speech, and mind. It is the main thing. Seal (*mudrā*) refers then to its nature of imagination. [It is as stated in the *Hevajra Tantra*]:

> In this karmamudrā the four joys arise—
> Divided according to the four moments.[489]

> It is from knowing the moments that blissful wisdom,
> Which is based in the syllable *evaṃ*, arises.[490] (2)

The four joys are: joy, supreme joy, coemergent joy, and the joy of no-joy. Otherwise, this passage would not make sense:

> Between supreme joy and the joy of no-joy,
> See the goal and stabilize it![491] (3)

The four moments are: the manifold, maturation, freedom from defining characteristics, and relaxation. The placement of freedom from defining characteristics between maturation and relaxation needs to be understood in the context of empowerment. In forceful yoga (*haṭhayoga*), however, freedom from defining characteristics and coemergent joy are put at the end. The Illustrious One taught this extensively in the context of empowerment and forceful yoga.

All that appears as coemergent is called coemergent because it duplicates the image of the real coemergent. This image of the coemergent leads the adept to realize a type of wisdom that is similar to the coemergent. The coemergent is thus [only in this limited sense] the wisdom based on a prajñā.[492] Therefore, there is no arising of the coemergent in the wisdom based on a prajñā. For inasmuch as the true nature of all phenomena, namely, what is called the coemergent, is the "actual reality" (*svalakṣaṇa*)[493] of the uncontrived, a fruit similar [to the real coemergent] is produced by relying on a karmamudrā.

A similar flow (i.e., the same liquid) is an outflow. Just as a reflection of a face cast from a mirror is similar, but not the real face (it did not exist before, nor does it exist now—this mirror creates a reflection of the face, one only resembling it), and nevertheless, in their delusion people are satisfied with the thought that they have seen their own face [rather than merely a reflection], so too masters of inferior intellect accomplish the wisdom that is based on a prajñā and are satisfied, thinking that they have experienced the real coemergent. Being satisfied [with what they have found], they have not even heard of the dharmamudrā.

How can the uncontrived wisdom called coemergent arise for those who have not even heard of the dharmamudrā? How can the uncontrived arise only through the contrived practice of uniting with a karmamudrā? Only from a cause of a specific kind does a fruit of this same specific kind arise, and not from another kind. Just as the sprout of a śālī tree and not a kodrava plant arises from a śālī seed, the uncontrived coemergent arises from the presence of the uncontrived dharmamudrā. Therefore, it is only the dharmamudrā that is the cause of mahāmudrā (to figuratively apply a distinction [between a cause and an effect] to what in fact admits of no such distinction).

Why, then, did the Illustrious One teach [the following in the *Hevajra Tantra*]?

> The divine reality, which has the form of the letter *e*
> And is ornamented with the letter *vaṃ* in its middle,
> Is the basis of everything blissful—
> The box of the buddha jewel.[494] (4)

As to the box of the buddha jewel, because it duplicates the image of the Buddha, the box is a basis, a foundation. Therefore, there is a lotus that is the source of abundant jewels, namely, the joy obtainable from a woman as a karmamudrā. When the relative bodhicitta has entered from the central channel (*avadhūtī*) into the jewel through the friction of the penis and the vagina in union, then the wisdom called the lower (i.e., the image of the) coemergent (also called the momentary coemergent) arises. But this is not the real coemergent; it is only similar[495] to it. By its nature it is endowed with the wisdom based on a prajñā, the three joys and the four moments. In the context of empowerment and forceful yoga, it is called the similar fruit of the karmamudrā. This concludes the first chapter, the presentation of the karmamudrā as a fruit that is only similar to the real one.

OṂ dharmamudrā. It has the nature of the dharmadhātu, is free from mental fabrications; it is nonconceptual, uncontrived, and without arising. It is compassionate by nature, and owing to the supreme joy associated with it, it has turned into a means of unique beauty. In the permanence of its continuous flow and given its coemergent nature, it is not different from the prajñā (i.e., the karmamudrā), because of the rise of the coemergent. All this is called dharmamudrā.

Another defining characteristic of the dharmamudrā needs to be known: it is like sun rays in the darkness of dense ignorance. One gets purged of the affliction of delusion—mere straw chaff—on account of the dharmamudrā also being the guru's pith instructions. The dharmamudrā is the unique nature of the threefold world, which consists of the great elements, namely, all earth, water, wind, and fire. It should be known to be without any waves of affliction, inseparable from emptiness and compassion.

Moreover, the Illustrious One said [in the *Hevajra Tantra*]:

> The *lalanā* channel has the nature of prajñā,
> And the *rasanā* channel has the nature of means.
> In the middle is the *avadhūtī* channel,
> Devoid of the duality of a perceived and perceiver.[496] (5)

By being skillful in this, the path should be understood to have the form of suchness as its immediate cause. Knowing the path, one attentively and constantly practices it; thereby cessation, which has the nature of the coemergent, is actualized.

In like manner, [the following dharmamudrā] has been taught [in the *Sublime Continuum*, for example]:

> There is nothing to be removed from it
> And nothing to be added.
> The real should be seen as real,
> And seeing the real, one becomes liberated.[497] (6)

The avadhūtī dwells in the middle of the other two, the lalanā and the rasanā. This is realized through one-pointed meditation on everything as having the nature of the coemergent, and through the pith instructions of a genuine guru. Far from being different from it, the dharmamudrā is the cause of mahāmudrā. This concludes the second chapter, the presentation of the dharmamudrā as the fruit of maturation.

ĀḤ mahāmudrā. It is both great (*mahā-*) and a seal (*mudrā*), hence, a "great seal" (*mahāmudrā*). It is devoid of an own nature, free from the hindrances of the knowable, and so forth. It is like an immaculate daytime sky in the middle of autumn and the basis of everything perfect. It has the identity of cyclic existence and nirvāṇa as its nature, consists of universal compassion, and has the unique form of great bliss.

Moreover, we have [in the *Ornament of Manifested Wisdom*?]:

> The mental factors of amanasikāra are virtuous.
> Those of manasikāra are not virtuous.[498]

In the same text it has been said:

> Homage to you, who is without imagined thoughts,
> Whose intellect is not based on anything, who is without
> recollection,

Whose realization is nonconceptual,
And who is without any cognitive object.[499] (7)

This, too, is called mahāmudrā.[500] Through this mahāmudrā, which is inconceivable by nature, the fruit called samayamudrā arises. This concludes the third chapter, the presentation of mahāmudrā as the fruit that is stainlessness.

HŪṂ samayamudrā. The manifestation of Vajradhara in the form of Heruka for the sake of sentient beings is taught to be the samayamudrā. This manifestation is by its nature the aspect of the sambhoga- and nirmāṇakāyas and appears clearly. Once they have adopted this samayamudrā,[501] once they have started to practice the fivefold wisdom in the form of a circle by way of the fivefold ritual,[502] the masters meditate on this circle of the samayamudrā in terms of the mirror-like wisdom, the wisdom of equality, the wisdom of discrimination, the wisdom of activity, and the wisdom that is the pure dharmadhātu. They do this through the initial yoga, the yoga of the supreme king of the maṇḍala (i.e., *ati yoga*), the yoga of the supreme king of activity (i.e., great ati yoga), the yoga of drops, and the subtle yoga.[503] By doing this they accumulate merit.

Through that alone, however, they do not attain the fruit of the dharmamudrā, for it has been said:

From a specific cause a specific fruit of the same kind arises.[504] (8)

Therefore, having broken through to the coemergent, with the taste of having realized it, things such as the immovable and movable that are imagined by immature beings become the cause of perfect enlightenment. Through this realization the threefold world is perfectly cultivated in the form of the circle. This has been stated by the Illustrious One [in *Hevajra Tantra*]:

> There is neither recitation of mantras, nor prescribed
> observances, nor fire offering,
> Neither the retinue of the maṇḍala nor the maṇḍala itself.
> The enlightened mind is the recitation of mantras, prescribed
> observances,
> The fire offering, the retinue of the maṇḍala, and the maṇḍala
> itself.[505] (9)

[The Illustrious One further said]:

> In brief, the yogin possesses the forms of the assembly in
> terms of the enlightened mind.[506] (10)

"In brief" refers to the unique form of all phenomena, that is to say, the form of great bliss. "Mind" is here the enlightened mind (bodhicitta). As to "possesses the forms of the assembly," the wisdom whose nature is the empowerment of the dharmamudrā and mahāmudrā[507] is called the true assembly. This concludes the fourth chapter, the presentation of the samayamudrā as a fruit made by persons [for the sake of others].[508]

This concludes the teaching on the four seals, a manual in four steps, as taught by the master Nāgārjuna.[509]

CHAPTER 20

A Summary of the Meaning of Empowerment

HOMAGE to the Buddha!

A certain superior one called spiritual friend,
Who has greatness and is unfathomable,
Holds inexpressible true reality
As if in the palms of his hands. (1)

With the knowledge of such a supreme vajra master,
We compose a summary of the meaning of empowerment,
Gathered from the many treatises on empowerment
And in accordance with canonical scripture. (2)

The first is the vase empowerment,
And the second, the excellent secret empowerment;
The third is the prajñā-wisdom empowerment,
And the fourth one is just like that.[510] (3)

The Six Vase Empowerments

The meaning of this is as follows: As for the line, "The first is the vase empowerment," the six empowerments whose distinctive features are water, crown, vajra, bell, name, and master are vase empowerments.

Empowerment (lit. "besprinkling") means that one is "besprinkled" in order to wash away the stains of ignorance, just as external stains are washed away by external water. Because all these empowerments are performed with a vase, they are called "vase empowerments." The six are also called irreversible empowerments, since they have the nature of the six tathāgatas. Furthermore, the water empowerment partakes of the nature of Akṣobhya, who embodies mirror-like wisdom. The crown empowerment partakes of the nature of Ratnasambhava, who embodies the wisdom of equality. The vajra empowerment partakes of the nature of Amitābha, who embodies discriminating wisdom. The lord (i.e., the bell)[511] empowerment partakes of the nature of Amoghasiddhi, who embodies the wisdom of activity. The name empowerment partakes of the nature of Vairocana, who embodies the wisdom of the very pure dharmadhātu, [such wisdom] conforming to a form of awareness that is the result of having put an end to ignorance. The master empowerment partakes of the nature of Vajrasattva. The first five of these empowerments are empowerments of the awareness-consorts (*vidyā*), for the action during them is performed by Locanā and the other awareness-consorts.

The Water Empowerment

Among these, in order to wash away the stains of ignorance, the vajra master, who is visualized by the disciple as having the form of Akṣobhya, must bestow the water empowerment upon the disciple, who depends on the form of Vairocana.[512] There is such a [vajra] pride at all times.

The Crown Empowerment

The crown empowerment is the seed of the thick protuberance on the head (*uṣṇīṣa*) appropriate for being the future buddha.

The Vajra Empowerment

In terms of the purification of the twelve factors of dependent arising, a vajra twelve fingers breadth in length is shown. In its middle part there is the syllable HŪṂ, which expresses the unsurpassable true nature of phenomena. Its meaning is as follows: The letter *ha* [in HŪṂ] stands for being uncaused, the vowel *ū* for being without conceptual understanding, and *aṃ* (i.e., the anusvāra) for phenomena that are not based on anything.

> This HŪṂ is the place where the five sages emerge in the form of
> The five spokes of the vajra from the calyxes of the lotuses of cyclic existence.
> They come forth in bodies of cyclic existence as a result of
> The purification of the five skandhas. (4)

Now, it is made clear here, through the fact that the spokes at the side face the spoke in the middle, that all forms and the other, the first four skandhas, have the nature of the fifth skandha, consciousness. In order to signal that everything has the nature of everything[513] the tip of the vajra is quadrangular throughout its length.

> Now, these five sages of the Dharma, whose nature
> Is represented by the roaring sound of HŪṂ,
> The five embodiments of liberation
> Have sprung forth at their respective side. (5)

Each of them has three flowers, meant to express emptiness, signlessness, and wishlessness. According to the instruction of the guru, it should be known that the five buddhas embody the five types of wisdom, whose defining characteristics are likeness to a mirror, realization of equality, discrimination, activity, and being the pure dharmadhātu. The following characterization [in the *Vajra Crown*] of indivisible wisdom is a [good] summary:

> Emptiness is called the vajra,
> Which is of a steadfast essence, not hollow;
> Incombustible and indestructible,
> And whose defining characteristics is to be indivisible and impenetrable. (6)

In the *Hevajra Tantra* too it is said: "The vajra is indivisible."[514]

This performance of the vajra empowerment is, as it were, the planting of the seed for the arising indivisible wisdom.

The Bell Empowerment

Likewise, the vajra bell has, given its purpose for the previous one (i.e., the vajra), the length of twelve fingers breadth. It is an upside down lotus. Its ringing sound stands for the union with the vajra—this in order to make one realize that it is the nature of all phenomena to lack an own nature. In order to demonstrate that the source of phenomena (*dharmodayā*) is the basis of indivisible wisdom, it is adorned with two bands of vajra, one on its upper and another on its lower part. In order to express its nature as a divine palace—the same nature as that of the threefold world—there is a fringed network with chains and loops in between. Therefore, it is also marked by the [seed syllables of the] five tathāgatas. In order to indicate that the bell is the cause of the wisdom of inseparably united emptiness and compassion, it displays on its top the face of the consort (*prajñā*).

In order to show that dharmadhātu wisdom consists of the five tathāgatas, beginning with Vairocana, that it has the nature of the five skandhas, beginning with form, and the nature as well of the five elements, beginning with earth, the bell's top is adorned with five spokes. The connection of the four spokes facing the central spoke of the bell and so forth is as explained before. May empowerment be conferred by this ringing vajra bell. It will produce awakening toward the entire unsurpassable true nature of phenomena. In order to demonstrate its preeminence, and to show that it is the main cause, the vajra empowerment is given first, that is, the vajra bell empowerment is first passed over, even though it is the instrumental cause.

The Name Empowerment

The name empowerment is given in order to demonstrate the namelessness of all phenomena and to acquire a basis for a proper name when the level of a buddha is reached in the future. The empowerment is given by removing the old name and bestowing a new name in accord with one's family and clan deity.

The Master Empowerment

The master empowerment has the defining characteristics of the vajra commitment, the bell commitment, and the seal commitment; suitableness; permission; [vajra] conduct; prediction; and reassurance. The vajra commitment makes the disciple realize: "Form now on, you have the requisite commitment to realize the continuous flow of the unconditioned indivisibility and indivisible union." The bell commitment makes the disciple understand: "Now you are a holder of the group of eighty-four thousand Dharma teachings." The seal commitment makes the disciple understand: "You have the nature of your chosen deity (*iṣṭadevatā*)." The reality of the maṇḍala, the defining characteristic of the maṇḍala's purity, the reality of the deity, the defining characteristic of the deity's purity, the performance of the master, the knowledge of the means of accomplishing the maṇḍala, the five lamps, and the food of five nectars, all this constitutes suitableness. And true reality here is that the maṇḍala, deities, and so forth lack an own nature, [as is realized and cultivated] during the completion phase. Permission is given to set the wheel of the Dharma in motion. Vajra conduct is prescribed in order for outer conduct to be abandoned. A prophecy is made in order to reveal that one will have the nature of earth and the other elements when one attains enlightenment. For, to explain, this is the meaning of the mantra BHŪR BHUVAḤ SVAḤ:[515] *Bhūr* means "may you be"; *bhuvaḥ* "of earth and the other elements"; and *svaḥ* "nature" (i.e., "May you have the nature of earth and the other elements!"). [It is declared:] "One is free from all hindrances, equal to all buddhas and bodhisattvas." This reassurance is given from now on for the sake of awakening.

The Secret Empowerment

The bestowing [of the two essences] of bodhicitta, which is performed by both the guru and his consort simultaneously, is the secret empowerment. It is conferred in order to transform the adept into a suitable cultivator of insight and faith, and in order to protect his commitments. The secret empowerment is given by means of these two secret essences of means and insight. This is the word formation [of *guhya*].

The Prajñā-Wisdom Empowerment

The compound prajñā-wisdom admits of two word formations here: "the wisdom from prajñā" and "the wisdom which is prajñā." As to the first of these, the intellect, which still retains the two aspects of cognition, namely, a perceived object and perceiving subject, is the prajñā that by its nature is a woman with well-rounded limbs and consisting of the four elements, five skandhas, and the six cognitive objects starting with matter.[516] The aspect of bodhicitta arisen from this [form of prajñā] as cause is wisdom. This is the first word formation. Precisely this prajñā, in its emptiness of the two aspects (i.e., the perceived and perceiver), is also wisdom. This is the other word formation.

The Fourth Empowerment

Some say that the goal characterized by prajñā-wisdom and endowed with the seven constituents[517] is the meaning of the fourth empowerment. Others say that that which is like the stainless autumn sky while becoming familiar with this very prajñā-wisdom is the meaning of the fourth empowerment. Others say that it is prajñā-wisdom itself; or the form of its true nature; or the forms of its deviation from the natural state, namely, natural arising; or the pure nature of nondual continuity in which emptiness and compassion are united as a pair is the meaning of the fourth empowerment. Other positions are not mentioned here for reasons of space.

Through the fame[518] and related merit that I have produced
By this summarized description of the very secret
    empowerment,
May the whole world have faith to acquire the endurance
Of the stainless and clear words well spoken by the Sugata. (7)

This Summary of the Meaning of Empowerment *is ended. This is a work by the paṇḍita and renunciant, the venerable Advayavajra. Translated, corrected, and finalized by the Indian paṇḍita Vajrapāṇi and the Tibetan translator Tsültrim Gyelwa.*[519]

CHAPTER 21

The Five Aspects of Vajrasattva

HOMAGE to the Buddha![520]

> Having venerated Vajrasattva,
> Who is unsurpassable in his freedom from mental fabrications,
> I will explain in brief, for the better understanding of disciples
> His five aspects. (1)

Once one has protected the abode, oneself, and the practice by saying OṂ ĀḤ HŪṂ, offerings should be made to the five tathāgatas and five yoginīs in the middle of a quadrangular or other maṇḍala in a place suffused with fragrant smells and so forth.

Akṣobhya

In the middle of it is the multicolored syllable PAṂ, which turns into a multicolored, eight-petalled, blossoming lotus. On its stamen is the red letter RAṂ,[521] which turns into a sun disk. From a blue syllable HŪṂ situated on this sun disk, arises Akṣobhya,[522] blue and with one face and two arms. He performs the earth-touching mudrā and sits in the cross-legged vajra posture. His body is adorned with the thirty-two major marks and the eighty excellent minor marks of a buddha. He is the unique abode of a multitude of qualities, such as the ten strengths and the four fearlessnesses, and is without porosity, flesh, or bones—a mere appearance like a reflection in a mirror—neither true nor false. Embodying great kindness, he is of a dark-blue color and his sign is a dark-blue vajra. He has the nature of the skandha of consciousness, which is the very pure dharmadhātu. His head and beard are shaven, and his body is covered with religious robes. The crown of his head displays a Vajrasattva, for he has the nature of Vajrasattva, being inseparable from emptiness and compassion.

Therefore, he has the nature of cause and effect and the defining characteristic of emptiness, which is endowed with all supreme forms. Being unconditioned and having the nature of suchness, he is also the dharmakāya. Being a mere reflection, he is the sambhogakāya. Given that he has the nature of imagined consciousness, he is the nirmāṇakāya. Possessing the single taste of all three kāyas, he is the svābhāvikakāya. This is stated [in *Twenty Verses on Mahāyāna*]:

> The unconditioned mind is the dharmakāya;
> Realization is the defining characteristics of the
> saṃbhogakāya;[523]
> Then there is that: A variegated body has been emanated (i.e., the nirmāṇakāya).
> The natural one (i.e., the nijakāya) is the nature of all three.[524] (2)

Untouched by thoughts and the like, he belongs to the vajra family. And this vajra family is not reached by worldly people. Anger, vajra water, the cool season, noon, a sharp taste, hearing, sky, sound, and the series [of palatal consonants starting with] *ca*—these purities emblematic of Akṣobhya are a presentation of outer and inner features. The presentation of the four kāyas here is as before. His mantra of recitation is: OṂ ĀḤ VAJRADHṚK HŪṂ.

Vajrasattva

Now, Vajrasattva [on Akṣobhya's crown] has arisen from a white HŪṂ. He has one face and two arms and holds a vajra and a vajra bell. He has the nature of mental consciousness, sealed with emptiness. He embodies the astringent taste and the purified autumn season. He has the nature of the letters *ya*, *ra*, *la*, *va*, and so forth. His time is from midnight until dawn. Another term for him is dharmadhātu.

Vairocana

On the eastern petal of the lotus, white Vairocana has arisen on a moon disk from a white OṂ. His sign is a white wheel, and he displays the mudrā of supreme enlightenment. He has the nature of the skandha of matter and embodies bewilderment. He is of the purity of excrement, belongs to the tathāgata family, and abides as mirror-like wisdom. He is the purified winter season and embodies a sweet taste. He is related to the series [of velar consonants starting with] *ka*, and his time is the morning. He has the nature of the body. His mantra is: OṂ ĀḤ JINAJIK HŪṂ.

Ratnasambhava

On the southern petal of the lotus, yellow Ratnasambhava has arisen on a sun disk from a yellow TRĀṂ. His sign is a jewel, and he displays the mudrā of generosity. He has the nature of the skandha of sensation, embodies slander, has the nature of ova, belongs to the *ratna* family, and has the wisdom of equality. He has the character of the spring season and embodies a salty taste. He is related to the series [of retroflex consonants starting with] *ṭa*, and his time is the afternoon. His mantra is: OṂ ĀḤ RATNADHṚK HŪṂ.

Amitābha

On the western petal of the lotus, red Amitābha has arisen on a sun disk from a red HRĪḤ. His sign is a lotus, and he displays the mudrā of meditative stabilization. He has the nature of the skandha of discrimination and embodies attachment. He has the nature of semen, belongs to the *padma* family, and has discriminative wisdom as a defining characteristic. His season is the summer, and he embodies a sour taste. He is related to the series [of dental consonants starting with] *ta*, and his time is the first part of evening. His mantra of recitation is: OṂ ĀḤ ĀROLIK HŪṂ.

Amoghasiddhi

On the northern petal of the lotus, green Amoghasiddhi has arisen on a sun disk from a green KHAṂ. He has the nature of flesh. His sign is a sword, and he displays the mudrā of fearlessness. He has the nature of the skandha of karmic formations and belongs to the karma family. He has the character of jealousy and the nature of the wisdom of activity. His season is the rainy season. He embodies a bitter taste. He is related to the purified series [of labial consonants starting with] *pa*. His time is midnight, and his mantra of recitation is: OṂ ĀḤ PRAJÑĀDHṚK HŪṂ.

The Five Tathāgatas

All of them sit in the cross-legged vajra posture and have one face, two arms, and a protuberance on the head (*uṣṇīṣa*). Their heads and beards are shaven. They wear religious robes, are adorned with the thirty-two major marks and the eighty excellent minor marks [of a buddha], and are the unique abode of the multitude of qualities—the ten strengths, the four fearlessnesses, and the rest. They are without porosity, flesh, or bones, like a reflection in a mirror. They have sambhogakāya forms, which are mere appearances without stains, beyond all concepts of true, false, and the like. Grounded in their svābhāvikakāya, which is the single taste of the three kāyas, they are inseparable from the dharmakāya, whose nature is unconditioned suchness, as well as the kāya of imagined consciousness (i.e., the nirmāṇakāya).

In order to realize that they are consciousness-only, Vairocana, Ratnasambhava, Amitābha, and Amoghasiddhi, who have the nature of respectively the skandhas of matter, sensation, discrimination, and karmic formation, are sealed with Akṣobhya, for which their heads are adorned with Akṣobhya. Now in order to realize the essencelessness of consciousness and the identity of emptiness and compassion, even Akṣobhya must be sealed with Vajrasattva. Through this it is realized that the world, whose nature partakes of cause and effect, merely has this single taste of emptiness, cyclic existence and nirvāṇa alike. This is as stated [in the *Vajra Tent of the Ḍākinīs*]:

> Wherever a mind of inseparable
> Emptiness and compassion is cultivated—
> There is indeed the teaching of
> The Buddha, Dharma, and Saṅgha.[525] (3)

[And in the *Exposition of the Enlightened Attitude* it is said:]

> I claim that the nature
> Of all phenomena is emptiness,
> In the same way as sweetness
> Is the nature of molasses, and hotness that of fire.[526] (4)

Likewise, [Nāgārjuna says in his *Sixty Verses on Reasoning*]:

Thorough knowledge of cyclic existence—
This is called nirvāṇa.[527] (5)

Locanā

On the petal in the southeastern direction, white Locanā has arisen on a moon disk from a white LĀṂ.[528] Her sign is an eye. She has the nature of the earth element, belongs to the tathāgata family, and is fond of bewilderment. Her seed syllables and mantra are: OṂ ĀḤ LĀṂ HŪṂ SVĀHĀ.

Māmakī

On the petal in the southwestern direction, dark-blue Māmakī has arisen on a moon disk from the dark-blue seed syllable MĀṂ. Her sign is a dark-blue vajra. She has the nature of the water element, belongs to the vajra family, and is fond of hatred. Her seed syllables and mantra are: OṂ ĀḤ MĀṂ HŪṂ SVĀHĀ.

Pāṇḍaravāsinī

On the petal in the northwestern direction, red Pāṇḍaravāsinī has arisen on a moon disk from the red seed syllable PĀṂ. Her sign is a red lotus. She has the nature of the fire element, belongs to the padma family, and is fond of attachment. Her seed syllables and mantra are: OṂ ĀḤ PĀṂ HŪṂ SVĀHĀ.

Tārā

On the petal in the northeastern direction, green Tārā[529] has arisen on a moon disk from the green seed syllable TĀṂ. Her sign is a blue lotus. She has the nature of the wind element, belongs to the karma family, and is fond of jealousy. Her seed syllables and mantra are: OṂ ĀḤ TĀṂ HŪṂ SVĀHĀ.

Vajradhātvīśvarī

These four goddesses are each sixteen years old, of extraordinary beauty, well-formed, and youthful, as if shaped in their beauty. They have the nature of the four kāyas, just as explained above. They are pleasant, the support of all the qualities of the victorious ones, and have the nature of the five tathāgatas. In their middle is their mistress, Vajradhātvīśvarī, who has the nature of vowels and the nature of Vajrasattva. She is said to be Bhagavatī, suchness, emptiness, the perfection of insight, the extreme of true reality, and essencelessness.

My intention here is not to demonstrate
My skillfulness in composing treatises;
What is it then? In short,
That I may make my students understand. (6)

The entire virtue attained by me
For having duly set forth, for the sake of sentient beings,
That which accords with all scriptures of the Victorious One
and with reasoning—
May all sentient beings become Vajrasattva through it! (7)

The Five Aspects [of Vajrasattva], *composed by Advayavajra,*[530] *is ended.*[531]

CHAPTER 22

A Discourse on Illusion

Homage to the Buddha![532]

If the learned ones realize
That the world, like an illusion, lacks an own nature,
Why are people then deluded,
Even though they know and are seeking bliss? (1)

A magician creates the illusion
Of the radiance of a burning house;
And to some it appears to be real,
Those knowing [the trick take] the illusion as an illusion. (2)

Seeing it as an illusion,
Everything one wishes comes without effort.
One enjoys it as illusion,
So that everything is realized as illusion. (3)

Alas, if you do not realize that they are false,
You will have to assert the permanence of illusions.
But since the dharmadhātu has not arisen,
There is not the undesired consequence of its destruction either. (4)

Since phenomena neither arise nor cease,
They cannot turn into the stiffness of matter either.

Phenomena arise from emptiness,
But the true nature of phenomena is not different from these
phenomena. (5)

Therefore, the omniscience
Of the Buddha is not impaired.
With his power to avoid superimposition,
He sets the *dharmacakra* completely in motion. (6)

Not even stretching his legs any more,
And abandoning pride and the like—
The yogin adopts such proper conduct,
And so is well established in the practice of nonabiding. (7)

Whoever does not adopt proper conduct,
Even after obtaining the best food and drink,
And having proclaimed what is pure,
Is not a fit vessel for perfect enlightenment. (8)

People talk about true reality
And approve proper conduct,
But it is difficult to find a person
Accomplished in the practice of awareness. (9)

Earth is the bed, nakedness are the clothes,
Food is the rice obtained in alms.
One endures the true nature of nonarising
And engages in effortless compassion. (10)

The very phenomena that conquer people
Are conquered by conduct;

The fruit of this is observable in this life—
The unsurpassable fruit to the same extent. (11)

The merit that I have gathered,
From having explained illusion with good intent,
May people reach the state of nonduality
And become established in the supramundane through it! (12)

The Discourse on Illusion, *composed by the learned master Advayavajra,*[533] *is ended. Translated and finalized by the Indian paṇḍita Vajrapāṇi and the Tibetan translator and monk Tsültrim Gyelwa.*

CHAPTER 23

A Discourse on Dream

Homage to the Omniscient One![534]

In the Vinaya, the Abhidharma, and the Sūtras,
Phenomena are said to be like a dream,
By the victorious supreme beings.
This is clearly proclaimed. (1)

Is the dream true or not?
Does it [illustrate the tenet that] the manifold forms of the mind are true or the one that only the mind itself is true?
Or [the one of nonduality in the sense that everything is like] an illusion? Or the one of nonabiding?
What is here maintained on behalf of the noble ones? (2)

[You may say:] When not realized for what it is, the dream is true.
When realized, it acquires the status of falsehood.
[Response:] In the first case, it would be wrongly known as permanent;
In the second, as nonexistent. (3)

While what is wrongly imagined is removed as a result of awakening,
Experience is not removed.

That whose nature is the manifestation of the truly existing
manifold forms of mind
Is a sublime experience. (4)

Its instantaneous perishing is due to the ground consciousness,
And its manifoldness to the active consciousnesses arising from
this root.
Here, the consciousnesses possesses the manifoldness as aspects.
It has indeed been claimed that this manifoldness is only mind. (5)

When a dream arises from a dream,
Then the manifoldness of the mind is seen to be false.
It is neither true, given the false perception of it,
Nor absolutely nothing, given its clarity. (6)

Why should the nameless be given a name?
Or is the name called an illusion?
But a name for a name is not proper,
And there is no basis in the nameless for a name. (7)

Of the six positions here, two must be abandoned;
Four are taken to lead to enlightenment.
The supreme buddhas say thus:
All this here is like a dream. (8)

Know then, moreover, that the position of nonabiding
Is the supreme wealth among Buddhists.
Know this in particular through self-awareness,
Attained thanks to the genuine guru's efforts, and through
proper conduct. (9)

The Discourse on Dream, *taught by the learned master and renunciant Advayavajra, is ended. Translated and finalized by the Indian paṇḍita Vajrapāṇi and the Tibetan translator Tsültrim Gyelwa.*

CHAPTER 24

An Elucidation of True Reality

Homage to the Buddha![535]

I pay homage to the embodiment of the Buddha's threefold kāya,
Which has the nature of insight and skillful means.
From its power the most supreme within
Cyclic existence and nirvāṇa is born. (1)

Just as somebody who is partially blind
Thinks that there are net-like apparitions in the sky,
So too the extremely foolish, those hindered
By the darkness of ignorance, have a false impression of the world. (2)

For somebody with a pure view, the net-like hairs that appear
Because of delusion are recognized as nothing but the sky;
For a yogin with pure vision,
All states of existence appear in such a way. (3)

Alas! Look into the sky!
I do see net-like apparitions!
Then somebody with a pure view would say:
"It is not so, your mind is confused." (4)

In order to abandon the confusion of those who are partially blind,
They say that in the future confusion will not exist anymore.
Because the manifestation is empty of being anything else,
There is in reality neither denial nor assertion. (5)

Likewise, activity for the sake of sentient beings
Unfolds from the undefiled dharmakāya
Through the saṃbhoga- and nirmāṇa-kāya,
Owing to dependent arising, former prayers. (6)

The two form kāyas are not different from the dharmakāya,
Because the two have the dharmakāya as their nature;
Their identity is established as the natural kāya.
The distinction made between them is for the sake of dispelling
the narrowness of the mind. (7)

If their nonarising were not maintained,
The kāyas would be different under the constraint of the
excluded opposite.
How would the meaning of Madhyamaka
Then be different from Yogācāra thought? (8)

If the meaning of Madhyamaka only stood out
By reason of its abandonment of the four extremes,
There would be the undesired consequence that this also applies
to Vijñānavāda,
For in this tenet, too, the four extremes are abandoned. (9)

The followers of Vijñānavāda know
A form of wisdom that is free from the four extremes.
Yet this wisdom exists as something real and is nondual,
Empty of thought and without cognitive object. (10)

From the extreme limit of reality,
The manifold world arises in dependence;
It is empty of real things, unborn,
Distinct from independent being and a name only. (11)

The Omniscient One taught making a distinction
Between self-empowerment and luminosity;
Teaching either of them,
The view of nihilism is abandoned. (12)

In whomever there is no attachment
To the fruit, true reality, or remedy,
For that one the level of a buddha is completed
Through a practice that is effortless. (13)

The true reality of phenomena is their nonarising.
This accords with the Dharma of the Buddha
And is maintained by the noble Nāgārjuna,
Who was prophesied by the Tathāgata. (14)

Whatever merit I have accumulated
From having composed the *Elucidation of True Reality*,
May the entire world become a worthy recipient
Of the teaching on indivisible union through it. (15)

The Elucidation of True Reality, *composed by the learned master Advayavajra, is ended. Translated and corrected by the Indian paṇḍita Vajrapāṇi and the Tibetan translator monk Tsültrim Gyelwa.*[536]

CHAPTER 25

An Elucidation of Nonabiding

Homage to the Buddha![537]

The entire wealth of a Buddhist can be taken to be
The nonabiding of awareness,
But only when such a realization is cultivated for the sake of sentient beings[538]
Through a yoga practice that is without effort. (1)

Once knowledge based on exclusion and affirmation has arisen,
There are the positions of nihilism and affirmation.
But there never is any such thing as arising and passing out of existence,
So that all talk of production and termination is ignorant talk. (2)

If self-awareness is a valid form of cognition,
The existence[539] of awareness can be falsely maintained.
But since all fabrications[540] have been abandoned,
Such an existence is not agreeable. (3)

If its existence is accepted in post-meditation,
Then certainly not as a mental substance.
In this case it is called "without fabrications," which means
That any wrong assertion has been annulled or invalidated. (4)

Even in actual meditation practice there is awareness,
Because it becomes manifest this way during post-meditation.
First it is nonconceptual,
And then this wisdom becomes a perceiving knower. (5)

Since the mental factors of the past,
Future, and present do not abide,
They have the nature of essencelessness.
This is what the Lord of the World taught. (6)

The very arising of phenomena is inconceivable,
Even through natural self-awareness.
This very arising is called emptiness,
Without falling into the extreme of nihilism. (7)

From the seed of nonabiding
Comes a nonabiding fruit:
The supreme reality of the protectors—
The way fabricated comes from fabricated. (8)

Thus we do not tell those whose conduct is nonattachment
That meditation does not exist;
For in terms of dependent arising,
It constantly arises in accord with its natural flow. (9)

Whatever arises in dependence,
Is the mind, mulitiplicity, and nonduality.
Accordingly, there is a division into emptiness, mind, and
multiplicity,
That is to say, the dharma-, saṃbhoga-, and nirmāṇa-kāya. (10)

Whatever virtue I have accumulated
From having taught nonabiding,
May people attain, thanks to it,
The state of nonabiding in all they experience. (11)

The Elucidation of Nonabiding, *composed by the learned master Advayavajra, is ended. Translated by the Indian paṇḍita Vajrapāṇi and the Tibetan translator Tsültrim Gyelwa.*[541]

CHAPTER 26

An Elucidation of Indivisible Union

Homage to the youthful Mañjuśri![542]

Whatever the appearance, it is pure.
Once that is realized, there is no more change.
Change means to have arisen from conditions, but these
conditions in turn arise from preceeding conditions;
Hence, nonarising applies. (1)

The form is not found in the form itself,
Nor is it found in the eye,
Or in the consciousness that arises in association with it.
It is as in the discussion of the rubbing sticks and the fire. (2)

At the beginning, fire exists neither in the rubbing sticks,
Nor in the block,
Nor in the person's hands,
It arises as something in dependence. (3)

Is mental darkness born before its own children,[543]
Or after the children have been born?
If the children were not born first,
Then it is not real. (4)

Given that they are thus only conditions,
Phenomena lack an own nature.
A yogin who abides in this view
Does not fall out of supreme bliss. (5)

Even though there is nothing to abandon or adopt at all,
The conventional unfolds.
Once dependent arising is understood,
[One realizes that the conventional,] like an illusion, lacks an own nature. (6)

Lacking an own nature, it has not truly arisen,
And due to conditions (i.e., dependent arising), there is no termination of it either.
Thus, there is neither existence nor nonexistence,
But their indivisible union nonetheless manifests. (7)

The unity of emptiness and compassion
Is not producible by one's own thought.
It is the natural indivisible union
Of emptiness and clarity. (8)

The good yogin directly realizes
The profound inborn emptiness
Endowed with all supreme aspects.
May they thereby pay homage to the buddhas. (9)

Once the wise person is always steeped in this realization,
With body, speech, and mind,
Whether they follow the prescribed conduct or not,
They will still be called an observer of proper conduct. (10)

The Elucidation of Indivisible Union, *composed by the renunciant Advayavajra, is ended. Translated and corrected by the Indian paṇḍita Vajrapāṇi and the Tibetan translator Tsültrim Gyelwa.*[544]

CHAPTER 27

The Manifestation of Great Bliss

Homage to youthful Mañjuśrī![545]

Having venerated Vajrasattva,
Whose nature is insight and means,
I will now explain in brief the nonduality of great bliss,
Which is the true reality of entities. (1)

The meditation of the creation phase is one form of meditation,
And the meditation of the completion phase a second;
Therefore, the meditation of both together
Is here called identity. (2)

It is settled that phenomena do not possess
Any such property as not arising in dependence.
Since all of them have arisen in dependence by their nature,
Is it not likewise so for that which has arisen from the syllables HŪṂ and MAṂ? (3)

From the awakening toward emptiness, a seed syllable arises.
From it, an image [of a deity and so forth].
And for such an image there are projection and dissolution phases.
Therefore, everything arises in dependence. (4)

What was taught by Śākyamuni
As the outer union of the couple,[546]
All that should be clearly known in the tantras,
To be for the sake of realizing something different. (5)

Without bliss there is no enlightenment,
Since the latter is considered to have the nature of bliss.
But if bliss actually existed, there would be great attachment,
Which would be the cause of saṃsāra arising. (6)

The bliss that has arisen in dependence—
Realize it as the bliss of primordial quiescence!
It does not represent an entity, though.
Therefore, we say that bliss neither exists nor does not exist. (7)

True reality is, first of all, the nonarising
Of phenomena on the level of ultimate truth.
The pure apparent truth should be known
To be something in which there is a false manifestation of bliss.[547] (8)

These two truths are pure:
Emptiness and the apparent truth of the yogin;
Their nonduality must be established,
Once what is worthless is abandoned. (9)

The gifted one, whose character is formed by the practice
Of mantras and visualized forms, becomes submerged in bliss.
Then they see in such a manner of practice the manifold world
To be like an illusion and nondual. (10)

By then, they will have penetrated to the extreme summit of true reality
And reached the level of the indivisible union.
A yogin abiding on this level
Strives solely for the sake of sentient beings. (11)

The blissful mind assumes the form of the chosen deity,
The circle of the manifold[548] being the means.
The consort (*prajñā*) is called emptiness;
Their identity is taken as the goal. (12)

True reality has the nature of insight and means
For its purity is both outer and inner.
Once it is realized, the mantra practitioner is, in short,
Delighted through the practice of nonabiding. (13)

Being mere dependent arising,
Bliss is neither existence nor emptiness;[549]
And its manifestation in the form of deities
Naturally lacks an own nature. (14)

No matter how bliss appears,
It will always have the nature of emptiness;
Whether bliss be taken as duality or not,
Here, [in tantric practice,] it is the fruit of mental imprints. (15)

The yogin is proud of becoming Heruka;
While striving to become Heruka.
Having transformed the factors of existence into gurus,
The divine yogin wanders about like a lion. (16)

For the victorious ones the multitude of the world appears in its natural purity, always and everywhere.
It never did arise, nor will it be terminated, and it is free from reckoning in terms of self and other throughout ten million eons.
It is indeed something in which there is the false manifestation of bliss, and whose nature is one of nonduality, that is, the equality of cyclic existence and peace.
The lord of the circle, to whom all this appears, who has the qualities of a victorious one as a base and is a vajra sky-goer and a buddha, made it. (17)

The Manifestation of Great Bliss, *composed by the glorious renunciant master Advayavajra,*[550] *is completed. Translated by Guru Vajrapāṇi and Maben.*

CHAPTER 28

The Twenty Verses on True Reality

Homage to the Omniscient One![551]

Prajñā [in the form of karmamudrā] is related to the moments of the manifold,
Maturation, relaxation, and freedom from defining characteristics.[552]
Therefore, you must realize true reality from her,
So that you will be the supreme ruler pervading the world. (1)

Prajñā [as dharmamudrā] is the same as cyclic existence.
She is the three kāyas and the three vehicles.
[As samayamudrā] she is the maṇḍala, the means of bliss,
And the yoginī. All this is myself and the other. (2)

She can appear as Mañjuvajra, Mahāmāyā,
A vajra sky-goer,[553] and as other deities as well.
She is the prajñā herself, though, appearing individually.
[As mahāmudrā] she is liberation, having the nature of the Victorious One. (3)

[Prajñā] is the inconceivable mind and nevertheless thought of;
Nonduality and nevertheless dual;

Endowed with all supreme forms;
Existence and nonexistence; perception and nonperception. (4)

The mind without consciousness,
Devoid of cognitive objects, unsurpassable,
Peaceful, pure, and devoid of appearances
Is the awareness known as prajñā. (5)

The means of access to her
Will become clear in the treatises of the mantra system,
For there are manifold means in them,
Corresponding to persons of inferior, average, and superior
faculties. (6)

Those with inferior capacities have perfectly cultivated the
maṇḍala[554]
With the help of the karma- and samayamudrās.
With a mind directed to the external in the matter of pure reality,
They meditate on enlightenment. (7)

In union with a jñānamudrā,
With Mañjuvajra or the like as chief deities,
All this being neither true nor a false appearance—
This is the practice of yogins with average faculties. (8)

To those unable to know
The level of self-empowerment as it really is,
The path is taught in gradual steps
Towards the attaining of enlightenment. (9)

Given your affection for deities,
How is there not a mental imprint?

Even if this mental imprint is pure,
Will it still be like all other imprints? (10)

The yogin who has seen true reality, however,
Is wholly devoted to mahāmudrā;
Their faculties being unsurpassable,
They abide in [the realization of] the nature of all entities. (11)

Bliss, naturally attained
And free from all imagining,
This is precisely what the world is;
Therefore, everything is free of confusion. (12)

This is because the outer entities perceived by the mind
Do not appear as delusion;
These vivid presences are just like a woman in a dream—
Mind-only—but still they serve a function. (13)

For one who has attained enlightenment there is mind only,
And mind is then taken as no-mind;
No-mind in turn is self-awareness,
And such an awareness depends on the guru. (14)

The emptiness of all things
Is not taken as the name of any one thing.
This emptiness, being the nature of all entities,
Is difficult to realize directly by oneself. (15)

Just as grains become boiled rice in this world,
Through the presence of fire and so forth,
Ignorance becomes awareness
When purified by suchness. (16)

They for whom thought is meditation,
For them nothing is inconceivable.
The buddhas declared to the world
That a yogin is someone whose nature is inconceivable.[555] (17)

The circle of the maṇḍala is the yogin,
And they themselves are mahāmudrā.
They are the dharma-, sambhoga-, and nirmāṇa-kāyas,
And they themselves are all forms. (18)

They who have done their duty and are without any wish,
Have turned away from all attachment,
And engage in the four modes of ascetic behavior[556]
Are a buddha and regarded as a buddha. (19)

Nonduality having been presented as nonduality,
May, by the merit I have accumulated,
The world experience this very day
Nonduality and great bliss. (20)

The Twenty Verses on True Reality, *composed by the renunciant and glorious Advayavajra,*[557] *is ended. From the mouth of the venerable Dhīra Śrī Jñāna and translated by the translator Sengkar Shakya Ö.*

CHAPTER 29

The Twenty Verses on Mahāyāna

Homage to the Svābhāvikakāya![558]

I prostrate to the natural kāya,
Which is unconditioned and without defining characteristics.
It is endowed with all supreme forms
And joined with the level indivisible union. (1)

The seeing of the natural kāya, which is contained
In the dharma-, saṃbhoga-, and nirmāṇa-kāyas as their true nature,
Is the appropriate practice
For the attainment of perfect enlightenment. (2)

The seeing of this natural kāya is deep insight,
Because of not superimposing anything.
This will be explained now
In accordance with the mantra system. (3)

The manifold world is not taken to be eternal,
Or said to be entirely annihilated either;
Nor is it a combination of both eternal and annihilated,
Nor can it be that neither is the case.[559] (4)

Knowers of reality know true reality
As being free from these four extremes.
It is clear of the four extremes,
While still being based on the four extremes.[560] (5)

It is equivalent to space, if not in reality;
It is quiescent, without beginning, middle, or end,
Inconceivable and still only mind,
It is the very nature of all entities. (6)

Once the one taste in everything,
Which is luminous and undefiled, is realized,
As long as one is not afraid of any thought,
One may abide as one pleases! (7)

Neither are defilements different from enlightenment,
Nor do defilements arise in the state of enlightenment.
The thought of defilement arises because of delusion,
But delusion is stainless by nature. (8)

For the wise who are free from concepts,
Activity on the level of the body is the ascetic life.
On the level of speech, it is the teaching of the Dharma.
Activity on the level of the mind is determination. (9)

This illusion, that the world is an illusion—
Do not think that an illusion is just an illusion!
[It is not that easy;] illusion is confusion, a great error,
And for the wise, an error remains an error. (10)

Thus, in short, for buddhas and other enlightened beings,
This is duly recognized.

Experiencing everything wholly in this way,
The knower of reality succeeds. (11)

Well, one may realize emptiness
In the thousand collections of teachings;
But it is not realized through analysis.
The meaning of emptiness[561] is learned, rather, from the guru. (12)

For a wise person, given that their thoughts have ceased,
All forms are blissful reality.
But emptiness is not this blissful reality.
Blissful reality is neither inconceivable nor the [ultimate,
emptiness-like] bliss.[562] (13)

Wherefore, it is realized without superimposition,
But not seen ultimately.
Only in the case of not truly seeing, its occurrence is justified.
After having accepted this, it is experienced in whichever
manner. (14)

They for whom there is neither duality nor nonduality,
And for whom enlightenment is not different from existence—
Such a great yogin is free from any expectations
And has reached the path of all forms. (15)

All yogins should perform
The initial activity as taught above;
Wisdom that is inseparable from emptiness and compassion
Is taken to be present in the state of enlightenment.[563] (16)

Emptiness is nothing else than loving kindness,
And loving kindness is another name of compassion.

We do not say this as if having made something up;
If we were to describe them, we would do so as their indivisible
union. (17)

They whose practice of continuous meditation remains
undisturbed, even
When apprehending forms, such as a vase,
Will become a great buddha,
Whose single body [of compassion and emptiness pervades] all
forms. (18)

The unconditioned mind is the dharmakāya;
Realization is the defining characteristics of the saṃbhogakāya.
Then there is that: A variegated body has been emanated (i.e., the
nirmāṇakāya).
The natural one (i.e., the nijakāya) is the nature of all three.[564]
(19)

Through whatever merit I, fortunate one, have accumulated
By having composed this treatise,
May the entire world become determined
To attain the enlightenment of the Buddha! (20)

The Twenty Verses on the Mahāyāna*, composed by Advayavajra,*[565] *is ended. From the mouth of the Indian paṇḍita Vajrapāṇi*[566] *and translated by the monk from Tsur Jñānākara.*[567]

CHAPTER 30

The Five Verses on Penetrating Insight

Homage to omniscience![568]

Once the buddha within is realized, the world becomes pure.
This is through the realization of the buddha within, this friend.
Oh, primordially pure great buddha!
Is the teaching of the Buddha understood? (1)

These are words relating to the nature of someone who has overcome all concepts about remedy, true reality, and fruit, and possesses penetrating insight into the coemergent.

Wisdom is not only spotless and empty,
But has also the nature of effortless compassion.
It arises in dependence
And is free from both an own nature and nonexistence. (2)

This explains the image of penetrating insight.

The emptiness of phenomena, amazing!
Compassion, even more amazing!

Amazing, the power of great bliss!
Amazing, the pure apparent! (3)

This teaches the roar of the profound coemergent.

Well, what shall we say, how shall we explain it,
And when we explain it, where are the people who
understand?
They, for whom realization occurs,
Possess it without effort. (4)

In this verse it is proclaimed that true reality is difficult to find for people who only believe in the profound Dharma, which is expressive of nonabiding [nirvāṇa, attained] through compassion.

My fruit, indeed, is the direct cutting of sentient beings
from the
Seed of the threads of their own karma.
The violent is not to be harmed by me.
Even such a person, alas, I endure! (5)

In this verse Maitrīpa has considered the compassionate heart of bodhisattvas. They assist all sentient beings whose intellect is fettered and afflicted by the threads of their karma.

The Five Verses on Penetrating Insight, *composed by the learned master Maitrīpa, is ended. Translated by the Indian paṇḍita Vajrapāṇi and the Tibetan translator Maben.*

CHAPTER 31

The Six Verses on the Middle Path

HOMAGE to the Buddha![569]

Sākāravāda

Nondual wisdom
That is free from the four extremes really exists.
It is empty of thoughts and devoid of cognitive objects.
This is what the Sākāravādins know. (1)

Nirākāravāda

Here, the right middle path according to them is upheld
Based on the belief that while self-awareness is not
invalidated,[570]
Blue and so forth do not appear
And characteristic signs do not arise. (2)

Māyopamādvayavāda

Clarity that is free from the four extremes
Has the defining characteristic of being false.

It is nonduality in the sense that everything is like an illusion.
This is an acceptable tenet. (3)

An awareness empty of entities,
Spotless and without aspects,
This is the middle path right for them.
After meditation it is the pure relative. (4)

Apratiṣṭhānavāda

Whether mind has clarity or not,
In reality neither is apprehended,
Since by nature it is entirely unarisen.
The superior ones take this to be the [right] middle path. (5)

Clarity that is free from the four extremes
Has the nature of deities.
It has the nature of nondual bliss
And is mere dependent origination. (6)

The Six Verses on the Middle Path *is ended. This work is by the great paṇḍita and renunciant, the glorious Advayavajra.*[571] *Translated by Guru Vajrapāṇi and Naktso.*

CHAPTER 32

The Five Verses on Transcendent Love

Homage to the venerable Vajrasattva!

Were it not for the handsome suitor of appearances,
Which are but dependent arising,
The beloved mistress of emptiness
Would be considered no better than dead. (1)

Emptiness is a most lovely mistress,
With an incomparable figure.
If they ever parted,
The handsome lover would be forlorn. (2)

Therefore, trembling with anxiety,
The man and woman are seated in front of the guru,
And through their natural pleasure,
The guru has generated the love belonging to coemergence. (3)

Marvelous! Such mastery on the part of this genuine guru!
So great his skill!
That these two are now inseparable from the natural state,
Beyond cognitive objects, and unsurpassable. (4)

All their qualities are complete,
And both of them are without the two extremes.
This couple is the nature of all that is,
Yet the two always manifest without an own nature. (5)

The Five Verses on the Love of Insight *and Means are ended.*

CHAPTER 33

The Ten Verses on True Reality

Homage to Vajrasattva![572]

Homage to you, suchness,
Which has no association with existence and nonexistence,
Because, when stainless, this very suchness
Has the form of enlightenment in virtue of realization. (1)

Somebody who wishes to know suchness does not find it
In [the Yogācāra tenets of] Sākāravāda or Nirākāravāda;
Even Madhyamaka, which is not adorned
With the words of a guru, is only middling. (2)

This state of being is indeed enlightenment.
This is what it naturally is once attachment is abandoned;
Attachment is born from confusion,
And confusion is without a basis—so it is claimed. (3)

What is true reality? It is the form (i.e., the nature) of entities,
And form is indeed no-form (i.e., emptiness),
Because no-form is also form, given its being by nature[573]
Both the fruit to be attained and the [coemergent] cause of suchness. (4)

Thus phenomena are all of one taste,
Unobstructed, and without an abode.

They are all realized as luminous
Through the samādhi of realizing true reality as it is. (5)

This samādhi of realizing true reality as it is, for its part,
Comes from engaging bodhicitta,
Since true reality arises without interruption,
For those who are aware of its abode. (6)

The world itself, which is free from knowledge and knowable objects,
Is taken to be nonduality.
But even vain clinging to a state free of duality
Is taken, in like manner, to be luminous. (7)

By the power of having realized this true reality,
The yogin, with eyes wide open,
Moves everywhere like a lion,
By any chosen means and in any chosen manner. (8)

The yogin who has left the eight worldly dharmas behind
And adopted yogic conduct that appears to be crazy
Does everything without any need for a reference point,
Being adorned with self-empowerment. (9)

What has been taught as stainless reality,
What has been called nonduality—
The gifted ones are worthy of its knowledge,
Having excluded from it sameness and difference. (10)

The Ten Verses on True Reality *is ended. This work is of the learned master and renunciant Advayavajra.*[574]

CHAPTER 34

A Justification of Nonconceptual Realization

HOMAGE to the Buddha![575]

The word *amanasikāra* is one that many are confused about.

[1. Objection:] Some say that it is an ungrammatical word, for in compound the appropriate form should be *amanaskāra*.

[Response: In Pāṇini's *Aṣṭādhyāyī* it is stated:] "In the case of *tatpuruṣa*s, when there is a [noun with a] *kṛt* [suffix, the locative ending] is often preserved."[576] Given that Pāṇini says "often" in this sūtra, the ending of the seventh case has not disappeared. When compounds are formed without the disappearance of the case ending, the forms *amanasikāra*, which means the same as *amanaskāra*; *tvacisāra* ("firmness in the skin"), which means the same as *tvaksāra* ("skin firmness"); and *yudhiṣṭhira* ("resolute in battle") result. Therefore, *amanasikāra* is not ungrammatical.

[2. Objection:] The next opponent says: This term, *amanasikāra*, can be accepted as having accurate features, but unfortunately it can hardly be established as a Buddhist one.

[Response:] Not so, for it is found in various sūtras and tantras. In the *Ornament of Manifested Wisdom* it is stated:

> The mental factors of amanasikāra are taken to be virtuous, and those of manasikāra not virtuous.[577]

Likewise it is stated in the same sūtra:

> Homage to you, who are without imagined thoughts,
> Whose intellect is not based on anything,
> Who are without mindfulness, whose realization is nonconceptual,
> And who are without cognitive object.[578]

And in the *Magic Formula for Entering the Nonconceptual* we find:

> A bodhisattva, a great being, abandons all characteristic signs, which are produced by thoughts and consist of mental forms through nonconceptual realization (amanasikāra).[579]

Various other passages are not recorded here for reasons of space.

[3. Objection:] Now, another opponent contends: *amanasikāra* may be a term used by those who follow the sūtras, but it is not used by those of the mantra system, it being found only in sūtras.

[Response:] That is not so, for it is stated in the *Hevajra Tantra*, in the chapter on reality:

> Neither . . . mind nor mental factors exist in terms of an own nature.[580]

And also [in the *Hevajra Tantra* it is said]:

> The whole world should be meditated upon in such a way
> That it is not produced by the intellect.[581]

By implication it is understood [that it is meditated upon] through nonconceptual realization (amanasikāra).

[4. Objection:] The next opponent says: True, the sense of *amanasikāra* is also [found] in the tantras, [but] what it refers to does not exist, since *manasikāra* is the object of the negative particle in a nonaffirming negation.

[Response:] That is not the case. A nonaffirming negation is a negation of what is relevant: Not to negate what is not applicable is [the defining characteristic of] a nonaffirming negation, like for instance "the wives of the king who do not see the sun." The meaning of this is as follows: The wives of the king are indeed kept secret,[582] so that they do not even see the sun. This does not imply the non-existence of the sun. Then what does it imply? What is applicable: that the wives of the king see the sun—that is what is negated. In the case of amanasikāra, too, it is what is applicable—namely, mental engagement (*manasikāra*) resulting in something perceived, a perceiver, and the like—that is negated by the privative *a*, and not the mind itself.[583] Therefore, there is no fault.

[5. Objection:] Someone may say that the Illustrious One approved of mental engagement, which has the defining characteristics of permanence and nihilism.

[Response:] Then we say: Are eternalism, nihilism, and so forth mental engagement or not? Through it the abandonment of all acts of clinging is referred to, by the very term *amanasikāra*. This has been stated by the Illustrious One in the *Magic Formula for Entering the Nonconceptual*:

> Son of a noble family, what is the reason the state of the nonconceptual sphere being called amanasikāra? It is in view of one's having gone beyond all characteristic signs created by conceptual thinking. In other words, the term *amanasikāra* denotes a state in which one has left all conceptual thinking behind.

Affirming Negation

Even when amanasikāra is taken in the sense of an affirming negation, there is no fault. When someone says "Bring a non-brahmin," the bringing of somebody similar to a brahmin, a kṣatriya or the like, is intended, not a low-caste person of base origin, such as a wagoner. Here, too, [where amanasikāra is taken as an affirming negation,] an awareness of essencelessness is maintained. Hence the tenet of Māyopamādvaya is established. From what, then, does the undesired consequence of the view of nihilism follow?

Amanasikāra as a Compound in Which the Middle Word Is Dropped

Or, alternatively, the negative particle (i.e., the privative *a*) is only used in its usual [metaphorical] sense. This word (i.e., this negation) has two meanings that require explaining. Everything being either like an illusion or something not truly established,[584] the privative *a* negates neither something existent nor something nonexistent. By this reasoning, it is ruled out that the privative *a* has the meaning of negating the world. I will explain the formation of the word. *Amanasikāra* means the *manasikāra* for which the letter *a* in front of it is the main focus. It is a compound in which the middle word is dropped, as in the case of a *śākapārthiva*, a "king for whom vegetables [are the main thing of his diet]." Accordingly, whatever mental engagement (*manasikāra*) there is, all of it is "*a*" which has the nature of nonorigination.[585]

[Objection:] Where did the Illustrious One teach that the letter *a* stands for nonorigination?

[Response:] This is also as taught in the *Hevajra Tantra*, in the chapter on mantras:

> The letter *a* is at the beginning because all phenomena have not arisen throughout beginningless time. . . .[586]

This means: Given that all phenomena have not arisen throughout beginningless time, the letter *a* is at the beginning; that is, it is the main thing. The letter *a* relates to the defining characteristic of nonorigination, and this is stated as such in the *Chanting the Names of Mañjuśrī*:

> The letter *a* is the beginning of the alphabet.
> Its significance is great. It is the supreme letter (*akṣara*),
> Of great strength, without arising,
> Beyond words and exemplification.[587]

Moreover, the letter *a* is the seed of the goddess Selflessness (Nairātmyā), and this is as stated in the *Hevajra Tantra*:

> The first vowel (i.e., *a*) is the seed syllable of Nairātmyā.[588]

Therefore, all mental engagement is said to lack a true self, an own nature. This is stated, moreover[, in *Hevajra Tantra*]:

> Nairātmyā has the nature of the first vowel.
> The buddhas conceive her as being wise.
> In the yoga of the completion phase, she is the female
> buddha,
> The personification of insight.[589]

Moreover, *a* stands for the word "luminous," and *manasikāra* for the word "self-empowerment." It is both *a* and *manasikāra*, so we get *amanasikāra*.[590] Because of that, the words *a*, *manasikāra*, and so forth,[591] refer to the inconceivable state of being luminous and the one of self-empowerment, that is, an awareness that continues as something that is not separate from emptiness and compassion, that is, not distinct (*advaya*) from the level of indivisible union.

The Justification of Nonconceptual Realization, *composed by the great learned master, the glorious Advayavajra,*[592] *is ended. Translated by the Indian paṇḍita Vajrapāṇi and the Tibetan translator Maben Chöbar.*[593]

CHAPTER 35

The Six Verses on the Coemergent

Homage to Vajradhara![594]

Buddhists take true reality
To be free from permanence and nihilism;
To engage in affirmation and exclusion,
When it comes to naturally arisen phenomena—this is the talk of fools. (1)

To those who claim that there is existence, we say
That, upon analysis, nothing exists.
To those who claim that there is no existence, we say
That, when no analysis is done, everything exists. (2)

In whatever manner superimpositions
Present themselves to the yogin of true reality,
In like manner, superimpositions
Are destroyed by the yogin of true reality. (3)

As the coemergent is not fabricated,
Attachment does not pertain to the coemergent.
Bliss is not different from the coemergent;
Bliss has the defining characteristic of freedom from attachment. (4)

Once the genuine bliss associated with realization is known,
Bliss whose nature it is to be free from attachment,
The manifold world is turned into self-realization
And is dissolved into the ocean of the coemergent. (5)

The yogin of mantra reality
Is thoroughly established in a state without attachment.
Having transformed the factors of existence into gurus,
He will be without attachment to objects. (6)

This work, the Six Verses on the Coemergent, *by the learned renunciant, the glorious Advayavajra,*[595] *is ended. Translated by the Indian paṇḍita and the Tibetan translator and monk from Tsur, Yeshé Jungné.*

CHAPTER 36

A Pith Instruction on True Reality Called *A Treasure of Dohās*

Homage to glorious Heruka!

The three ways (*yānas*) are explained in terms of four positions.[596]
It should be known that the Vaibhāṣikas are the first two ways.[597]
The inferior and average śrāvakas are from the West;
The superior ones and the Pratyekabuddhas, from Kashmir. (1)

The five skandhas are the tenet of all,
But only the two schools from the West assert an inexpressible person.
All of them take refuge for life in the three jewels,
While the self-compassion of wishing to discipline themselves arises exceedingly. (2)

For those on the inferior Śrāvakayāna, the notion of clinging to the purity of the body
Must be understood as a stain, with the help of the meditation on the repulsive.
Exhaling and inhaling is the meditation of the average śrāvakas.
The stain of this meditation is breath retention. (3)

The meditation of superior śrāvakas is focused on the four truths,
The eightfold path, and the emptiness of a personal self.
Suffering is saṃsāra, origination attachment,
Cessation nirvāṇa, and freedom from bad influences the path. (4)

To apprehend so called permanence is known as a stain.
Pratyekabuddhas meditate by themselves on the inconceivable.
The stains of their meditative equipoise should be known to be twofold:
They should be known to be excitement and lack of attention. (5)

The world is an accumulation of suble atoms, this according to the tradition of the Sautrāntika.
Their meditation is on the inconceivable, and their stains are like the previous ones.
Their view is centered on the six perfections,
And with the power of compassion they dedicate their merit to others. (6)

The world is only mind. There are no subtle atoms.
The Yogācāras claim that the world is like a dream.
The manifold appearances of blue, yellow, and the rest,
Claim them to be what you want—everything has the nature of mind. (7)

Everything is for them as experienced in the meditation of self-awareness.
Their view of permanence should be known as their stain of meditation.
Moreover, they maintain that there are mental imprints of our existence.
All the forms they produce appear to be opposed to mind. (8)

Space-like nonduality is inconceivable and pure.
It has the nature of compassion, lacks mental forms, and is the perfect buddha.
The two form kāyas arise from this root.
The stains of their meditation and view are like the previous ones. (9)

Mere self-awareness beyond the four extremes, everything being
Like the reflection of the moon in the water, an illusion, and a dream—
The meditation of this view has been taught [in Madhyamaka].
The nihilism of abandoning self-awareness is their stain of meditation. (10)

People go further and further afield and attain something else.
But all forms are naturally pure:
This is the matchless tenet of nonabiding.
The stains of meditation and view boil down to perceiving reality in extremes. (11)

This aspect is the outer pāramitā system.
Using experiences of one's blissful nature is the great secret mantra system.
It is the blissful mind that results from the uniting of the vajra and lotus.
The moon and sun[598] of supreme attachment unite. (12)

Through the power of the means, compassion, all sentient beings
Can abide in this desire while realizing it as suchness.
Wherever there is the one taste whose nature is bodhicitta,
This is coemergent bliss. (13)

At this time two drops have actually fallen into the lotus.[599]
Moreover, emptiness and compassion have become equal there.
The entire world is realized as having an aspect of the
coemergent,
In accordance with the teachings of the supreme guru. (14)

The Pith Instruction on Reality Called a Treasure of Dohās, *composed by the great learned master and renunciant, the glorious Advayavajra, is ended. Translated by the reverend Dhīra Śrī Jñāna.*

CHAPTER 37

A Pith Instruction on Settling the Mind

A Genuine Secret

Homage to the genuine gurus!

Practitioners of inconceivable yoga
Awaken their mind of compassion instantaneously;
It is sealed with unborn insight
And is characterized by inconceivable nonduality. (1)

Appearances simply remind them of the unborn.
The nature of mindfulness is without a perceived object.
Through the nature of entities, form and the other skandhas,
They experience the taste of great bliss
And realize the inconceivable yoga. (2)

Through the kindness of the guru, in turn,
One's practice acquires the nature of discriminating awareness. (3)

Since mind produces everything in conformity with one's experience,
Mindfulness produces neither a perceived object nor the opposite.

Since cause and fruit are inseparable,
I do not have gradual levels of meditation. (4)

Tasting the taste of emptiness,
Even meditation is realization;
This is because through meditation with insight
Everything becomes mahāmudrā. (5)

Even in what is opposed to liberation,
There is nothing but mahāmudrā,
No matter for however long the duality of diversity arises.
In this naturally relaxed and carefree state,
Everything melts [back] into what it has arisen from. (6)

Possessing blissful wisdom as a result of that,
There is no hope for any fruit.
The yogin of nonconceptual realization
Has nothing to think about emptiness, the essential nature. (7)

Insight into nonduality rests in itself
And categories such as "absorption" or "subsequent attainment"
no longer apply.
The practitioner of a yoga that is a continuity of the
inconceivable
Rests in himself, not becoming engaged with duality. (8)

He truly awakens to nonarising,
All entities having evaporated into the nonarisen.
What in reality is nondual accords with vajra emptiness;
States of being overpowered by faults are only adventitious. (9)

Therefore, the yogin is straight and fresh,
This world and true reality being experienced directly.
May the yogin who sees nonarising
Not clutch at knowledge but rest in natural clarity! (10)

Why gather anything in or project anything onto
The nonarisen true nature of mind?
Pith instructions are the supreme means! (11)

Notes

1. The translation mirrors Maitrīpa's two levels of understanding: Besides its standard meaning of not conceptualizing duality, Maitrīpa understands *amanasikāra* also as the realization of emptiness, luminosity. See pp. 3–4.
2. Rus pa'i rgyan can: *Rnal 'byor gyi dbang phyug chen po mi la ras pa'i rnam mgur*, 464–65. The verses are found at the end of the first *Tshe ring ma* story, the "Rosary of Pearls of Poetry," which is part of "A Test by the Five Sisters of Long Life and a Sequence of Questions and Answers."
3. Roerich (1949–53: 842) settled on 1007/10–1084/87, while Tatz (1994: 65) suggested ca. 1007–ca. 1085. Roberts (2014: 4 and 212, n. 8) rightly points out, however, that the *Blue Annals* do not specify the year elements, and that the life stories of Maitrīpa's disciples require that their master already had to have passed away before Vajrapāṇi reached Nepal in 1066.
4. Dpa' bo Gtsug lag phreng ba, *Chos byung mkhas pa'i dga' ston*, vol. 1, 772.
5. See Isaacson and Sferra 2014: 65.
6. See Maitrīpa's life story in the *'Bri gung bka' brgyud chos mdzod*, translated in chapter 1.
7. On the difficulties in providing dates that are more precise, see Schaeffer 2005: 13–14. The *terminus ante quem*, at least for Saraha's *Dohākoṣa*, can be narrowed down now to the middle of the tenth century, because in his *Catuṣpīṭhanibandha* (CPN 39b) on *Catuspīṭhatantra* III.4.11, Bhavabhaṭṭa (mid-tenth century) quotes verse 74 of the *Dohākoṣa*: "As long as you pour [only] water into water, its taste remains the same. The mind is a mine of faults and qualities. Fools! There is nothing that can oppose it" (*jattiu païsaï jalehi jalu tattiuṃ samarasa hoi* | *doṣaguṇāaracittao baḍha paḍibakkha ṇa ko bi* ||). Thanks to Péter Dániel Szántó for this reference. The *terminus post quem* is when the *Hevajratantra* (which some take to be around 900 CE) was composed, because the *Hevajratantra* shines through different parts of Saraha's *Dohākoṣa*. Saraha thus uses, for example, the tantric

code word *kunduru* exactly as in the *Hevajratantra* (where it had for the first time the meaning of "sexual union").

8. Supernatural manifestations of Śavaripa are said to have appeared not only to Maitrīpa, but also centuries later to Vibhūticandra (twelfth/thirteenth century) and Vanaratna (1384–468). See Mathes 2008: 248–50.
9. The first six lines are identical with Saraha's *Dohākoṣa* (Shahidullah 1928: 139).
10. Mathes 2011: 106.
11. TV 9.
12. According to some Tibetan sources, Maitrīpa did not leave Vikramapura, but was expelled from Vikramaśīla Monastery for being involved with alcohol (see below).
13. Dpa' bo Gtsug lag phreng ba, *Chos byung mkhas pa'i dga' ston*, vol. 1, 774.
14. SNP, p. 192. For a fine edition and translation of the entire *Sekanirdeśapañjikā*, see Isaacson and Sferra 2014: 165–203 and 255–333.
15. See Mathes 2015:218.
16. SN 26.
17. Isaacson and Sferra 2014: 307. Key technical terms have been replaced for consistency.
18. Isaacson and Sferra 2014: 307.
19. It should be noted that I follow here the reading of Dwags po Bkra shis rnam rgyal's *Phyag chen zla ba'i 'od zer* (148.19–149.3).
20. See Mathes 2019: 145.
21. See Mathes 2009: 89 and 117.
22. SN 40.
23. See pp. 134–36.
24. See Mathes 2019: 137–38.
25. Roberts 2014: 6.
26. Mathes 2008: 248.
27. *Deb ther sngon po*, vol. 2, 1133. First translated in Mathes 2014: 372.
28. *Deb ther sngon po*, vol. 1, 632–33. First translated in Mathes 2016: 488.
29. Seyfort Ruegg 1988: 1255–56.
30. Mi bskyod rdo rje, *Dbu ma la 'jug pa'i kar ṭī ka*, 10: "In this Dharma tradition [of Sgam po pa], calm abiding and deep insight [tend to] be overstated as the exemplifying and actual wisdoms, which are known as the third and fourth empowerments explained in the unsurpassable Mantra[yāna] of this and other precious lineages. Whatever experience of calm abiding and

deep insight may have arisen in one's mindstream, it cannot indisputably eradicate most of what must be abandoned, i.e., the three hindrances. Thus, when one reaches conclusive certainty about the meaning of signs [and words] in this Dharma tradition, this is praised as the supreme progress towards realization."

31. Mi bskyod rdo rje, *Shing rta chen po*, 532–33.
32. SRS XXXII.92–97.
33. SRS XXXII.98–105.
34. According to *Abhidharmakośa* I.14cd, a *saṃjñā* has the nature of apprehending a *nimitta*. However, Sahajavajra treats the two terms as interchangeable aspects of the mental event (see Mathes 2015: 232).
35. Mathes 2015: 114 and 232–36.
36. Mi bskyod rdo rje, *Dgongs gcig lta sgom spyod pa'i tshogs kyi kar ṭik smad cha*, vol. 2, 304.
37. The *guhyābhiṣeka* is thus conferred by bestowing upon the adept a drop of alcohol from a skull (*kapāla*), instead of the sexual fluids from the guru and his consort; and the *prajñājñānābhiṣeka* is performed by showing the adept a small drawing (Tib. *tsak li*) with a tantric couple, and not the adept's union with an actual consort. See Mathes 2019: 137.
38. GPKU (B 290b, D 164b, P 184b). First quoted and translated in Mathes 2015: 77–78.
39. I.e., *Dpal 'bri gung bka' brgyud kyi chos mdzod chen mo*. See Sørensen and Sonam Dolma 2007: 9.
40. See Bstan 'dzin padma'i rgyal mtshan 2000: 183.
41. Kun dga' rin chen, *'Bri gung bka' brgyud chos mdzod*, vol. *ka*, 173b–178a.
42. Kun dga' rin chen., vol. *ka*, 178a3–vol. *kha* 89a. The *sa bcad* of the *Sekanirdeśapañjikā* is on fols. 80b–82a.
43. Kun dga' rin chen, vol. *kha*, 177b–186a.
44. Roerich 1949–53: 857.
45. See Bu ston Rin chen grub, *Bu ston gsan yig*, 114–15, and Roerich 1949–53: 857.
46. I.e., MS 1095 of the Tucci Tibetan Fund.
47. Passavanti 2014: 433–42.
48. This version of the life story was first translated in Mathes 2015: 24–40. Reprinted with permission from the Austrian Academy of Sciences Press.
49. Tib. *'Bar ba'i gtso bo*. The name Jvālapati ("Chief Blazer") appears to be used in reference to Kṛṣṇācārya as an honorific term reflecting the high

degree of yogic practice he had attained in mahāmudrā. Maitrīpa was thus a reincarnation of Kṛṣṇācārya (Templeman 1989: 83). Templeman (1997: 213) identifies Kṛṣṇācārya also with Jvālanātha.

50. Tucci 1971: 212.

51. According to Tāranātha's life story of Kṛṣṇācārya (i.e., Jvālapati), this was the malicious ḍākinī Viśvarūpi, who had five hundred *rākṣasī* attendants. Each day they were said to devour a hundred thousand men and animals in Jambudvīpa and the small islands. In order to subdue them, Kṛṣṇācarya crossed the ocean by magical means (Templeman 1989: 21).

52. In his life story of Kṛṣṇācārya, Tāranātha reports, however, that Viśvarūpi and her attendents were successfully tamed. (Templeman 1989: 22).

53. For Na bu and Tse dhe. In the Sanskrit life story edited by Isaacson and Sferra (2014: 424–26) we find:... *brāhmaṇajātir nānūko nāma brāhmaṇī ca sāvitrī nāma prativasati sma* |.

54. Lit. *bha rin te*. See Passavanti 2014: 433.

55. According to the Sanskrit life story, Maitrīpa had studied for five years under the tantric master Rāgavajra before studying Nirākāravāda under Ratnākaraśānti at Nālandā for one year (see Isaacson and Sferra 2014: 424–25).

56. Brunnhölzl (2007: 126) reports on the basis of the Sanskrit manuscript, however, that Maitrīpa "practiced the meditation and recitation of Tārā. Finally, at the age of fifty, Tārā told him in a dream to go east in order to receive a prophecy from Avalokiteśvara at Khasarpaṇa. Accordingly, he quit Vikramapura and stayed in Khasarpaṇa for one year. Then, again in a dream, Avalokiteśvara encouraged him to proceed to the southern twin mountains Manobhaṅga and Cittaviśrama." In a footnote, Brunnhölzl (2007: 511) remarks that no Tibetan source speaks about Vikramapura.

57. For O te sha. See Isaacson and Sferra 2014: 425.

58. This vajra song is normally attributed to Śavaripa himself (Mathes 2008a: 247).

59. Bal po Asu was a Nepalese disciple of Vajrapāṇi. See Schaeffer 2005: 63.

60. Śavaripa's song is fully in line with the tradition of Saraha's dohās. In fact, the first six lines are found in Saraha's *Dohākoṣa*, while the lines 7 and 8 are nearly identical with Saraha's *Mahāmudropadeśa* (DKMU 79b). While Bal po Asu's version of the story requires a more tantric context, Ti pu pa's account suggests that in his empowerment, Śavaripa merely pointed out the true nature of mind. This depends on the guru's qualities and the

purity of the disciple's mind and not necessarily on the four seals. The fact that two contradictory versions of Śavaripa's empowerment are reported in the *History of the Twenty-Five Texts of the Amanasikāra Cycle* convincingly suggests that in India there was already a Mahāmudrā tradition that was not specifically tantric. See Mathes 2014: 375.

61. For Natekara. In his *Blue Annals*, 'Gos Lo tsā ba Gzhon nu dpal reports that one of Maitrīpa's four great disciples, named Sahajavajra, first was the heretic Natekara (Roerich 1949–53: 842). Brunnhölzl (2007: 130) refers to this former heretic as Natikara.
62. According to the Sanskrit biography from the Kaiser Library in Kathmandu, only half of the Samāveda, though.
63. Isaacson and Sferra (2014: 63) consider the (in my opinion unlikely) scenario that Maitrīpa did not give up Brahmanism all together, as no account of conversion can be found in the Sanskrit biography.
64. Brunnhölzl 2007: 511, n. 445.
65. See Roerich 1949–1953:731 and Isaacson and Sferra 2014: 71.
66. See Tatz 1987: 709–10 and Brunnhölzl 2007: 131.
67. Roerich 1949–53: 731–32.
68. Isaacson and Sferra 2014: 65.
69. According to Brunnhölzl (2007: 125–26) referring to Padma dkar po.
70. Isaacson and Sferra 2014: 65 and 427.
71. Passavanti 2014: 433.
72. According to Tatz (1987: 700) all Tibetan sources seem to conflate Vikramapura with Vikramaśila.
73. Isaacson and Sferra 2014: 65–66.
74. Isaacson and Sferra 2014: 71.
75. Brunnhölzl 2007: 511.
76. Tatz 1988: 474.
77. I.e., the *Jo bo rje dpal ldan mar me mdzad ye shes kyi rnam thar rgyas*. For a German translation see Eimer 1979, vol. 1.
78. Based on oral communication with Khenpo Tamphel, Vienna, June 4, 2020.
79. See Eimer 1979, vol. 2: 139–40.
80. Padma dkar po, *Chos 'byung bstan pa'i padma rgyas pa'i nyin byed*, 288.2–6. First tranlated by Tatz 1987: 700.
81. A corresponding practice is described in the second chapter of the *Hevajratantra*'s first part: "Those who wish to cause someone to throw up

alcohol, visualize the syllable *maṃ* in [his] navel. Visualize that from the transformed syllable *maṃ* his stomach will be full of alcohol. It will be seen that this causes him to vomit. He vomits alcohol." (HT p. 36.5–7).

82. Padma dkar po, *Chos 'byung bstan pa'i padma rgyas pa'i nyin byed*, 296.5–297.4.
83. Brunnhölzl 2007: 511, n. 448.
84. Where it was catalogued and microfilmed by the Nepal-German Manuscript Preservation Project.(NGMPP reel no. C 14/6).
85. See https://www.manuscript-cultures.uni-hamburg.de/mom/2012_04_mom_e.html, accessed June 3, 2020.
86. I.e., following the translation of Harunaga Isaacson, Rangjung Yeshe Institute handout "Indian Buddhist Tantric Literature, Session 11 (March 1, 2011, The Fourth Consecration)."
87. Passavanti 2014: 441.
88. Pad ma dkar po, *Chos 'byung bstan pa'i padma rgyas pa'i nyin byed*, 297.5–6.
89. Tatz 1987: 709.
90. Roerich 1949–53: 843.
91. Dpa' bo Gtsug las phreng ba, *Chos byung mkhas pa'i dga' ston*, vol. 1, 774.16–21.
92. Padma dkar po, *Chos 'byung bstan pa'i padma rgyas pa'i nyin byed*, 298.1–2.
93. Mathes 2011: 111–13.
94. Tatz 1987: 710.
95. When taken as the fourth moment, *vilakṣaṇa* refers to a moment "different" from the first three.
96. This hermeneutic stance is demonstrated in his commentary on HT II.8ab: "Then teach Yogācāra followed by Madhyamaka" (*yogācāraṃ tataḥ paścāt tad anu madhyamakaṃ diśet*). Ratnākaraśānti (HP 223) provides the following definitions: "Yogācāra means that all that [world] is mind-only. Even in the absence of an object, the very mind itself arises with an object as its appearance through the power of mental imprints, just as in a dream. Madhyamaka means the right middle path, in the sense that the mind does not exist in its form of duality, nor is it nonexistent, in its form of [something that is] empty of duality."
97. HT I.1.10–12.
98. Lindtner 1990: 110–11. This Yogācāra interpretation requires taking *taj* and *jñāne* not in compound, so that the demonstrative pronoun *taj* can take up "the great elements" from the first part of the verse as the subject

of the new sentence. Otherwise, one would have to read "Once they are understood (*tajjñāne* [*prāpte*]), they disappear." See Isaacson 2013: 1042.

99. MMK XXIV.18 (p. 426).
100. Thus, Ratnākaraśānti does not simply equate dependent designation with false imagining, as Moriyama (2013: 53) claims.
101. This is clear from *Madhyāntavibhāga* I.5. See Mathes 2000: 208.
102. MAVṛ/MPS 104b–105a.
103. For this equation, see *Saṃdhinirmocanasūtra* VI.5 (SNS 60).
104. In MAVBh I.5, false imagining is related to the dependent nature. (MAVBh 19: *abhūtaparikalpaḥ paratantraḥ svabhāvaḥ*). In his subcommentary, Sthiramati explains: "'False imagining is the dependent nature' means that [false imagining] is other-dependent (*paratantraḥ*, otherwise translated as dependent), inasmuch as it is ruled (*tantryate*) or produced by other (*parair*) causes and conditions, and hence does not exist in its own right." (MAVṬ, p. 23).
105. MAVṬ, p. 13: "The past, future, and present mind and mental factors, which are cause and result, which belong to (i.e., constitute) the beginningless threefold world, which end in nirvāṇa, and which conform with saṃsāra, are precisely false imagination."
106. MAVṬ 13: "False imagining is that in which or by which false duality is imagined."
107. MABh VI.97.
108. MMK XV.2cd
109. The emendation of *ma rig par* to *ma reg par* is based on the Sanskrit original of this sentence, which Anne MacDonald kindly provided me from her forthcoming edition: *kṛtakapadārthāsaṃsparśena kevalasya svabhāvasya sākṣātkāraṇāt tasyaiva buddhatvād buddha ity ucyate* |. La Vallée Poussin's (1911: 255) reconstruction *avidyāsvabhāva* thus is not tenable anymore.
110. Translated on the basis of the Sanskrit provided by Anne MacDonald: *paratantre tayoḥ parikalpitatvaṃ cintyam* (em., text: *centyam*).
111. MABh, pp. 201–2.
112. In his *gZhan stong snying po*, Tāranātha reaches a similar conclusion (see Mathes 2000: 219–20).
113. *Madhyamakālaṃkāropadeśa* (D 231a, P 266b).
114. *Yid la mi byed tho yig*, 79b.
115. See Roerich 1949–53: 842.
116. GPKU (B 290b, D 164b, P 184b).

117. There is no Sanskrit title. The Tibetan according to the Tōhoku catalogue is as follows: *Chos thams cad rab tu mi gnas par ston pa'i de kho na nyid tshigs su bcad pa byed kyi 'grel pa* (Derge Bstan 'gyur, no. 2296).
118. Attributed to Avadhūtipa in the Tōhoku catalogue but Advayavajra in the title in the Dpal spungs edition of the *Phyag chen rgya gzhung*.
119. Derge Bka' 'gyur, no. 128, *mdo sde*, vol. *da*, 172a–b.
120. Probably the Vātsīputrīya-Sāṃmatīyas, who were the southern neighbours of the Sarvāstivādin (Frauwallner 1956: 85).
121. Frauwallner 1956: 85. The *Jewel Garland of True Reality* describes pudgala as being free from permanence and impermanence.
122. This follows Gzhon nu dpal's explanation in his commentary on the *Ratnagotravibhāga* (see Mathes 2008: 174–75).
123. The other option of "matter only" has never been seriously discussed in any Buddhist system.
124. See Burton 1999: 90 and Rospatt 1995: 69ff.
125. This is clear from the Yogācāras' introduction of a ground consciousness as the solution of a philosophical problem posed by the commonly accepted meditative absorption of the complete cessation (*nirodhasamāpatti*) of anything mental. The problem arises from the Abhidharma axioms that (a) something mental must be caused by something mental and (b) that the cause must immediately precede the effect. What causes then the first mental event after *nirodhasamāpatti*? Either it is caused by material seeds produced from the last mental event before meditation and stored in the sense faculties, or the last mental event before meditation directly causes the first mental event after meditation. In the former case (a) is violated, and in the latter (b). The solution the Yogācāras had to offer was a cognitively inactive ground consciousness that can store mental seeds even during *nirodhasamāpatti*. For a detailed discussion see Griffith 1999.
126. Viṃś 12ab.
127. See Frauwallner 1956: 77–86 for an explanation of this process according to the *Abhidharmakośa*; and Mathes (1996: 146–47) for an explanation in the *Dharmadharmatāvibhāgavṛtti*.
128. Viṃś 9 (pp. 5–6).
129. See Frauwallner 1956: 375–76.
130. Viṃś 12ab.
131. I.e., mental imprints taken the place of external objects.

132. Lit. "What does an external object have as justification?" If there was an external object, there would be two forms of it, the one in the mind and the one consisting of the external object itself.

133. This is how Maitrīpa quotes the verse in his *Jewel Garland of True Reality*. In *Pramāṇavārttika* III.432 (PV, p. 98) we find, though: "If the mind has forms of something blue and the like, what is the reason for an external object? If the mind does not have forms of something blue and the like, how can there be an experience of it (i.e., the outer object)?"

134. The Tibetan has *ye shes* for *citta*.

135. See Oberhammer 1983.

136. MMK II.1 (p. 32): "There is no movement in what has been traversed. Then there is also no movement in what has not yet been traversed. A present motion apart from what has been and not yet been traversed cannot be understood." The Greek philosopher Zenon uses similar arguments against motion.

137. See Rāmapāla's commentary on *Presentation of Empowerment*, 29a (see Isaacson and Sferra 2014: 311).

138. A number of Tibetan masters, such as Bcom ldan rig pa'i ral gri (1227–1305), Stag tshang Lo tsā ba, Mkhas grub rje (1385–1438), and 'Ju Mi pham rnam rgyal rgya mtsho (1846–1912) thus equated Apratiṣṭhāna with Prāsaṅgika. Klong chen pa (1308–1364), on the other hand, subsumed it under Svātantrika (Almogi 2010: 170).

139. SNP 36 (p. 197). The translation of Isaacson and Sferra (2014: 322) is only slightly adopted in consideration of consistent terminology.

140. See Mathes 2007: 547.

141. Almogi 2010: 170.

142. MMK XXIV.16–17 (p. 424): "If you see the true existence of things as coming from a [supposed] own nature (*svabhāva*), then in that case you see things as being without either causes or conditions. You exclude result, cause, agent, doing, action, arising, passing out of existence, and fruit."

143. Mathes 2014: 367.

144. Ti pi 'bum la 'bar, *Rin chen phreng ba'i bshad pa*, 195b.

145. APP 7.

146. MMK I.1 (p. 12).

147. Bohr 1961.

148. Particles, which have interacted physically, remain under certain conditions entangled (such that they are mysteriously twisted together), even

after they have become separated over large distances. The shared state of polarization or spin, for example, remains indefinite until measurement.

149. Ricard and Trinh Xuan Thuan 2001: 73.
150. Ricard and Trinh Xuan Thuan 2001: 69–70.
151. Ricard and Trinh Xuan Thuan 2001: 70.
152. Held at the University of Vienna on May 26, 2012.
153. I.e., a space in which all possible states of a system are represented.
154. TRĀ 27.
155. I.e., TRĀ 28, which defines Apratiṣṭhāna Madhyamaka.
156. Priest (2018: 66–67) refers to this inconceivable value as the "fifth corner," and distinguishes a semantic tetralemma of four values, all negated by Nāgārjuna and Maitrīpa, from an ontological tetralemma in which the inconceivable ultimate remains after deconstructing the four values.
157. MV 5ab.
158. TD 5: "Thus, phenomena are [all] of one taste, unobstructed, and without an abode. They are all [realized as] luminous through the samādhi of realizing true reality as it is."
159. See pp. 3–4.
160. MV 3.
161. Ui Hakuju (1952) reads *sarvasminn apratiṣṭhāne* (which is supported by the Tibetan): "While not abiding in anything."
162. TRĀ 29.
163. TRĀ 30–31.
164. TRĀ 31 is identical with SN 30.
165. SNP p. 193. The English translation follows Isaacson and Sferra 2014: 313.
166. TRĀ 33.
167. See Mathes 2016a: 331–32.
168. See *Samādhirājasūtra* XXXII.8ab (SRS p. 195), where phenomena (*dharmas*) are in reality buddha qualities (*buddhadharmas*): "All dharmas are buddhadharmas [for those] who are trained in dharmatā." (*sarvadharmā buddhadharmā dharmatāyāṃ ya śikṣitāḥ*). Note that *ya* is used for *ye* or the like for metrical reasons.
169. BV 73. Lindtner 1990: 206.
170. See Nakamura 1989: 281. For a good summary of the debate, see Cabezón and Dargay 2006: 19–21, and Karmey 2007: 87–89.
171. This is fully in line with Jayāditya's and Vāmana's *Kāśikāvṛtti* on *Aṣṭādhyāyī*

II.1.60, in which Maitrīpa's example of "vegetable king" is analyzed as a "king for whom vegetables are the main thing." (see KV, vol. 2, 84).

172. See Padma dkar po, *Phyag chen rgyal ba'i gan mdzod*, 40–41.
173. DKMU 75b.
174. *Majjhimanikāya* III.104–9.
175. CSS pp. 104–8.
176. Schmithausen 2007: 215–19.
177. ŚBh p. 395. First quoted and translated in Mathes 2010: 7.
178. See Schmithausen 1969: 46–47.
179. See Mathes 2010: 7.
180. See JĀA 146: "Homage to you, who are without imagined thoughts, whose intellect is not based [on anything], who are without mindfulness, who become mentally disengaged, and who are without any cognitive object." First quoted and translated in Mathes 2007: 555.
181. I.e., the *nimitta*s associated with the natural imagination (*prakṛtivikalpa*) (which constitute the duality of the ordinary world) along with those associated with the three types of interpretative imagination (*nirūpaṇa-vikalpa*), relating to the remedy, reality (or suchness), and the fruit. For in the process of abandoning the mistaken projections of an ordinary mind, which operates under the influence of desire, hatred, and so forth, one tends to cultivate mistaken notions of the remedy, reality, and the fruit. The latter must likewise be abandoned by becoming mentally disengaged. See Mathes 2005: 19–20.
182. The abandonment of the four *nimitta*s in the *Dharmadharmatāvibhāga* is one of the six points that specify the means by which nonconceptual wisdom is cultivated (see Mathes 2005: 12).
183. This is described in point seven, concerned with comprehending the transformation of the basis (see Mathes 1996: 146–49).
184. DhDhVV, line numbers 485–88.
185. See Mathes 1996: 87 and 143.
186. See Mathes 2005: 11–16 and 19–24.
187. APDh p. 95. First quoted and translated in Mathes 2010: 7.
188. APDhṬ, fol. 157b. First quoted and translated in Mathes 2009a: 9.
189. It should be noted that such a type of amanasikāra is not accepted as nonconceptual wisdom in the *Dharmadharmatāvibhāga* (see p. 75).
190. See above and Mathes 2019: 154.

191. RGV I.9 (RGVV 10–11). See Schmithausen 1971: 136.
192. RGVV 21.
193. TD 5c–6b.
194. Tib. *rgyun chags su 'jug pa* (DRSM 55). The Dpal spungs, and Derge and Peking Bstan 'gyur editions have: *lhun gyis grub pa rgyun* (D, P: *rgyan*) *gyis 'jug pa*.
195. Skt. *bhāvanā* can be translated as both "production" and "meditation."
196. HT I.8.44cd (p. 197).
197. Following DRSM.
198. Lit. "destruction."
199. MV 12.
200. MV 18.
201. Not quoted by Sahajavajra.
202. TD 6.
203. TDṬ (B 19b–20b, D 172b–173a, P 189a). See also Mathes 2008: 266–67.
204. HT I.8.44cd.
205. According to Thrangu Rinpoche, it is possible to ascertain the true status of phenomena (including mental events) by investigating their color, shape, etc., with the help of direct cognition within one's introverted mental consciousness during vipaśyanā.
206. TDṬ (B 21b, D 173b, P 190b).
207. This is also observed by Gzhon nu dpal in his commentary on the "abandoning of characteristic signs" in the *Dharmadharmatāvibhāga* (DRSM 114): "Kamalaśila maintains that the [interpretative] imagination that must be given up can only be given up through the insight of thorough investigation. [By contrast,] it is maintained in the commentary on Maitrīpa's *Ten Verses on True Reality* that it is not given up by thorough investigation, but by the 'meditative stabilization which [experiences] reality exactly as it is.' The latter knows as luminosity [even] the own nature of that which must be given up. Here it is reasonable to follow Maitrīpa, who [re]discovered this treatise [known as the *Dharmadharmatāvibhāga*]." See Mathes 2008: 390.
208. TDṬ (B 20b, D 21a, P 189b).
209. The Dpal spungs edition, Derge, and Peking have *gnyen po'i phyogs*, not *snying po*, and Gzhon nu dpal has the syllable *gnyen* in his commentary on this quotation (DRSM 464).
210. TD 7cd.

211. SN 36
212. My translation is based here on the the Dpal spungs edition, Derge, and Peking.
213. According to TDṬ (B, D, P) and MV 5cd: "[True reality] is clear of the four extremes while still being based on the four extremes."
214. TDṬ (B 20b–21b, D 173a–173b, P 189b–190b).
215. Mathes 2009: 116.
216. For a translation of the relevant passages see Mathes 2005: 19–20.
217. The passage of Rāmapāla's commentary on verse 36 and the corresponding passages from the *Avikalpapraveśadhāraṇī* have been first quoted and translated in Mathes 2016a: 328–31.
218. See preceding note.
219. See AKBh, p. 54.
220. SRS XXXII.93–98ab. For a critical edition of the Sanskrit and Tibetan, see Thomas 2020: 66–69. The English translation is my own.
221. TDṬ (B 21b–22a, D 173b–174a, P 190b–191a); DRSM 463.
222. TD 8.
223. TDṬ (B, 23a–b; D 174b, P 191b).
224. TDṬ (B 24a–b, D 175a, P 192a–b). First quoted and translated in Mathes 2006: 220–21.
225. It should be added that Jñānakīrti structures his *Tattvāvatāra* around the distinction among three approaches to reality, namely, those of the Mantranaya, Pāramitānaya, and "the path of freeing oneself from attachment" (i.e., Śrāvakayāna). Each of these three has again three distinct forms, for adepts with sharp, average, and inferior capacities. See Mathes 2008: 36.
226. LAS 10.257d. See Mathes 2008: 36.
227. For a detailed discussion, see Mathes 2019: 157–59.
228. Buswell and Lopez 2014: 714.
229. Mathes 2020: 275.
230. Since Akṣobhya embodies mirror-like wisdom, it makes sense that his seal is that of nondual mind, because when looking into a mirror, what you are seeing is yourself seeing yourself.
231. *'Bri gung bka' brgyud chos mdzod*, vol. *kha*, 18a.
232. GPKU (B 304b–305a, D173a, P 195a).
233. Mathes 2009:99–106.
234. Kvaerne 1986: 34–35.
235. See HT II.3.7–8 (p. 156), which is translated below.

236. CMU (B 11b, D 213a, P 232b).
237. As elaborated in Rāmapāla's commentary on *Presentation of Empowerment*, 36 (see p. 84–87).
238. See Isaacson 2010: 268–74.
239. See Mathes 2009: 93–94.
240. In his *Mkhas grub nā ro mai tri dbang gi bzhed pa mthun par grub pa*, 839, Zhwa dmar Chos kyi grags pa explains: "In forceful yoga, the generation stage and so forth, venerable Maitrīpa places coemergent [joy] at the end. This accords with Nāropa. . . ." (*rje mai tri pas drag po'i sbyor ba'i dbang bskur dang bskyed rim sogs la lhan skyes mthar 'don pa ni nā ro pa dang 'thun* . . .). In other words, *haṭhayoga* stands here for a Buddhist practice or empowerment, in which coemergent joy is taken as the last of the four joys (as explained, for example, in Nāropa's *Sekoddeśaṭīkā*). In the same text (826), Chos kyi grags pa tells us: "'Forceful yoga' means the stabilization of the element (i.e., the drop of bodhicitta) in the jewel of the vajra through the forceful yoga of bodily exercise and the power of the subtle winds. Before, in the *Caturmudrānvaya*, it is referred to as *haṭhayoga*."
241. Written in old Brāhmī, *e* looks like a vagina, and *va* like a penis.
242. CMAṬ (B 258b–259a, D 286a, P 321a–b).
243. See Mathes 2009: 94.
244. See Rāmapāla's *Sekanirdeśapañjikā* (Isaacson and Sferra 2014: 191 and 310).
245. This is clear from the following passage of Kāropa's commentary on the *Caturmudrānvaya*. See Mathes 2009: 99.
246. This is made utterly clear in Kāropa's commentary on the definition of *mahāmudrā*. See Mathes 2009: 116.
247. See Isaacson and Sferra 2014: 263ff.
248. SN 2.
249. HT II.3.7–8 (HT 156).
250. Zhwa dmar Chos kyi grags pa, *Mkhas grub nā ro mai tri dbang gi bzhed pa mthun pa grub pa*, p. 826.
251. MNS 107.10 (p. 107).
252. CMU (B 11b–12a, D 213b, P 233a). First quoted and translated in Mathes 2009: 89.
253. According to some tantric sources, sexual fluids, semen virile and sometimes also menstrual blood, are called bodhicitta. This type of bodhicitta is not only physiological, though, but has also a psychical aspect (see Wangchuk 2007: 218).

254. Zhwa dmar Chos kyi grags pa, *Mkhas grub nā ro mai tri dbang gi bzhed pa mthun par grub pa*, p. 840.
255. In forceful yoga, *vimarda* and *virama* mean "interruption" and "intensification of joy" (instead of "relaxation" and "the joy of no-joy"). See Zhwa dmar Chos kyi grags pa, "*Mkhas grub nā ro mai tri dbang gi bzhed pa mthun par grub pa*, 840: "In the third moment of interruption (*vimarda*: *rnam nyed*) one [gets] free from the manifest joy of clinging to an external attractive body and coarse thoughts disappear. This leads to the joy in the cessation of joy."
256. GPKU (B 305b–306a, D 174a, P 195b–196a).
257. Mathes 2019: 158–59
258. CMU (B 12a, D 213b).
259. SN 3–4.
260. Mathes 2009: 99. See the explanation of karmamudrā in the *Caturmudrānvaya*.
261. HT II.5.70cd (p. 214). First quoted and translated in Mathes 2009: 102.
262. HT I.10.18cd (p. 118). First quoted and translated in Mathes 2009: 102.
263. See Isaacson and Sferra 2014: 275–76.
264. This follows from the third verse of the *Presentation of Empowerment* (SN 3).
265. SN 5.
266. See Zhwa dmar Chos kyi grags pa, *Mkhas grub nā ro mai tri dbang gi bzhed pa mthun par grub pa*, p. 843.
267. SUṬ, p. 107.
268. CMU (B 11b, D 213a–b, P 232b–233a).
269. CMU (B 12a, D 13b, P 233a).
270. ŚBhG II.16.
271. The verse is part of Kṛṣṇa's famous sermon to Arjuna about the nonexistence of the body and the existence of the soul (ātman). The idea is that Arjuna should not be afraid of killing his relatives in battle, for it is only the body, which has never really existed in the first place, that gets killed (ŚBhG 54).
272. See Isaacson and Sferra 2014: 183 and 292.
273. LAS X.256–57 (pp. 298–299).
274. I.e., the vagina.
275. SN 22.
276. MNS X.3b.
277. See my remarks on SN 2.

278. HT II.3.10 (p. 156).
279. HT II.3.11 (p. 156).
280. This follows from HT II.3.14c–15b (HT 157–158), where the final part of the second empowerment is clearly described: "He must drop it with the thumb and ring finger into the disciple's mouth. The identical taste [of insight and means] needs to be produced here as an experiential object of the disciple." (*jyeṣṭānāmikābhyāṃ ca śiṣyavaktre nipātayet | kāritavyaṃ tu tatraiva samarasaṃ śiṣyagocaram ||*). This leads to the third empowerment, as presented in HT II.3.15c–16b (p. 158): "The teacher must worship the prajñā, and having honoured her, offer her [to the disciple] saying: 'O great being take this [karma]mudrā who will bring you bliss.'" (*prajñāṃ pūjayec chāstā arcayitvā samarpayet | śāstā brūyāt mahāsattva gṛhṇa mudrāṃ sukhāvahām*).
281. I.e., vagina and penis.
282. HT II.3.13 (p. 157).
283. GPKU (B 309a, D 176a, P 198a).
284. See Mathes 2011: 109–10.
285. Maitrīpa elaborates here on the differences between forceful, base, and genuine empowerments.
286. Mathes 2009: 109.
287. CMU (B 11a–12b, D 213a–214a, P 232b–233b).
288. See CMA, karmamudrā.
289. See CMA, karmamudrā.
290. Zhwa dmar Chos kyi grags pa, *Mkhas grub nā ro mai tri dbang gi bzhed pa mthun par grub pa*, p. 849.
291. Mathes 2009: 94.
292. Maitrīpa explains here the four joys on the level of the dharmamudrā (see pp. 120–21).
293. CMU (B 12b, D 214a, P 233b).
294. See Mathes 2016a: 318.
295. Maitrīpa explains here how the four seals can be taken as the four joys in their relation to mahāmudrā (see p. 120).
296. CMU (B 12b–13a, D 214a–214b, P 233b–234a).
297. This can be compared to the *ekakṣaṇābhisamaya* in the *Abhisamayālaṃkāra*, which refers to the bodhisattva's simultanenous realization of all aspects of the three knowledges in the vajra-like samādhi during the last moment of the tenth *bhūmi*, which is immediately followed by the attainment of

buddhahood (Brunnhölzl 2010: 60). To be sure, "perfect enlightenment in a single moment" does not mean that it only lasts for a single moment, for once mahāmudrā is attained, it will never be lost.

298. Maitrīpa explains here the four joys on the level of the samayamudrā.
299. CMU (B 13a, D 214b, P 234a).
300. SN 28.
301. For a similar description of the first moment, see Rāmapāla's *Sekanirdeśapañjikā* (Isaacson and Sferra 2014: 191 and 310).
302. CMU (B 12b, D214a, P 233b).
303. See HT II.3.7ab (p. 156): "[The moment of the] manifold is called variety" (*vicitraṃ vividhaṃ khyātam āliṅgacumbanādikam* |).
304. See Mathes 2009: 89.
305. For a detailed description of the third moment on the level of karmamudrā see Mathes 2016a: 314–16.
306. SN 29.
307. See JĀA p. 146.
308. Quoted from Mathes 2007: 555.
309. See more on p. 116–17.
310. MSP 8cd.
311. For the different completion stages in Maitrīpa's system, see p. 132–33.
312. GPKU (B 299b–300a, D 170a–b, P 191a–b).
313. I.e., a visualized consort.
314. TV 7–11.
315. The quote is at the end of the description of the first deity, and should be taken to apply implicitly to all remaining deities of the maṇḍala.
316. Tib. *de nyid* is a wrong translation of Skt. *ata eva*. See Mathes 2015: 416.
317. I.e., taking *kalpita* in the sense of *parikalpitasvabhāva*.
318. This sentence is missing in the Tibetan. See PĀ 417.
319. Mi bskyod rdo rje, *Sku gsum ngo sprod rnam bshad,* vol. 1, 203–4. First quoted and translated in Mathes 2020: 286–87.
320. Mi bskyod rdo rje. First quoted and translated in Mathes 2020: 288.
321. HT I.8.24cd–25ab (pp. 81 and 87): "The dharma teachings of the Adamantine One are based on two stages, the *utpattikrama* and the *utpannakrama*."
322. See Mathes 2009: 92.
323. See Isaacson and Sferra 2014: 329.
324. Wedemeyer 2007: 49.
325. See Isaacson and Sferra 2014: 327.

326. Thurman (1988: 132) writes: "One has died as a coarse body and mind, and one has entered an internalized realm of the subtle body and mind, a 'microverse' where one perceives pure patterns of interconnection of all beings and things, patterns of pure light and energy. Once one has reached the first taste of clear light, one has reached Candrakīrti's second stage, 'mind-objective.'"
327. Wedemeyer 2007: 56.
328. Tomabechi 2006: 34.
329. See Mimaki and Tomabechi 1994: ix–x.
330. GPKU (B 300a; D 170b, P 191b).
331. See Kṛṣṇapāda's Hevajra commentary (HP 143) on HT II.4.25, where the fifteen yoginīs are said to be the ones of Nairātmyā. In Kashmir Shaivism, the fifteen yoginīs preside over the moon's phases and are also identified with the fifteen vowels of the Sanskrit alphabet. See also Brooks 1992: 127.
332. Lit. "... the colors black, red, yellow, green, blue, and white must be cultivated in that order."
333. These first two paragraphs were first quoted and translated in Mathes 2014: 373–74.
334. NP 262–64. Unpublished edition of the Nairātmyaprakāśa by Harunaga Isaacson, quoted from "*Sekanirdeśapañjikā*: Notes (3), Handout 4 July, 2007."
335. First presented in Mathes 2014: 373–74.
336. For the Apabhraṃśa and Tibetan, see Shahidullah 1928: 139.
337. See more on p. 85–88.
338. Mathes 1996: 142–43.
339. Thrangu Rinpoche (Thrangu 2006: 88) describes self-awareness in terms of direct realization as follows: "This freedom from existence is not a nothingness or a voidness, because cognitive lucidity is present at the same time. Since mind's nature has this inherent wisdom, it can cognize, and therefore it can cognize itself. In that this nature knows itself, it is without the duality of viewer and viewed."
340. Together with the closely related *Ratnagotravibhāga*, another text attributed to Maitreya. See Mathes 2008: 162.
341. Mathes 1996: 153.
342. DhDhVV (Sanskrit), lines 83–94. (Mathes 1996: 103)
343. DhDhVV, lines 701–2.
344. *Theg chen rgyud bla ma la gdams pa*.

345. Mathes 2015a: 317–18.

346. The *Dharmadharmatāvibhāgakārikā* (DhDhVK, lines 18–19 of the Tibetan translation) is quoted in *Jñānaśrīmitranibandhāvali* (JNĀ, p. 432), while *Ratnagotravibhāga* I.9 is summarized in JNĀ, p. 478.

347. See Mathes 1996: 163–68.

348. DRSM 4.

349. Skyo ston Smon lam tshul khrims, *Chos nyid kyi khrid*, 315. First quoted and translated in Mathes 2015a: 308.

350. Mathes 2005: 16–19.

351. Mathes 2008: 300.

352. These four aspects are explained in RGVV I.25 as: (1) the mind is simultaneously pure and defiled; (2) suchness, which is free from stains, i.e., purified of stains; (3) all sentient beings possess inseparable buddha qualities; (4) and buddha activity unfolds everywhere simultaneously. See Mathes 2008: 407–8.

353. See Karma Phrin las pa, *Btsun mo do ha'i ṭī ka 'bring po*, p. 120: "E ma! The secret ḍākinī language is the basis of mahāmudrā, whose nature is nonduality" (*e ma mkha' gsang ba'i skad* || *gnyis med rang bzhin phyag rgya chen po'i gnas* |). The commentary on these lines is as follows: "*Ḍāka*s and yoginīs magically fly through the sky, and their secret language, communicated in a language of 'signs' (*brda*), such as 'mindfulness' and 'beyond mindfulness,' is difficult for ordinary people to understand. Therefore, it is amazing" (*dpa' bo dang rnal 'byor ma rnams ni nam mkha' la rdzu 'phrul gyi bgrod pas 'gro bas nam mkha' 'gro de rnams kyi gsang ba'i skad ni dran pa dran med sogs brda'i skad du gsungs pa phal gyis rtogs dka' bas na ngo mtshar che ba'o*).

354. *dran pa*, *dran med*, *skye med*, and *blo 'das*.

355. BhPHṬAP (D 286b–287a, P 309b). My translation differs from the one of Lopez, Jr. (1996: 202–3) only in terminology.

356. DKSGṬ (D 92b, P 124b).

357. DKSGṬ (D 92b, P 124a).

358. DKSGṬ (D 92b, P 124b).

359. *gaṇacakra*; *tshogs 'khor*.

360. Karma Phrin las pa, *Dmangs do ha*, 30 (see also Shahidullah 1928: 134). The manuscript photographed by Sāṃkṛtyāyana (DKG 3a–b) with the Apabhraṃśa root text reads: "Eating, drinking, enjoying intercourse, summoning the 'assembly [of adepts]' (*[gaṇa]cakra*) with plenty of alcohol (*ali*) and food (*bali*)—by means of these fortunate people attain [supreme]

siddhi. [The master] stamps on the heads of those in the deluded world. He is one of whom the world is greatly afraid." (*khāantem̥* pībantem̥ *suraa ramantem̥ / alibalibahala cakka pasarantem̥ | emaï siddhi jāṇa paraloaha / matthahi pāva deï pasulobaha* ||). Thanks to Péter Dániel Szántó for providing the Apabhraṁśa verse quoted in this footnote. The Apabhraṃśa version finds resonance in Advayavajra's *Dohākoṣapañjikā* (DKP, p. 98): "By this [Saraha] teaches a conduct of excess, just like that engaged in by Indrabhūti: Among the five forms of sensual pleasures, the play of intercourse must be performed with food and drink. With the skull and so forth in his hands, [the master] offers the [alcohol and] food (*bali*), and stands as the deity in the middle of the great assembly. By means of this, [these] fortunate people will attain the accomplishment of wisdom, the accomplishment of mahāmudrā."

361. It should be noted that the cakras of the vajra body become here the metaphor of a wheel (*cakra*) to express continuous practice.
362. Karma Phrin las pa, *Dmangs do ha*, 31.
363. Karma Phrin las pa, *Dmangs do ha*, 32.
364. See Isaacson and Sferra 2014: 310.
365. DKP, p. 138: "First, I [could] read [the sentence]: 'May there be realization!' [Later,] I drank the essence [of its meaning] and forgot [the words. At first,] I only understood the letters but not the words based on them, my friend." (*siddhir atthu maï paḍame paḍhiaü | maṇḍa pivantem̥ visaraa e maïu | akkharam ekka ettha maï jāṇiu | tāhara ṇāma ṇa jāṇami e saïu* |).
366. Karma Phrin las pa, *Dmangs do ha*, 101.
367. See also Zhwa dmar Chos kyi grags pa, *Mkhas grub nā ro mai tri dbang gi bzhed pa mthun par grub pa*, p. 843, who takes the third and fourth as the coemergent joy: "Since the terms 'no-joy' and 'joy of no-joy' are freely used with the same meaning in the *Hevajratantra*, the two realized masters are forced to explain, following [this] meaning, both the third and the fourth joy as the coemergent [one]."
368. The English translation and summary of the amanasikāra cycle presented here was first published in Mathes 2015, and I thank the Austrian Academy of Sciences Press for their permission to reprint. The gaps in *A Fine Blend* (Mathes 2015), where I had translated only parts of the *Destruction of Wrong Views* and the *Presentation of Empowerment*, are filled now. The respective editions of the Sanskrit and Tibetan are from Mathes 2015: 319–509.

369. This title is not found in any of the available manuscripts and is probably an invention of Shastri.
370. Even though contained in the *Advayavajrasaṃgraha*, an author is not mentioned in the colophon. Maitrīpa's disciple Rāmapāla attributes *Succession of the Four Seals* to the tantric Nāgārjuna (Mathes 2009: 90–91). This is corroborated by the colophon to it in the Tibetan translation and the *Bu ston gsan yig* (116).
371. I.e., the *Thabs dang shes rab rtse ba lnga pa* (D 2246, P 3091) and the *dGa' gcugs lnga pa* (D 2237, P 3082)
372. *Dbang gi bya ba mdor bsdus pa* (D 2244, P 3089).
373. The *Dbang gi bya ba mdor bsdus pa* reminds of Vajrapāṇi's *Instructions on the Stages Handed Down by the Lineage of Gurus*, which is a commentary on Maitrīpa's *Jewel Garland of True Reality*, *Sekatātparya*, and *Presentation of Empowerment*, and Vajrapāṇi's commentary on the *Heart Sūtra* (D 3820, P 5219). Vajrapāṇi gave the commentary in the form of special instructions upon hearing Tibetan friends reciting the *Heart Sūtra*. In the Peking Bstan 'gyur we find that "the Indian abbot himself and the translator, the monk Seng ge rgyal mtshan, revised the text." (Lopez 1996: 214–15). It is thus possible that a Sanskrit original never existed in written form, an oral teaching having been directly translated and written down in Tibetan.
374. For an explanation of the four seals, see p. 5–6.
375. One of the four main disciples of Maitrīpa, the other three being Rāmapāla, Vajrapāṇi, and Kāropa (see Roerich 1949–53: 842–47). See also Sanderson 2009: 233, n. 536.
376. See Mathes 2006: 222–23.
377. In the colophon of Vajrapāṇi's commentary on the *Prajñāpāramitāhṛdaya* (D 3820, P5219), it is stated that this disciple of Maitrīpa taught a special instruction on this sūtra to the translator Seng ge rgyal mtshan in Patan, Nepal (Lopez 1996: 215). It is possible that the *Instructions on the Stages Handed Down by the Lineage of Gurus* was composed under similar circumstances.
378. The full verse RGV II.61 is as follows: "Here, the first one is the dharmakāya, and the latter two the form kāyas. These latter appear on the basis of the former, just as visible forms appear in space (for the Sanskrit, see the English translation of PTMV below).
379. See Mathes 2009: 91.

380. In the *Hevajra Tantra* (HT II.3.7–8, p. 156) we find the following explanation of the four moments: "[The moment of the] manifold is called variety, since it involves embracing, kissing, and so forth. [The moment of] maturation is the reverse of the [first moment] in that it is the enjoyment of blissful wisdom. [The moment of] relaxation is said to be the reflecting upon [the fact] that one has experienced bliss. [The moment of] *vilakṣaṇa* is something other than these three, being free from both passion and absence of passion" (*vicitraṃ vividhaṃ khyātam āliṅgacumbanādikam | vipākaṃ tadviparyāsaṃ sukhajñānasya bhuñjanam || vimardam ālocanaṃ proktaṃ sukhaṃ bhuktaṃ mayeti ca | vilakṣaṇaṃ tribhyo 'nyatra rāgārāgavivarjitam ||*).
381. CMU (B 11b, D 213, P 232b).
382. Zhwa dmar Chos kyi grags pa, *Mkhas grub nā ro mai tri dbang gi bzhed pa mthun pa grub pa*, p. 826.
383. See Kvaerne 1986: 34–35.
384. See Mathes 2011: 111–12.
385. See Mathes 2009: 91.
386. *Bu ston gsan yig*, 116.
387. This I conclude from Maitrīpa's statement in the *Jewel Garland of True Reality* that tantra can only be practiced on the basis of Yogācāra and Madhyamaka, and thus not Vaibhāṣika and Sautrāntika (see p. 154).
388. MMK XV.3ab (Ye Shao Yong 2011: 236): "Where, in the absence of an own nature, will there be an other-being?" (*kutaḥ svabhāvasyābhāve parabhāvo bhaviṣyati ||*).
389. I.e., taking *pratiṣṭhāna* in the sense of *sthiti* (APP 6b), as referring to the "object-side," so to speak.
390. These attributes follow from the fact that one's vision is supposed to be without superimposition.
391. See Mathes 2008: 35.
392. See RGV I.9 (RGVV, p. 10–11) and RGVV on I.25 (RGVV, p. 21). See Schmithausen 1971: 136.
393. See my analysis of the Ten Verses on True Reality on pp. 165–66.
394. See Mathes 2015: 333.
395. Lit. "the excellence of all aspects." What is meant are the first five perfections.
396. MV 16.
397. HT I.6.19ab.

398. HT II.8.9ab. From here on until the end of the *Kudṛṣṭinirghātana* the translation is new (not from Mathes 2015). For the Sanskrit, see *Annual of the Institute for Comprehensive Studies of Buddhism*, Taisho University 10 (March 1988), 225–99 (10–36).
399. HŪṂ is missing in the Sanskrit.
400. Translated in accordance with the Tibetan.
401. The Tibetan has the extra line: "and will be engaged in virtuous deeds."
402. I.e., Bodhgayā.
403. I.e., merit.
404. Tib.: "The *Kudṛṣṭinirghātana* composed by the great learned master Advayavajra is ended. Translated, corrected, and finalized by the Tibetan translator mTshur ston Ye shes 'byung gnas as taught by the Indian learned master and guru Vajrapāṇi."
405. MAV V.5.
406. There is no Tibetan translation of this text, nor is an author mentioned in the colophon.
407. This causal ablative is not literally translated, nor are the following ones in the enumeration.
408. Of this text that lists eight gross offenses, there is no Tibetan translation, nor is there any reference to an author in the colophon.
409. This verse is quoted in the *Subhāṣitasaṃgraha* (SBhS 388). Bendall seems not to have understood *jaḍīyase* as the dative of the comparative of *jaḍa* and remarks: "The verbal form *jaḍīye* ('talk like an idiot') is new." The Tibetan translation of *jaḍīyase* (*'gro ba shin tu rmongs pa la'o*) is in the last line of the stanza and thus difficult to construe.
410. Tib.: "fat."
411. Tib.: "heart."
412. Skt.: "weariness."
413. Tib.: "stomach."
414. BCA V.62–63.
415. Even though they claim that it is neither impermanent nor permanent (see p. 194).
416. I.e., Śāriputra and Maudgalyāyana.
417. Mostly translated as "self-arisen wisdom."
418. A follower of Vedānta who lived around 800 CE (see Tatz 1994: 102, n. 25).
419. The first two lines of this verse accord with *Vijñānabhairava* 75ab; the second part in the *Vijñānabhairava* (VBh, p. 65) is as follows: "This state

must be realized by one's mind. [Then] the supreme goddess shines forth" (*sāvasthā manasā gamyā parā devī prakāśate*). Sferra (2003: 64–65) charges Maitrīpa for having changed the second part of the verse from the *Vijñānabhairava* with the intention to conceal the unfolding of the supreme reality in its active, female principle. I do not see why Maitrīpa should have done so. Maitrīpa simply quotes this verse to show that the faults of a Pratyekabuddha's meditation are similar to those of a heterodox system.

420. I.e., on symbols, gestures, and the like.
421. PV III.247. This is the chapter on *pratyakṣa* (the numbering of chapters and verses follows Steinkellner's (1977) *Verse Index*.
422. This verse is contained in Munidatta's commentary on the *Caryāgiti* (song no. 29 by Luipāda). See Kvaerne 1986: 192.
423. Lit. "on the tip of the nose."
424. I.e., the ones of the pratyekabuddhas.
425. Viṃś 12ab.
426. The compound *cittākāradhāri* has not been translated into Tibetan. The meaning in this system is that there are images of external objects without any external correlate at all.
427. Lit. "What does an external object have as justification?" If there was an external object, there would be two forms, the one in the mind, and the one of the external object.
428. Cf. PV III.432 (p.98): "If the mind has forms of something blue and the like, what is the reason for an external object? If the mind does not have forms of something blue and the like, how can there be an experience of it (i.e., the outer object)?" (*dhiyo nīlādirūpatve bāhyo 'rthaḥ kiṃpramāṇakaḥ | dhiyo 'nīlādirūpatve sa tasyānubhavaḥ katham* ||).
429. See Lhalungpa 1993: 9 and Tatz 1994: 105.
430. LAS X.154c–155b.
431. The masculine endings of the compounds in this line suggest that the subject has already changed here from "mind" to "dharmakāya." This is no problem, because for Maitrīpa the dharmakāya is the true nature of mind.
432. PTMV 4.
433. This means that the manifold appearances or aspects of mind are real, but beyond the duality of a perceived object and a perceiving subject.
434. Ascribed to Āryadeva, but probably composed by a Mādhyamika later than Bhavya (see Nakamura 1989: 245).

435. ĀM 53.
436. Vasubandu, *Thirty Verses* (*Triṃśikā*), 27–28.
437. This is the form the term commonly takes. The Sanskrit has *bhagavataḥ saṃsthita*.
438. SN 15.
439. See also Mimaki 1982: 194. Dvivedī and Vajrācārya (1986: 86) claim that this stanza is by Sarahapāda.
440. Ui treats this quotation as verse 26.
441. MV 4.
442. Ui reads *sarvasminn apratiṣṭhāne* (which is supported by the Tibetan): "While not abiding in anything."
443. SN 32.
444. SN 30.
445. SN 34.
446. AA VIII.33, AA VIII.12, and AA VIII.1, respectively.
447. ĀM 176.
448. NS 21.
449. The Tibetan has an extra line: "Not knowing it, one is bound."
450. PV II.253cd.
451. NS 7.
452. KDN 4.
453. LAS X.458.
454. Tib.: "self-awareness."
455. RGVV II.61b (88).
456. TRĀ 20.
457. Tib.: "self-awareness."
458. If vajra and sattva are not experienced as being inseparable, then emptiness (i.e., vajra) would be a mere nothingness disconnected from compassion. Rising from meditation on Yogācāra emptiness means to rise from something, i.e., nondual mind, but rising from meditation on Madhyamaka emptiness means to rise from nothing, i.e., a state in which everything including compassion is destroyed.
459. The extra line (*med na mi 'byung nges phyir ro*) at the beginning of the Tibetan translation of this verse correponds to *avinābhāvaniyamāt* in the verse above (PTMV 9).
460. I.e., consciousness.
461. Tib.: "self-awareness."

462. Tib.: "self-awareness."

463. YṢ 19.

464. I.e., the *Samādhirājasūtra*. But the verse cannot be found there. Brunnhölzl (2007: 525, n. 553) identified this verse in the *Anavataptanāgarājaparipṛcchasūtra* (Derge Bka' 'gyur no. 156, 230b). See also La Vallée Poussin 1903–13: 239.

465. LAS II.169.

466. ĀM 248. See Lindtner 2003: 96–97.

467. HT II.3.36ab.

468. ĀM 247.

469. PĀ 3.

470. This verse is quoted in Muniśrībhadra's *Pañcakramaṭippaṇī Yogīmanoharā*, 24a. See Zhongxin Jiang and Toru Tomabechi 1996: 34.

471. HT II.4.34ab (p. 179).

472. The author is not mentioned in the Sanskrit.

473. Tib.: "Homage to the youthful Mañjuśrī!"

474. I.e., that which has as its city, i.e., place, the jewel, which is held to have the nature of pleasure (oral information from Harunaga Isaacson).

475. VBh 69.

476. *Mahābhārata* XII.316.40.

477. ŚBhG II.6.

478. I.e., Akṣobhya.

479. HT II.3.7.

480. HT II.3.11.

481. The Tibetan has at the tip of the jewel.

482. TRĀ 31.

483. PTMV 22.

484. TRĀ 30.

485. TRĀ 32.

486. Lit. "been caused to arise/appear." I follow here 'Gos Lo tsā ba Gzhon nu dpal, who has in his quotation of SN 35 *'byed pa* instead of *bsgom pa* (DRSM 463).

487. My translation of the karmamudrā verses and the introductory verse of the *Presentation of Empowerment* profited from Harunaga Isaacson and Francesco Sferra's *Sekanirdeśapañjikā* class in the summer semester 2007 in Hamburg and English translation in Sferra and Isaacson 2014: 255–306.

488. Missing in the Tibetan.

489. This sentence was HT II.3.5ab, *karmamudrāyām* having originally been a gloss or an oral commentary by the author.

490. HT II.3.5.

491. A passage from an attested but unrecovered tantra. This recognition of *sahaja* during the third moment was also maintained by Maitrīpa's teacher Ratnākaraśānti. Abhayākaragupta and Kamalanātha took sahaja as the fourth (see also Kvaerne 1986: 34–35). This latter view, i.e., *virama* ("the [joy of] no-joy") in the third position, goes back to a tradition that takes virama as "intensification of joy" and not its cessation (the [joy of] no-joy). In the *Sekoddeśaṭīkā* (SUṬS, p. 106), for example, virama is in the third position and also understood this way as can be seen from the Tibetan translation *khyad par dga' ba* (SUṬT, p. 272). For a reliable Italian translation see Gnoli and Orofino 1994: 204.

492. *Prajñā* must be taken here as referring to a karmamudrā, i.e., a tantric partner.

493. I.e., taking *svalakṣana* in a way similar to Dignāga, as a bare particular, i.e., a given actuality as such (see Arnold 2003: 142).

494. HT II.3.4

495. Lit. "an outflow" (see p. 232).

496. HT I.1.14

497. RGV I.154. For a list of Mahāyāna works in which this stanza occurs, see Takasaki 1966: 300.

498. I could not locate this quotation in the *Jñānālokālaṃkāra* itself, but the same passage is also quoted in Rāmapāla's *Sekanirdeśapañjikā* (Mathes 2007: 555), and Maitrīpa's *Amanasikārādhāra*.

499. See JĀA 146.

500. After the two quotations from the *Jñānālokālaṃkāra*, the construction *yā sā* is no longer suitable. Its presence implies, as in the description of dharmamudrā earlier, the directly preceding feminine attributes at the beginning of the definition. In other words, the original text did not contain the sūtra quotations.

501. I.e., the vajrācārya empowerment (CMAṬ B 291b, D 309a, P 349a).

502. This second *pancavidhaṃ* is taken in the sense of *pañcavidhinā*. Kāropa (CMAṬ B 293b, D 310b, P 350a) equates *cho ga lngar btags pa* (*pañcavidhi-parikalpa*) with *mngon par byang chub pa lnga*. The fivefold ritual perfor-

mance is identified in the *Bod rgya tshig mdzod chen mo* (s.v.) as: "chanting the ritual melodies, visualizing during the mantra recitation, assuming different hand gestures, playing the drum, dancing."

503. Kāropa specifies the "initial yoga" as "yoga" and "yoga attained after [meditation]"; the "supreme king of the maṇḍala" as "ati yoga"; the "supreme king of activity" as Great ati yoga; the "drop" as the "semen of bodhicitta"; and the "subtle" as the "wind" and "channel." See (CMAṬ B 294a, D 310b–311a, P 350b).
504. The commentary (CMAṬ B 294b, D 311a, P 351a) informs us that "the samayamudrā is a manifold fabrication (i.e., visualization), the experiential object of the conceptual accompanied by clinging, the cause of saṃsāra, and contrived."
505. HT I.10.43.
506. HT I.10.44.
507. I.e., the fourth empowerment. See CMAṬ (B 316a, D 325b, P 367a).
508. CMAṬ (B 316a, D 325b, P 367a).
509. This sentence is not found in the Sanskrit and is supplied from the Tibetan translation.
510. This is similar to a verse in the eighteenth chapter of the *Guhyasamāja Tantra* (GST, p. 160).
511. Sanskrit *adhipati* and *ghaṇṭā* are used interchangeably (oral information from Harunaga Isaacson).
512. I.e., the disciple is visualized by the master as having the form of Vairocana.
513. I.e., that everything arises in dependence (Thrangu Rinpoche).
514. HT I.1.4a.
515. An old Vedic mantra (oral information from Harunaga Isaacson).
516. In order to establish the equation of prajñā with "woman," Maitrīpa proposes here the bridging link of the intellect, which creates all perceived objects (including women). In fact, the yoga involving a karmamudrā mainly works on the level of imagination, whence it can also be performed with a visualized consort (*jñānamudrā*). See the definition of *karmamudrā* in the *Succession of the Four Seals* above, where karmamudrā is said to have the nature of imagination.
517. I.e., enjoyment, union, great bliss, devoid of own nature, full of compassion, uninterrupted, without cessation (oral information from Harunaga Isaacson).

518. I.e., taking *śloka* in its meaning of "fame."

519. P: Mtshur ston [Ye shes 'byung gnas].

520. Tib: "Homage to Vajrasattva!"

521. According to the Tibetan; the Sanskrit reads *-repha-*.

522. According to the Tibetan; *akṣobhya* is missing in the Sanskrit.

523. Based on the Tibetan, I suggest reading *bodhaḥ sambhogalakṣaṇam*.

524. MV 19.

525. PTMV 23.

526. BV 57.

527. YṢ 6cd. The two lines in Lindtner's edition (1990: 104) differ only slightly: *parijñānaṃ bhavasyaiva nirvāṇam iti kathyate*.

528. Tib.: *laṃ*.

529. Lit. *tāriṇī*.

530. The author is not mentioned in the Sanskrit.

531. The colophons of the Derge and Peking Bstan 'gyur and the Dpal spungs edition mention neither an Indian paṇḍita nor a Tibetan translator.

532. Tib.: "Homage to the youthful Mañjuśrī!"

533. The author is not mentioned in the Sanskrit.

534. Tib.: "Homage to the Buddha!"

535. Tib.: "Homage to the youthful Mañjuśrī!"

536. Peking Bstan 'gyur: "Translated by paṇḍita Vajrapāṇi and the translator Rma ban chos 'bar."

537. Tib.: "Homage to the youthful Mañjuśrī!"

538. The use of the term *sattva* in the *Elucidation of Nonabiding* is ambiguous. The context of verses 3 and 4 requires taking *sattva* as "existence," but still the Tibetan continues to render *sattva* as "sentient being" (*sems can*).

539. Even though the context requires "existence," *sattvaṃ* is translated into Tibetan as "sentient being" (*sems can*). It should be noted, however, that the existence of awareness is the main characteristic of a sentient being.

540. Lit. "carved manifestions."

541. Peking Bstan 'gyur: *nag tsho*.

542. Missing in the Sanskrit.

543. I.e., hatred and so forth.

544. According to the Peking Bstan 'gyur the Tibetan translator was Nag tsho.

545. Missing in the Sanskrit.

546. I.e., the physical union of a yoginī and a yogin.

547. Tib. *mi gsal ba* is difficult to construe. In the *Succession of the Four Seals* the bliss or coemergent arisen from a karmamudrā is an imitation of an image of the real coemergent bliss. Mathes 2009: 107.
548. *viśvacakra*. According to Kuladatta's *Kriyāsaṃgrahapañjikā*, chapter 6 (VI.6.6), prose after verse 14, the term is listed as the last of four *cakra*s: *vajracakraṃ ratnacakraṃ padmacakraṃ viśvacakraṃ*.
549. I.e., nothing at all.
550. The author is not mentioned in the Sanskrit.
551. Tib.: "Homage to the venerable Buddha!"
552. It is noteworthy that the sequence of the third and fourth moments here does not accord with Maitrīpa's system. It may have been inverted, though, for metrical reasons.
553. *vajraḍāka*.
554. Implying the union with a consort and so forth.
555. I.e., the yogin sees everything as not being different from the inconceivable.
556. I.e., walking, standing, sitting, and lying down. (see *īryāpatha* in Edgerton: *Buddhist Hybrid Sanskrit Grammar and Dictionary*, vol. 2, s.v.).
557. The author is not mentioned in the Sanskrit.
558. Missing in the Sanskrit.
559. TRĀ 28.
560. See Mathes 2015: 194.
561. Lit. "destruction."
562. See MSP 7–8.
563. KDN 8.
564. PĀ 2.
565. The author is not mentioned in the Sanskrit.
566. Peking Bstan 'gyur: "Translated and finalized by the learned Indian man Divākaracandra and the Tibetan translator-monk Śākya brTson 'grus."
567. I.e., Yeshé Jungné.
568. Tib.: "Homage to the Buddha!"
569. Missing in the Sanskrit.
570. Lit. "cut off."
571. Tib.: ". . . by the learned master and paṇḍita Maitrīpa."
572. Tib.: ". . . the youthful Mañjuśrī!"
573. Sahajavajra in TDṬ (B 16b) takes "nature" as "dependently arisen self-awareness."
574. Tib.: "The *Ten Verses on True Reality*, composed by the great learned master

and renunciant Advayavajra, is ended. Translated by the Indian paṇḍita Vajrapāṇi and the Tibetan translator Tshul khrims rgyal ba." P: "Translated by the guru Vajrapāṇi and Mtshur [Ye shes 'byung gnas]. Later, translated [again] by Tshul khrims rgyal ba."

575. Tib.: "Homage to the glorious Vajrasattva!"

576. *Aṣṭādhyāyī* VI.3.14. See Böthlingk 1998: 336.

577. I could not locate this quotation in the *Jñānālokālaṃkāra* itself, but the same passage is also quoted in Rāmapāla's *Sekanirdeśapañjikā* (Mathes 2007: 555) and the *Succession of the Four Seals* (Mathes 2009: 115).

578. See JĀA, p. 146.

579. See APDh, p. 95.

580. HT I.5.1.

581. HT I.8.44ab. The second part of the same stanza (HT I.8.44cd): "When one thoroughly knows all phenomena, meditation is actually nonmeditation." (*sarvadharmaparijñānaṃ bhāvanā naiva bhāvanā* ||) is also quoted in Sahajavajra's *Tattvadaśakaṭīkā* in order to provide doctrinal support for the nonanalytical meditation of the samādhi that realizes true reality as it is. Reading amanasikāra into the *Hevajratantra* thus prepares the way for extending its semantic range from a pure negation of mental activity and objective support to include direct realization of phenomena, which in the *Ten Verses on True Reality* are said to be luminous by nature.

582. I.e., protected from other men.

583. It is interesting that such a defintion of nonaffirming negation allows for a distinction between what is meant to be negated ("what is applicable") and a luminous nature or emptiness of the mind, to which the yogin directs his attention (*manasikāra*), as we shall see further below. This distinction could be well taken as a forerunner of the Tibetan *gzhan stong* ("empty of other") interpretation of emptiness. Likewise, in the case of taking amanasikāra as an affirming negation, only a particular aspect of the mind, namely, that part of it which is engaged in the normal dualistic process of conceptualization, is negated. This does not entail the negation of all mental processes.

584. This means that the negation must be taken as implying the mode of emptiness asserted by the Māyopamādvayavādins or that asserted by the Apratiṣṭhānavādins.

585. Maitrīpa analyzes *amanasikāra* as a compound in which the component *pradhāna* ("the main thing") has been dropped. This is fully in

line with Jayāditya's and Vāmana's *Kāśikāvṛtti* on *Aṣṭādhyāyī* II.1.60, in which Maitrīpa's example of "vegetable king" is analyzed as a "king for whom vegetables are the main thing" (see KV, vol. 2, 84: *śākapradhānaḥ pārthivaḥ śākapārthivaḥ*). "When it is understood thus—that one directs one's attention (*manasikāra*) to the letter *a* as the main [focus]—'*a*' can no longer be the simple privative, but must stand for a more profound negation, such as the one implied by emptiness or nonorigination (*anutpāda*)." In other words, the first analysis, in accordance with the *Kāśikāvṛtti*, implies a second analysis of *amanasikāra*, in which *a* is taken as having the nature of *anutpāda*. This suggests that a form of *manasikāra* that is aware of its true nature of nonorigination or emptiness is not excluded by the term *amanasikāra*. Padma dkar po's remarks in this regard are as follows: "The letter *a* being taken to mean nonorigination, [the remaining] *manasikāra* is [then] explained as mental engagement. Thus, the correct mental engagement [of realizing] the meaning of the letter *a* is 'the mental engagement of *a*' (*a-manasikāra*). The middle word [of the compound] has been dropped, just as in the case of calling a king who is fond of vegetables a 'vegetable king.' *A* stands here for the 'perfection of insight' (*prajñāpāramitā*), 'not arisen' (*an-utpanna*), and 'not obstructed' (*a-nirodha*)." (*Phyag chen rgyal ba'i gan mdzod*, 40–41). Padma dkar po's analysis of the compound "vegetable king" is in accord with Jayakṛṣṇa's *Subodhinī* commentary on the *Siddhāntakaumudī* (no. 739), where we find: *śākapriyaḥ pārthivaḥ śākapārthivaḥ* (SB, p. 178). Maitrīpa's own analysis of the compound as "*manasikāra* for which the letter *a* is the main thing" shows, however, that he followed the *Kāśikāvṛtti*.

586. HT I.2.1.
587. MNS V.1c–2b.
588. HT II.4.22a.
589. HT II.4.44.
590. This means that *amanasikāra* is taken here as a *karmadhāraya* compound.
591. I.e., luminosity and self-empowerment.
592. The author is not mentioned in the Sanskrit.
593. The Tibetan translator is not mentioned in the Peking Bstan 'gyur.
594. Missing in the Sanskrit.
595. Tib.: "Maitrīpa."
596. I.e., schools of thought.
597. I.e., Śrāvakayāna and Pratyekabuddhayāna.

598. I.e., prajñā and means.

599. In his *Instructions on the Four Seals*, Maitrīpa explains that coemergent joy is experienced when "two of what is present in the form of four drops are at the tip of the jewel and two in the middle of the lotus." See Mathes 2011: 108.

Bibliography

Primary Sources (Indian)

Abhidharmakośa (AK). See AKBh.

Abhidharmakośabhāṣya (AKBh). Edited by Prahlad Pradhan. Tibetan Sanskrit Works Series 8. Patna: 1967.

Abhisamayālaṃkāra (AA). Edited by Ramshankar Tripathi (together with the *Abhisamayālaṃkāravṛttiḥ Sphuṭārthā*). Bibliotheca Indo-Tibetica Series 2. Sarnath: Central Institute of Higher Tibetan Studies, 1993.

Ālokamālā (ĀM). Edited by Christian Lindtner. See Lindtner 2003.

Amanasikārādhāra (AMĀ). See edition of the Sanskrit and Tibetan texts in Mathes 2015, 489–97.

Apratiṣṭhānaprakāśa (APP).
See edition of the Sanskrit and Tibetan texts in Mathes 2015, 443–46.

Avikalpapraveśadhāraṇī (APDh). Edited by Kazunobu Matsuda. See Matsuda 1996, 93–99.

Avikalpapraveśadhāraṇīṭīkā (APDhṬ). Tibetan translation. D: Derge Bstan 'gyur 4000, *mdo 'grel*, vol. *ji*, 123a–145b. P: Peking Bstan 'gyur 5501, *mdo sna tshogs 'grel pa*, vol. *ji*, 146b–174b.

Bhagavatīprajñāpāramitāhṛdayaṭīkārthapradīpanāma (BhPHṬAP). D: Derge Bstan 'gyur 3820, *shes phyin*, vol. *ma*, 286b–295a. P: Peking Bstan 'gyur 5219, *mdo 'grel*, vol. *tsi*, 309b–319b.

Bodhicittavivaraṇa (BV). Tibetan translation. Edited by Christian Lindtner. See Lindtner 1990, 184–216.

Catuḥpīṭhanibandha (CPN). Kaiser Library, Kathmandu: 134.

Caturmudrānvaya (CMA). See edition of the Sanskrit and Tibetan text in Mathes 2015, 389–402.

Caturmudrānvayaṭīkā (CMAṬ). Tibetan translation. B: Dpal spung block print of the *Phyag rgya chen po'i rgya gzhung*, vol. *oṃ*, 255a–317a. D: Derge Bstan

’gyur 2259, *rgyud*, vol. *wi*, 283b–326a. P: Peking Bstan ’gyur 3104, *rgyud ’grel*, vol. *mi*, 317b–367b.

Caturmudropadeśa (CMU). Tibetan translation. B: Dpal spung block print of the *Phyag rgya chen po’i rgya gzhung*, vol. *hūṃ*, 9a–13b. D: Derge Bstan ’gyur 2295, *rgyud*, vol. *shi*, 211b–214b. P: Peking Bstan ’gyur 3143, *rgyud ’grel*, vol. *tsi*, 231a–234a.

Cūḷasuññatasutta (CSS). In *Majjhiimanikāya*, vol. 3, 104–9. Ed. by Robert Chalmers. London: Pali Text Society, 1899.

Dharmadharmatāvibhāgakārikā (DhDhK). Edited by Klaus-Dieter Mathes. See Mathes 1996, 104–14.

Dharmadharmatāvibhāgavṛtti (DhDhVV). Edited by Klaus-Dieter Mathes. See Mathes 1996, 69–98.

Dohākoṣa (DK). Edited by Shahidullah 1928, 125–65.

Dohākoṣa (DKG). Göttingen manuscript photographed by Sāṃkṛtyāyana.

Dohākośanāmamahāmudropadeśa (DKMU). Tibetan translation. B: Dpal spung block print of the *Phyag rgya chen po’i rgya gzhung*, vol. *āḥ*, 73b–76b. D: Derge Bstan ’gyur 2273, *rgyud*, vol. *shi*, 122a–124a. P: Peking Bstan ’gyur 3119, *rgyud ’grel*, vol. *tsi*, 95a–97a.

Dohākoṣapañjikā (DKP). Eb: The Sanskrit of DKP edited by Prabodh Chandra Bagchi. Calcutta Sanskrit Series No. 25c, 1938, 72–148. Esh: The Sanskrit of DKP edited by Haraprasad Shastri on the basis of his transcript made from an unknown Nepalese manuscript in 1897 or 1898 in Kathmandu (Shastri 1916, 4–5). The edition is from Shastri 1959, 84–118. N: DKP on NGMPP Reel No. A 932/4, 17b3–102b5. The Nepalese manuscript of Hemraj Sharma (now at the National Archives, Kathmandu). P: The Tibetan translation of DKP in Peking Bstan ’gyur, no. 3101, *rgyud ’grel*, vol. *mi*, fols. 199a–231a.

Dohākoṣasārārthagītāṭīkā (DKSGṬ). D Derge Bstan ’gyur 2268, *rgyud*, vol. *zhi*, 65b–106b. P Peking Bstan ’gyur 3120, *rgyud ’grel*, vol. *tsi*, 97a–138a.

**Dohānidhināmatattvopadeśa* (DN). Tibetan translation. See edition of the Sanskrit and Tibetan texts in Mathes 2015, 503–5.

Guhyasamājatantra (GST). Edited by Benoytosh Bhattacharya. Gaekward’s Oriental Series 53. Baroda: Oriental Institute, 1967.

**Guruparamparākramopadeśa* (GPKU). Tibetan translation. B: Dpal spungs block print of the *Phyag rgya chen po’i rgya gzhung*, vol. *hūṃ*, 290b–320b. D: Derge Bstan ’gyur 3716, *rgyud*, vol. *tsu*, 164b–183a. P: Peking Bstan ’gyur 4539, *rgyud ’grel*, vol. *nu*, 184b–206b.

Hevajrapañjikā (HP). See HT.

Hevajratantra (HT). Edited (together with the *Hevajrapañjikā Muktāvalī*) by Ram Shankar Tripathi and Thakur Sain Negi. Bibliotheca Indo-Tibetica 48. Sarnath: Central Institute of Higher Tibetan Studies, 2001.

Jñānālokālaṃkāra (JĀA). Edited by the Study Group on Buddhist Sanskrit Literature. The Institute for Comprehensive Studies of Buddhism, Taisho University. Tokyo: Taisho University Press, 2004.

Jñānaśrīmitranibandhāvali (JNĀ). Edited by Anantalal Thakur. Tibetan Sanskrit Series 5. Patna: Kashi Prasad Jayaswal Research Institute, 1987.

Kāśikāvṛtti (KV). Edited by Śrīnārāyaṇa Miśra. Varanasi: Ratna Publications, 1985.

Kriyasaṃgrahapañjikā (KSP). Edited by Ryugen Tanemura. Leiden: Brill, 2004.

Kudṛṣṭinirghātana (KDN). See edition of the Sanskrit and Tibetan texts in Mathes 2015, 323–31 (up to verse 15).

Kudṛṣṭinirghātavākyaṭippinikā (KDNṬ). See edition of the Sanskrit and Tibetan texts in Mathes 2015, 333–36.

Laṅkāvatārasūtra (LAS). Edited by Bunyiu Nanjio. Bibliotheca Otaniensis 1. Kyoto: Otani University Press, 1923.

Madhyamakālaṃkāravṛtti or *Madhyamapratipadāsiddhi* (MAVṛ/MPS). Tibetan translation. D: Derge Bstan 'gyur 4072, *sems tsam*, vol. *hi*, 102a–120b.

Madhyamakālaṃkāropadeśa (MAU). Tibetan translation. D: Derge Bstan 'gyur 4085, *sems tsam*, vol. *hi*, 223b2–231a7. P: Peking Bstan 'gyur 5586, *sems tsam*, vol. *ku*, 257b2–267a4.

Madhyamakaṣaṭka (MṢ). See edition of Sanskrit and Tibetan texts in Mathes 2015, 477–79.

Madhyamakāvatārabhāṣya (MABh). Tibetan translation. Edited by Louis de la Vallée Poussin. Bibliotheca Buddhica 9. Reprint (first published in 1907–1912). Delhi: Motilal Banarsidass, 1992.

Madhyāntavibhāga (MAV). See MAVBh.

Madhyāntavibhāgabhāṣya (MAVBh). Edited by Gadjin M. Nagao. Tokyo: Suzuki Research Foundation, 1964.

Madhyāntavibhāgaṭīkā (MAVṬ). Edited by S. Yamaguchi. Nagoya: Librairie Hajinkaku, 1934.

Mahāsukhaprakāśa (MSP). See edition of the Sanskrit and Tibetan texts in Mathes 2015, 451–56.

Mahāyānaviṃśikā (MV). See edition of the Sanskrit and Tibetan texts in Mathes 2015, 465–71.

Mañjuśrīnāmasaṃgīti (MNS). Edited by Alex Wayman. In *Chanting the Names of Mañjuśrī*. Delhi: Motilal Banarsidass, 2006.

Māyānirukti (MN). See edition of the Sanskrit and Tibetan texts in Mathes 2015, 427–31.

Mūlamadhyamakakārikā (MMK). Edited by Ye Shaoyong. Beijing: Research Institute of Sanskrit Manuscripts and Buddhist Literature, 2011.

Mūlāpattayaḥ (MĀ). See edition of the Sanskrit and Tibetan texts in Mathes 2015, 337–38.

Nairātmyaprakāśa (NP). Unpublished edition by Harunaga Isaacson, quoted from "*Sekanirdeśapañjikā*: Notes (3), handout, July 4, 2007."

Niraupamyastava (NS). Edited by Guiseppe Tucci. *Journal of the Royal Asiatic Society* 1932, 309–25.

Nirvedhapañcaka (NVP). See edition of the Sanskrit and Tibetan texts in Mathes 2015, 473–76.

Pañcakrama (PK). Edited by Katsumi Mimaki and Tōru Tomabechi. Bibliotheca Codicum Asiaticorum 8. Tokyo: The Centre for East Asian Cultural Studies for Unesco, 1994.

Pañcatathāgatamudrāvivaraṇa (PTMV). See edition of the Sanskrit and Tibetan Texts in Mathes 2015, 371–84.

Pramāṇavārttika (PV). Edited by Yūsho Miyasaka (Sanskrit and Tibetan). In *Acta Indologica* 2: 1972, 2–206.

Prasannapadā (PrPa). Edited by Louis de la Vallée Poussin. Bibliotheca Buddhica 4. Reprint (first published in 1903–1913). Delhi: Motilal Banarsidass, 1992.

Premapañcaka (PP). See edition of the Sanskrit and Tibetan texts in Mathes 2015, 481–84.

Ratnagotravibhāga Mahāyānottaratantraśāstra (RGV). Edited by Edward H. Johnston. Patna: Bihar Research Society, 1950. Includes the *Ratnagotravibhāgavyākhyā*.

Ratnagotravibhāgavyākhyā (RGVV). See RGV. The manuscripts RGVV (A) and RGVV (B) on which Johnston's edition is based are described in Johnston 1950, vi–vii. See also Bandurski, et al. 1994, 12–13.

Sahajaṣaṭka (SṢ). See edition of the Sanskrit and Tibetan texts in Mathes 2015, 499–501.

Samādhirājasūtra (SRS). Gilgit Manuscripts: Edited by Nalinaksha Dutt and Vidyavaridhi Shiv Nath Sharma. Delhi: Sri Satguru Publications, 1984.

Edited by P.L. Vaidya. Darbhanga: The Mithila Institute of Post-Graduate Studies and Research in Sanskrit Learning, 1961.

Saṃdhinirmocanasūtra (SNS). Tibetan translation. Edited by Étienne Lamotte. Louvain, Belgium: Bureaux du Recueil, 1935.

Sekanirdeśa (also *Sekanirṇaya*) (SN). See edition of the Sanskrit and Tibetan texts in Mathes 2015, 385–88, verses 26–36.

Sekanirdeśapañjikā (SNP). Tibetan translation. Edited by Harunaga Isaacson and Francesco Sferra in *The* Sekanirdeśa *of Maitreyanātha (Advayavajra) with the* Sekanirdeśapañjikā *of Rāmapāla. Critical Edition of the Sanskrit and Tibetan Texts with English Translation and Reproductions of the MSS*. Manuscripta Buddhica 2. Naples: Università degli Studi Napoli "L'Orientale," 2014, 165–204.

Sekoddeśaṭīkā (SUṬS). Edited by Francesco Sferra. Serie Orientale Roma 99. Rome: Istituto Italiano per l'Africa e l'Oriente, 2006, 61–207.

Sekoddeśaṭīkā (SUṬT). Tibetan translation. Edited by Stefania Merzagora. Serie Orientale Roma 99. Rome: Istituto Italiano per l'Africa e l'Oriente, 2006, 211–398.

Śrāvakabhūmi (ŚBH). Edited by Karunesha Shukla. Tibetan Sanskrit Works 14. Patna: K.P. Jayaswal Research Institute 1973.

Śrīmadbhagavadgītā (ŚBHG). Edited by Wāsudev L.S.P. Bombay: Niṇaya-Sāgar Press, 1936.

Subhāṣitasaṃgraha, Part 1 (SBHS).
Edited by Cecil Bendall. In Le Muséon 4 (1903), 375–402.

Subodhinī (SB). Edited by Wāsudev L. Paṇśīkar. Mumbai: Nirṇaya-Sāgar Press, 1933.

Sthūlāpattayaḥ (SĀ). See edition of the Sanskrit and Tibetan texts in Mathes 2015, 339.

Svapnanirukti (SvN). See edition of the Sanskrit and Tibetan texts in Mathes 2015, 433–36.

Tattvadaśaka (TD). See edition of the Sanskrit and Tibetan texts in Mathes 2015, 485–88.

Tattvadaśakaṭīkā (TDṬ). Tibetan translation. B: Dpal spung block print of the *Phyag rgya chen po'i rgya gzhung*, vol. *ā*, 1a–27a. D: Derge Bstan 'gyur 2254, *rgyud*, vol. *wi*, 160b–177a. P: Peking Bstan 'gyur 3099, *rgyud 'grel*, vol. *mi*, 176a–195a.

Tattvaprakāśa (TP). See edition of the Sanskrit and Tibetan texts in Mathes 2015, 437–41.

Tattvaratnāvalī (TRĀ). See edition of the Sanskrit and Tibetan texts in Mathes 2015, 341–69.

Tattvāvatāra (TA). Tibetan translation. B: Dpal spung block print of the *Phyag rgya chen po'i rgya gzhung*, vol. *hūṃ*, 320b–377a. D: Derge Bstan 'gyur 3709, *rgyud*, vol. *tsu*, 39a–76a. P: Peking Bstan 'gyur 4532, *rgyud 'grel*, vol. *nu*, 42b–84b.

Tattvaviṃśikā (TV). See edition of the Sanskrit and Tibetan texts in Mathes 2015, 457–63.

[Vajrasattva-]Pañcākāra (PĀ). See edition of the Sanskrit and Tibetan texts in Mathes 2015, 415–25.

Vijñānabhairava (VBh). Edited by Mahāmahopādhyāya Paṇḍit Mukunda Rāma Shāstrī. Bombay: Tatva-Vivechaka Press, 1918.

Vijñaptimātratāsiddhi (VMS). Edited by Sylvain Lévi. Bibliothèque de l'École des Hautes Études, Sciences historiques et philologiques 245. Volume I. Paris: Librairie Ancienne Honoré Champion, 1925.

Viṃśatikā (Viṃś). See VMS.

Yuganaddhaprakāśa (YNP). See edition of the Sanskrit and Tibetan texts in Mathes 2015, 447–50.

Primary Sources (Tibetan)

Author unknown

Yid la mi byed tho yig. In *'Bri gung bka' brgyud chos mdzod*, vol. *kha*, 79b–80a.

Karma pa VIII Mi bskyod rdo rje

Sku gsum ngo sprod rnam bshad: Sku gsum ngo sprod kyi rnam par bshad pa mdo rgyud bstan pa mtha' dag gi e vaṃ phyag rgya. 3 vols. Sarnath: Vajra Vidya, 2013.

Dgongs gcig chos 'khor dang rten 'brel gyi tshoms kyi kar ṭī ka. Vol. 4. Kathmandu: Karma Lekshay Ling Institute, 2012.

Dgongs gcig lta sgom spyod pa'i tshoms kyi kar kar ṭī ka smad cha. Vol. 2. Kathmandu: Karma Lekshay Ling Institute, 2012.

Dbu ma la 'jug pa'i kar ṭī ka: Dwags brgyud grub pa'i shing rta. Seattle: Nitartha International Publications, 1996.

Shing rta chen po. In *Collected Works of the Eighth Karmapa*. Vol. 2, 514–67.

Karma Phrin las pa

Dmangs do ha'i rnam bshad. In *Do ha skor gsum gyi tshig don kyi rnam bshad sems kyi rnam thar ston pa'i me long zhes bya ba bzhugs so*, 1–118. Sarnath: Vajra Vidya Institute Library, 2009.

Kun dga' rin chen (ed.)

Grub pa sde bdun dang snying po skor gsum yid la mi byed pa'i chos skor bzhugs so (*'Bri gung bka' brgyud chos mdzod*, vol. *ka*). No place, no date.

'Phags yul bka' brgyud grub chen gong ma'i do ha'i skor bzhugs so (*'Bri gung bka' brgyud chos mdzod*, vol. *kha*). No place, no date.

Skyo ston Smon lam tshul khrims

Chos nyid kyi khrid. In *Bka' gdams pa'i gsung 'bum*. Edited by Dpal brtsegs bod yig dpe rnying zhib 'jug khang. Chengdu: Si khron mi rigs dpe skrun khang, 2007. vols. 31–60, vol. 50, 311–16.

Theg chen rgyud bla ma'i gdams pa. In *Bka' gdams pa'i gsung 'bum*. Edited by Dpal brtsegs bod yig dpe rnying zhib 'jug khang. Chengdu: Si khron mi rigs dpe skrun khang, 2007. vols. 31–60, vol. 50, 147–56.

'Gos Lo tsā ba Gzhon nu dpal

DRSM. *Theg pa chen po rgyud bla ma'i bstan bcos kyi 'grel bshad de kho na nyid rab tu gsal ba'i me long*. Edited by Klaus-Dieter Mathes. Nepal Research Centre Publications 24. Stuttgart: Franz Steiner Verlag, 2003.

Deb ther sngon po, 2 vols. Si khron mi rigs dpe skrun khang, 1985.

Ti pi 'bum la 'bar

Rin chen phreng ba'i bshad pa. In *'Bri gung bka' brgyud chos mdzod*, vol. *ka*, 182b–199b.

Bstan 'dzin padma'i rgyal mtshan (Skyabs mgon Che tshang sku phreng bzhi pa)

'Bri gung gdan rabs: *Nges don bstan pa'i snying po mgon po 'bri gung pa chen po'i gdan rabs chos kyi byung tshul gser gyi phreng ba zhes bya ba bzhugs so. 'Bri gung bka' brgyud* 6. Dehra Dun: Drikung Kagyu Institute, 2000.

Dwags po Bkra shis rnam rgyal

Phyag chen zla ba'i 'od zer. Sarnath: Vajra Vidya Institute Library, 2005

Padma dkar po

Chos 'byung bstan pa'i padma rgyas pa'i nyin byed. Ed. by Prof. Dr. Lokesh Chandra with a forward by E. Gene Smith. Śata-Piṭaka Series 75. Delhi: International Academy of Indian Culture, 1968.

Phyag chen rgyal ba'i gan mdzod. Sarnath: Vajra Vidya Institute Library, 2005.

Dpa' bo Gtsug lag phreng ba

Chos byung mkhas pa'i dga' ston, 2 vols. Beijing: Mi rigs dpe skrun khang, 1986.

Phyag chen ryga gzhung
See Phun tshogs rgyal mtshan (ed.).
Phun tshogs rgyal mtshan (ed.):
Phyag rgya chen po'i rgya gzhung. 3 vols (*oṃ, āḥ, hūṃ*). dPal spungs block print. No date.
Bu ston Rin chen grub
Bu ston gsan yig: Bla ma dam pa rnams kyis rjes su gzung ba'i tshul bka' drin rjes su dran par byed pa zhes byar bzhugs so. In *Bu ston thams cad mkhyen pa'i bka' 'bum*, vol. *la*, 1–142. Śata-Piṭaka Series 66. New-Delhi: International Academy of Indian Culture, 1971.
'Bri gung bka' brgyud chos mdzod
See Kun dga' rin chen.
Maitrīpa
Shes pa spro bsdu med par 'jog pa'i man ngag gsang ba dam pa. See edition of the Sanskrit and Tibetan texts in Mathes 2015, 507–09.
Rus pa'i rgyan can (Gtsang smyon He ru ka)
Rnal 'byor gyi dbang phyug chen po mi la ras pa'i rnam mgur. Mtsho sngon zhing hwa dpe khang, 1989.
Zhwa dmar IV Chos kyi grags pa:
Mkhas grub nā ro mai tri dbang gi bzhed pa mthun par grub pa zhes bya ba bzhugs so. In *gSung 'bum*, 6 vols, vol. 2, 800–50. Beijing: Krung go'i bod rig pa dpe skrun khang, 2009.

References

Almogi, Orna. "Māyopamādvayavāda versus Sarvadharmāpratiṣṭānavāda: A Late Indian Subclassification of Madhyamaka and its Reception in Tibet." *Journal of the International College for Postgraduate Buddhist Studies* 14 (2010): 135–212.

Arnold, Dan. "Candrakīrti on Dignāga on *Svalakṣaṇas*." *Journal of the International Association of Buddhist Studies* 26, no. 1 (2003): 139–74.

Bandurski, Frank et al. "Untersuchungen zur buddhistischen literatur." Edited by Bearbeitet von Frank Bandurski, Bikkhu Pāsādika, Michael Schmidt, und Bangwei Wang. *Sanskrit-Wörterbuch der buddhistischen Texte aus den Turfan-Funden* 5. Göttingen: Vandenhoeck and Ruprecht in Göttingen, 1994.

Böthlingk, Otto. *Pāṇini's Grammatik.* Delhi: Motilal Banarsidass, 1998.

Brooks, Douglas Renfrew. *Auspicious Wisdom: The Texts and Traditions of Śrīvidyā Śākta Tantrism in South India.* Albany: State University of New York, 1992.

Brunnhölzl, Karl. *Gone Beyond.* Vol. 1 of *Prajñāpāramitā Sūtras, The* Ornament of Clear Realization, *and Its Commentaries in the Tibetan Kagyü Tradition.* Ithaca, NY: Snow Lion, 2011.

——. *Straight from the Heart: Buddhist Pith Instructions.* Ithaca, NY: Snow Lion, 2007.

Burton, David. *Emptiness Appraised: A Critical Study of Nāgārjuna's Philosophy.* Richmond, UK: Curzon Press, 1999.

Buswell Jr., Robert E., and Donald S. Lopez Jr. *The Princeton Dictionary of Buddhism.* Princeton, NJ: Princeton University Press, 2014.

Cabezón, José Ignacia, and Lobsang Dargay. *Freedom from Extremes: Gorampa's "Distinguishing the Views" and the Polemics of Emptiness.* Boston: Wisdom Publications, 2006.

Chattopadhyaya, Alka. *Atīśa and Tibet: Life and Works of Dīpaṃkara Śrījñāna (alias Atīśa) in relation to the History and Religion of Tibet with Tibetan Sources.* Delhi: Motilal Banarsidass, 1981.

Dvivedī, Vrajavallabha, and Mahendraratna Vajrācārya. "Advayavajrasaṃgraha ke pāṃc pariśiṣṭa." *Dhīḥ* 2 (1986): 82–107.

Eimer, Helmut. *rNam thar rgyas pa: Materialien zu einer Biographie des Atiśa (Dīpaṃkaraśrījñāna).* Vol. 1: Einführung, Inhaltsverzeichnis, Namensglossar. Vol. 2: Textmaterialien. Wiesbaden: Harrassowitz, 1979.

Frauwallner, Erich. *Die Philosophie des Buddhismus.* Berlin: Akademie Verlag, 1956.

Gnoli, Raniero, and Giacomella Orofino. "Nāropā: Iniziazione." *Biblioteca Orientale* 1. Rome: Adelphi Edizioni S.P.A., 1994.

Griffith, Paul J. *On Being Mindless: Buddhist Meditation and the Mind-Body Problem.* Delhi: Sri Satguru Publications, 1999.

Isaacson, Harunaga. "Observations on the Development of the Ritual of Initiation (*abhiṣeka*) in the Higher Buddhist Tantric Systems." In *Hindu and Buddhist Initiations in India and Nepal.* Edited by Astrid Zotter and Cristof Zotter, 261–79. Wiesbaden: Harrassowitz, 2010.

——. "Yogācāra and Vajrayāna according to Ratnākaraśānti." In *The Foundation for Yoga Practitioners: The Buddhist* Yogācārabhūmi *Treatise and Its Adaption in India, East Asia, and Tibet.* Edited by Ulrich Timme Kragh, 1036–51. *Harvard Oriental Series* 75. Cambridge: Harvard University, 2013.

Isaacson, Harunaga, and Francesco Sferra, eds. *The* Sekanirdeśa *of Maitreyanātha (Advayavajra) with the* Sekanirdeśapañjikā *of Rāmapāla. Critical Edition of the Sanskrit and Tibetan Texts with English Translation and Reproductions of the MSS* (Manuscripta Buddhica 2). Naples: Università degli Studi Napoli "L'Orientale," 2014.

Jiang Zhongxin and Tōru Tomabechi. *The* Pañcakramaṭippaṇī *of Muniśrībhadra: Introduction and Romanized Sanskrit Text*. Schweizer Asiatische Studien (monographies 23). Bern: Peter Lang, 1996.

Kvaerne, Per. *An Anthology of Buddhist Tantric Songs*. 2nd ed. Bangkok: White Orchid Press, 1986.

La Vallée Poussin, Louis de. "*Madhyamakāvatāra*, Introduction au traité du milieu de l'ācārya Candrakīrti avec le commentaire de l'auteur. Traduit d'après la version tibétaine." *Le Muséon* 12 (1911): 1903–13.

Lhalungpa, Lobsang P. *Mahāmudrā: The Quintessence of Mind and Meditation*. Delhi: Motilal Banarsidass, 1993.

Lindtner, Christian. *A Garland of Light. Kambala's Ālokamālā*. Fremont, CA: Asian Humanities Press, 2003.

———. *Nagarjuniana: Studies in the Writings and Philosophy of Nāgārjuna*. Delhi: Motilal Banarsidass, 1990. Reprinted by Motilal Banarsidass (*Buddhist Tradition Series* 2). First published 1982.

Lopez Jr., Donald S. *Elaborations on Emptiness. Uses of the Heart Sūtra*. Princeton, NJ: Princeton University Press, 1996.

Mathes, Klaus-Dieter. "bKa' brgyud Mahāmudrā: 'Chinese rDzogs chen' or the Techings of the Siddhas?" In *Zentralasiatische Studien* 45 (2016a): 309–40.

———. "Blending the Sūtras with the Tantras: The Influence of Maitrīpa and his Circle on the Formation of *Sūtra Mahāmudrā* in the Kagyu Schools." Edited by Ronald M. Davidson and Christian K. Wedemeyer. In *Tibetan Buddhist Literature and Praxis: Studies in its Formative Period 900–1400* 10/4. Proceedings of the Tenth Seminar of the IATS, Oxford 2003. Leiden: Brill, 2006: 201–27.

———. "Can *Sūtra Mahāmudrā* Be Justified on the Basis of Maitrīpa's Apratiṣṭhānavāda?" Edited by B. Kellner, H. Krasser, H. Lasic, M.T. Much, and H. Tauscher. In *Pramāṇakīrtiḥ. Papers Dedicated to Ernst Steinkellner on the Occasion of His 70th Birthday. Wiener Studien zur Tibetologie und Buddhismuskunde* 70, no. 2 (2007): 545–66.

———. "The Collection of 'Indian Mahāmudrā Works' (*phyag chen rgya gzhung*)

Compiled by the Seventh Karma pa Chos grags rgya mtsho." Edited by Roger R. Jackson and Matthew T. Kapstein. In *Mahāmudrā and the Bka'-brgyud Tradition* (Königswinter 2006): 89–130. *Proceedings of the Eleventh Seminar of the International Association for Tibetan Studies, Konigswinter 2006*. Andiast, Switzerland: International Institute for Tibetan and Buddhist Studies, 2011.

———. *A Direct Path to the Buddha Within: Gö Lotsāwa's Mahāmudrā Interpretation of the Ratnagotravibhāga*. Boston: Wisdom Publications, 2008.

———. *A Fine Blend of Mahāmudrā and Madhyamaka: Maitrīpa's Collection of Texts on Nonconceptual Realization* (Amanasikāra). Vienna: Österreichische Akademie der Wissenschaften, 2015.

———. "'Gos Lo tsā ba Gzhon nu dpal's (1392–1481) Analytical and Direct Approaches to Ultimate Reality." In *Journal of the International Association of Buddhist Studies* 39, no. 2 (2016): 391–422.

———. "'Gos Lo tsā ba Gzhon nu dpal's Commentary on the *Dharmatā* Chapter of the *Dharmadharmatāvibhāgakārikās*." In *Studies in Indian Philosophy and Buddhism, University of Tokyo* 12 (2005): 3–39.

———. "Maitrīpa's *Amanasikāra*-Based Mahāmudrā in the Works of the Eighth Karma pa Mi bskyod rdo rje." Edited by Roger R. Jackson and Klaus-Dieter Mathes. In *Mahāmudrā in India and Tibet* (Leiden/Boston: Brill, 2020): 269–301.

———. "Maitrīpa's *Amanasikārādhāra* ('A Justification of Becoming Mentally Disengaged')." In *Journal of the Nepal Research Centre* 13 (2009a): 5–32.

———. "The Pith Instructions on the Mahāyāna Uttaratantra (Theg chen rgyud bla'i gdams pa). A Missing Link in the Meditation Tradition of the Maitreya Works." Edited by Olaf Czaja and Guntram Hazod. In *The Illuminating Mirror: Tibetan Studies in Honour of Per Sørensen on the Occasion of his 65th Birthday* (Wiesbaden: Ludwig Reichert Verlag, 2015a): 303–20.

———. "*Sahajavajra's Integration of Tantra into Mainstream Buddhism: An Analysis of his **Tattvadaśakaṭīkā* and **Sthitisamāsa*." Edited by Nina Mirnig, Marion Rastelli, and Vincent Eltschinger. In *Tantric Communities in Context* (Vienna: Austrian Academy of Sciences Press, 2019): 137–69.

———. "The *Śrī-Śabarapādastotraratna* of Vanaratna." Edited by Dragomir Dimitrov, Michael Hahn et al. In *Bauddhasāhityastabakāvalī: Essays and Studies on Buddhist Sanskrit Literature Dedicated to Claus Vogel by Colleagues, Students, and Friends* 36 (2008a): 245–67.

——. "The 'Succession of the Four Seals' (*Caturmudrānvaya*) Together with Selected Passages from Karopa's Commentary." In *Tantric Studies* 1 (2009): 89–130.

——. "A Summary and Topical Outline of the *Sekanirdeśapañjikā* by 'Bum la 'bar." In *The* Sekanirdeśa *of Maitreyanātha (Advayavajra) with the* Sekanirdeśapañjikā *of Rāmapāla. Critical Edition of the Sanskrit and Tibetan Texts with English Translation and Reproductions of the MSS. Manuscripta Buddhica* 2: 367–84. Naples: Università degli Studi Napoli "L'Orientale," 2014.

——. "Tāranātha's Presentation of *trisvabhāva* in the *gŹan stoṅ sñiṅ po*." In *Journal of the International Association of Buddhist Studies* 23, no. 2 (2000): 195–223.

——. *Unterscheidung der Gegebenheiten von ihrem wahren Wesen* (*Dharmadharmatāvibhāga*). *Indica et Tibetica* 26. Swisttal-Odendorf: Indica et Tibetica Verlag, 1996.

Mimaki, Katsumi. *Blo gsal grub mtha'*. Kyoto: Zinbun Kagaku Kenkyusyo, 1982.

Mimaki Katsumi and Tōru Tomabechi. *Pañcakrama. Sanskrit and Tibetan Texts Critically Edited with Verse Index and Fascimile Edition of the Sanskrit Manuscripts.* (Bibliotheca Codicum Asiaticorum 8). Tokyo: The Centre for East Asian Cultural Studies for Unesco, 1994.

Moriyama Shinya. "Ratnākaraśānti's Criticism of the Madhyamaka Refutation of Causality." In *China Tibetology* 20, no. 1 (2013): 53–66.

Nakamura, Hajime. *Indian Buddhism: A Survey with Bibliographical Notes*. Delhi: Motilal Banarsidass, 1989. First published 1980 (*Buddhist Tradition Series* 1).

Oberhammer, Gerhard, ed. *Inklusivismus. Eine indische Denkform.* Vienna: Institute for Indology, University of Vienna, 1983.

Passavanti, Marco. "The Life of Maitrīpā/Maitreyanātha from a Thirteeth-Century Tibetan Hagiography (MS 1095 of the Tucci Tibetan Fund)." In *The* Sekanirdeśa *of Maitreyanātha (Advayavajra) with the* Sekanirdeśapañjikā *of Rāmapāla. Critical Edition of the Sanskrit and Tibetan Texts with English Translation and Reproductions of the MSS. Manuscripta Buddhica* 2: 431–48. Naples: Università degli Studi Napoli "L'Orientale," 2014.

Priest, Graham. *The Fifth Corner of Four: An Essay on Buddhist Metaphysics and the Catuṣkoṭi.* New York: Oxford University Press, 2018.

Ricard, Matthieu and Trinh Xuan Thuan. *The Quantum and the Lotus: A Journey to the Frontiers where Science and Buddhism Meet*. Translated from the French by Ian Monk. New York: Crown Publishers, 2001.

Roberts, Peter Alan. *The Mind of Mahāmudrā. Advice from the Kagyü Masters*. Boston: Wisdom Publications, 2014.

Roerich, George N. *The Blue Annals*. 2 vols. Kalkota: Royal Asiatic Society of Bengal, 1949–53.

Rospatt, Alexander. "The Buddhist Doctrine of Momentariness." In *Alt- und Neu-Indische Studien* 47. Stuttgart: Franz Steiner Verlag, 1995.

Schaeffer, Kurtis R. *Dreaming the Great Brahmin: Tibetan Traditions of the Buddhist Poet-Saint Saraha*. Oxford: Oxford University Press, 2005.

Schmithausen, Lambert. "Aspects of Spiritual Practice in Early Yogācāra." In *Journal of the International College for Postgraduate Buddhist Studies* 11 (2007): 213–44.

——. "Der Nirvāṇa-Abschnitt in der Viniścayasaṃgrahaṇī der Yogācārabhūmiḥ." In *Veröffenlichungen der Kommission für Sprachen und Kulturen Süd-und Ostasiens* 8, *Sitzungsberichte* 2, no. 264. Vienna: Österreichische Akademie der Wissenschaften, 1969.

——. "Philologische Bemerkungen zum Ratnagotravibhāga." In *Wiener Zeitschrift für die Kunde Südasiens* 15 (1971): 123–77.

Seyfort Ruegg, David. "A Kar ma bKa' brgyud Work on the Lineages and Traditions of the Indo-Tibetan dBu ma (Madhyamaka)." Edited by G. Gnoli and L. Lanciotti. In *Orientalia Iosephi Tucci Dedicata. Rome Oriental Series* 56, no. 3: 1249–80. Rome: Istituto Italiano per il Medio ed Estremo Oriente, 1988.

Sferra, Francesco. "Some Considerations on the Relationship between Hindu and Buddhist Tantras." In *Buddhist Asia* 1. Papers from the First Conference of Buddhist Studies Held in Naples in May 2001, 57–84. Kyoto: Italian School of East Asian Studies, 2003.

Shahidullah, M. *Les chants mystiques de Kāṇha et de Saraha: Les Dohākoṣa (en apabhraṃsa, avec les versiọns tibétaines) et les Caryā (en vieux-bengali)*. Paris: Adrien-Maisonneuve, 1928.

Sørensen and Sonam Dolma. *Rare Texts from Tibet: Seven Sources for the Ecclesiastic History of Medieval Tibet*. Bhairahawa: Lumibini International Research Institute, 2007.

Steinkellner, Ernst. "Verse-Index of Dharmakīrti's Works." In *Wiener Studien zur Tibetologie und Buddhismuskunde* 1. Vienna: Arbeitskreis für tibetische und buddhistische Studien, 1977.

Takasaki Jikido. *A Study on the* Ratnagotravibhāga *Uttaratantra Being a Treatise on the* Tathāgatagarbha *Theory of Mahāyāna Buddhism*. In *Rome Oriental Series* 33. Rome: Istituto Italiano per il Medio ed Estremo Oriente, 1966.

Tatz, Mark. "The Life of the Siddha-Philosopher Maitrīgupta." In *Journal of the American Oriental Society* 107 (1987): 695–711.

———. "Maitrī-pa and Atiśa." Edited by Helga Uebach and Jampa L. Panglung. In *Tibetan Studies: Proceedings of the 4th Seminar of the International Association for Tibetan Studies*, 473–82. Munich: Bayerische Akademie der Wissenschaften, 1988.

———. "Philosophic Systems according to Advayavajra and Vajrapāṇi." In *The Journal of Buddhist and Tibetan Studies* 1 (1994): 65–120.

Templeman, David. *Tāranātha's Life of Kṛṣṇācārya/Kāṇha*. New Delhi: Indraprastha Press, 1989.

———. "Memories of a Past Life." Edited by Donald Lopez. In *Religeons of Tibet in Practice*, 212–22. Princeton, NJ: Princeton University Press, 1997.

Thomas, Paul. "The *Samādhirājasūtra* and "Sūtra Mahāmudrā": A Critical Edition and Translation of Verses 1–118 from Chapter 32 of the *Samādhirājasūtra*." Edited by Roger R. Jackson and Klaus-Dieter Mathes. In *Mahāmudrā in India and Tibet*, 10–89. Leiden/Boston: Brill, 2020.

Thrangu Rinpoche, Khenchen. *A Song for the King: Saraha on Mahāmudrā Meditation*. Boston: Wisdom Publications, 2006.

Thurman, Robert A. F. "Vajra Hermeneutics." Edited by Donald S. Lopez. In *Buddhist Hermeneutics*, 119–48. Honolulu: University of Hawaii Press, 1988.

Tomabechi Tōru. "*Étude du Pañcakrama: Introduction et Traduction Annotée*." Unpublished PhD thesis, Lausanne: Faculté des Lettres, Université de Lausanne, 2006.

Tucci, Guiseppe. *Animadversiones Indicae, Opera Minora* I (Studi Orientali Publicati a cura della Scuola Orientale 6). Rome: Università di Roma, 1971.

Ui Hakuju. "Shinri no Hokan (*Tattvaratnāvalī*)." In *Nagoya Daigaku Bungakubu Kenkyuronshu* 3 Tetsugaki 1 (1952): 1–31.

Wallis, Glenn. "Advayavajra's Instructions on the Ādikarma." In *Pacific World: Journal of the Institute of Buddhist Studies*. Third Series 5 (2003): 203–30.

Wangchuk, Dorji. *The Resolve to Become a Buddha: A Study of the Bodhicitta Concept in Indo-Tibetan Buddhism*. Tokyo: The International Institute for Buddhist Studies, 2007.

Wedemeyer, Christian. *Āryadeva's Lamp that Integrates the Practices (*Caryāmelāpakapradīpa*): The Gradual Path of Vajrayāna Buddhism According to the Esoteric Community Noble Tradition*. New York: Columbia University Press, 2007.

Index

LIVES OF THE MASTERS

"Since the time of Buddha Shakyamuni himself, Buddhists have been accustomed to recollect the lives of great teachers and practitioners as a source of inspiration from which we may still learn. The Lives of the Masters series continues this noble tradition, recounting the stories, wisdom, and experience of many accomplished Buddhists over the last 2,500 years. I am sure readers will find the accounts in this series inspirational and encouraging."

His Holiness the Dalai Lama

"The lives of the most important Buddhist masters in history written by the very best of scholars in elegant and accessible prose—who could ask for more?"

Jose Cabezón, *Professor of Tibetan Buddhist Studies, University of California Santa Barbara*

BOOKS IN THE SERIES

Atiśa Dīpaṃkara: Illuminator of the Awakened Mind
Dogen: Japan's Original Zen Teacher
Gendun Chopel: Tibet's Modern Visionary
Maitrīpa: India's Yogi of Nondual Bliss
S. N. Goenka: Emissary of Insight
The Third Karmapa Rangjung Dorje: Master of Mahāmudrā
Tsongkhapa: A Buddha in the Land of Snows
Xuanzang: China's Legendary Pilgrim and Translator

Please visit www.shambhala.com for more information on forthcoming titles.